By Small
& Simple
Things

Other volumes in the
BYU WOMEN'S CONFERENCE Series

BY SMALL
& SIMPLE
THINGS

TALKS *from the* 2011
BYU WOMEN'S CONFERENCE

DESERET
BOOK

SALT LAKE CITY, UTAH

Images on page 157 (*The Denial of Peter*, by Carl Bloch), page 158 (*Victory O Lord!* by John Everett Millais), page 161 (*Good Shepherd*, by Bernhard Plockhurst), and page 163 (*The Annunciation*, by Carl Bloch) are all public domain, via Wikimedia Commons.

Library of Congress Cataloging-in-Publication Data
Women's Conference (2011 : Brigham Young University)
   By small and simple things : talks from the 2011 BYU Women's Conference.
      pages cm
   Includes index.
   ISBN 978-1-60908-898-9 (hardbound : alk. paper)
   1. Mormon women—Religious life—Congresses.   2. The Church of Jesus Christ of Latter-day Saints—Congresses.   3. Mormon Church—Congresses.   I. Title.
   BX8641.W73 2011
   289.3'32082—dc23   2011041215

Printed in the United States of America
Publishers Printing, Salt Lake City, UT
10   9   8   7   6   5   4   3   2   1

CONTENTS

CONTENTS

"By Small and Simple Things Are Great Things Brought to Pass"

David A. Bednar

A Pattern in All Things

In a revelation given through the Prophet Joseph Smith in June of 1831, the Lord declared that "I will give unto you a pattern in all things, that ye may not be deceived; for Satan is abroad in the land, and he goeth forth deceiving the nations" (D&C 52:14). I invite you to consider a specific phrase in this verse—"a pattern in all things."

A pattern is a guide or a model. Patterns are used in sewing and knitting, in wood- and metalworking, and in a wide variety of other productive pursuits, activities, and jobs. Patterns help to avoid waste and unwanted deviations and facilitate uniformity that is appropriate and beneficial. Imagine the difficulty of sewing a blouse or building a table without an appropriate pattern.

Vital spiritual patterns are evident in the life of the Savior, in the scriptures, and in the teachings of living prophets and apostles. These spiritual patterns are now and always have been important aids to discernment and sources of direction and protection for faithful Latter-day

Elder David A. Bednar was ordained and set apart as a member of the Quorum of the Twelve Apostles of The Church of Jesus Christ of Latter-day Saints on 7 October 2004. Prior to his call to the Quorum of the Twelve, Elder Bednar served as an area seventy, area authority seventy, regional representative, twice as a stake president and as a bishop. Elder Bednar married Susan Kae Robinson in 1975. They are the parents of three sons.

Saints. Spiritual patterns are essential in avoiding the deception that is so pervasive in our world today.

A powerful pattern the Lord uses to advance His work and to tutor Heavenly Father's children upon the earth is the theme for this Women's Conference—"by small and simple things are great things brought to pass" (Alma 37:6). Let me briefly explain what I mean.

Many people in our contemporary world are drawn to promises of big results that occur quickly and all at once. Consider, for example, all of the money spent on lottery tickets. Recall the claims of advertising messages you have received that pledge immediate weight loss, instant health, fast hair growth, and a more youthful appearance in just fourteen days. We are bombarded constantly with messages from a multiplicity of sources promoting speedy supersizing, instant gratification, and outstanding performance that will impress our families and friends.

In a similar way, the adversary made impressive assertions about big results in premortality: "And I, the Lord God, spake unto Moses, saying: That Satan, whom thou hast commanded in the name of mine Only Begotten, is the same which was from the beginning, and he came before me, saying—Behold, here am I, send me, I will be thy son, and I will redeem all mankind, that one soul shall not be lost, and surely I will do it; wherefore give me thine honor" (Moses 4:1). Lucifer's grandiose pledge, however, was hollow and empty because he "sought to destroy the agency of man" (Moses 4:3).

EXAMPLES OF SMALL AND SIMPLE THINGS
THAT BRING GREAT THINGS TO PASS

In contrast to what we so often observe in the world, the Lord typically ministers "one by one" (3 Nephi 11:15). He enables us to learn "line upon line, precept upon precept, here a little and there a little" (2 Nephi 28:30). And He accomplishes His work by bringing to pass great things through small and simple means.

I believe many, if not all, of the most satisfying and memorable accomplishments in our homes, in the Church, in our jobs and professions, and in our communities will be the product of this important spiritual pattern—of simple and small things. We should find great comfort in the fact that ordinary people who faithfully, diligently, and consistently do simple things that are right before God will bring forth extraordinary results.

The following three examples illustrate this truth:

EXAMPLE 1. GUSTAVUS ADOLPHUS PERRY

Several years ago, Elder L. Tom Perry described in a Brigham Young University devotional message the legacy of Gustavus Adolphus Perry, the first member of the Perry family to join The Church of Jesus Christ of Latter-day Saints. Gustavus, his wife, Eunice, and their seven children lived on a beautiful farm in New York. The Perry family first heard the message of the restored gospel in 1830 and were baptized in 1832. After joining the Church, the family moved from New York to Ohio, from Ohio to Missouri, from Missouri to Illinois, and from Illinois across the plains to the Great Salt Lake Valley. The town of Perry, Utah, is named after the oldest son of Gustavus and Eunice, the first bishop to serve in that community.

In 1997, the Perry family celebrated the 200th birthday of Gustavus Perry. In preparation for that celebration, Elder L. Tom Perry's brother conducted extensive research and identified as many of the descendants of Gustavus and Eunice as he could.

In your mind, please try to guess the number of descendants Elder Perry's brother found. The answer: more than 10,000 family members had come from this faithful man and woman.

Elder Perry stated: "The number overwhelmed me. I could not believe that there could be more than 10,000 descendants of Gustavus Adolphus Perry. . . . In seven to eight generations, his family had sufficient numbers to organize three stakes of [the Church]."[1]

In this illustration we witness the power of a profound spiritual pattern—small and simple things bringing great things to pass. A faithful husband and wife did their best to rear children in righteousness; testimony and deepening conversion to Christ persisted across the generations to grandchildren, great-grandchildren, and thousands more. Many seemingly ordinary family prayers, common experiences working together, gospel conversations, tragedies and triumphs, and Sabbath days in scores of families across the generations produced a legacy of faithfulness. By small and simple things are great things brought to pass.

EXAMPLE 2. LUKE SYPHUS AND CHRISTIANA LONG

Luke Syphus and Christiana Long were born in 1827 and 1832, respectively, and lived in England. Both Luke and Christiana received and studied the restored gospel of Jesus Christ and were baptized. Following their conversions, they met, courted, and were married on Christmas Day of 1851. Approximately one year after their marriage, they boarded the ship *Java* and set sail for Australia.

During the five-month voyage, Luke and Christiana became good friends with Joseph and Adelaide Ridges. The Ridgeses likewise were emigrating to Australia from their native country of England. When the ship arrived at its destination in April 1853, the Syphus and Ridges families lived and worked together at Pennant Hills, approximately fifteen miles northwest of Sydney.

Luke and Christiana introduced Joseph and Adelaide to the restored gospel of Jesus Christ. During their journey from England, the Ridgeses had grown to admire Luke and Christiana for their good habits, for their kindly ways, and for their example of strength and devotion as Brother and Sister Syphus faced the heartache associated with the death of their firstborn child. Luke loaned Joseph a copy of the Book of Mormon and a text of the teachings of Elder Orson Pratt. Both Joseph and Adelaide ultimately became convinced of the truthfulness of the gospel and were baptized in 1853.

As a child in England, Joseph Ridges had been fascinated by an organ factory near his home. He had spent long hours watching and learning how organs are constructed. In his spare time in Australia and using the skills he had developed in England, Joseph began to build a small, seven-stop pipe organ. The mission president, Augustus Farnham, suggested Brother Ridges donate the organ to the Church in Salt Lake City. Joseph agreed, and with the help of the members and missionaries he dismantled the organ, packed the parts into six large tin cases and stowed the instrument in the cargo hold of a sailing vessel, the *Jenny Lind*. A company of approximately 120 people set sail for Utah in 1856, including the Ridges and the Syphus families and the organ Joseph had constructed.

After landing in California, the organ was hauled across the desert by mule teams and arrived in Salt Lake City in June 1857. Brother Ridges installed the small organ in the old adobe tabernacle on Temple Square, where the Assembly Hall now stands. That simple instrument was the forerunner of a great organ Brother Ridges later was to build.

Construction began in the 1860s on the Tabernacle that stands today on Temple Square. Brigham Young asked Joseph, who at the time was farming in Provo, if he could build a large organ for the new building. Brother Ridges responded that he could, and the work began. Eventually the organ would have two manuals, twenty-seven pedals, and thirty-five stops, with approximately 2,000 pipes—and would measure twenty feet by thirty feet by forty feet high. The organ took more than ten years to construct.[2]

Again in this example we witness the power of a profound spiritual pattern—small and simple things bringing great things to pass. Acts of kindness, of righteous influence, and of Christian compassion by Luke and Christiana were instrumental in bringing to pass the conversions of Joseph and Adelaide. A small and simple organ in Australia helped to bring forth the great Tabernacle organ that today is one of the iconic symbols of The Church of Jesus Christ of Latter-day Saints. No big results occurred quickly or all at once. Rather, by small and simple things great things were brought to pass.

EXAMPLE 3. BEDNAR BOYS

The lessons I learned from my great-great-grandfather Luke Syphus about the power of small and simple things in setting a righteous example came into greater focus for me in 1980 after I completed my studies at Purdue University. Sister Bednar and I and our sons moved to Fayetteville, Arkansas. Susan and I were excited to learn if life truly existed after graduate school. We anticipated with great excitement the adventure of a new start for our family in a wonderful community.

One of our sons had a challenging learning experience at his elementary school one day as several children told him they could not play with him during recess because he was a Mormon and not a Christian. This little boy came home after school and asked why the other children had said such things and acted as they did. We simply told him that they did not know much about our beliefs and church—and that he would have a terrific opportunity to be a missionary.

In the months and years that followed, this son and his two brothers, along with a small number of other Latter-day Saint youth who lived in the area, endeavored to be good examples as they participated in a wide range of school activities, countless athletic contests, and many community events. Our sons certainly were not perfect, as I previously have described in general conference. They were quite normal, fun-loving, and often rambunctious boys.[3] But our boys did strive to live the gospel and to be "example[s] of the believers, in word, in conversation, in charity, in spirit, in faith, in purity" (1 Timothy 4:12). They declined invitations to play on all-star athletic teams if Sunday practices and play were expected. And they did not participate in activities or events that would compromise their standards.

As these three young men progressed through both junior high and high school, Susan and I were intrigued to learn that the parents of our sons' friends frequently would ask their children if the Bednar boys were going to attend a party or some other activity. Interestingly, if the answer were yes, then those parents would permit their children to attend. If the answer were no, then many parents often would not allow their children to participate. We continue to cherish the associations and friendships we developed with the parents of our sons' friends—good and God-fearing men and women who were not members of our Church.

In 1997 we moved from Fayetteville to Rexburg, Idaho, so I could assume my new responsibilities as president of Ricks College, now Brigham Young University–Idaho. As we were preparing to relocate, I called upon and talked with a number of friends with whom we had associated for many years. I asked a favor of one good friend to whom I previously had given a copy of the Book of Mormon and with whom I had often talked about the Savior's restored Church. I indicated to my friend that falsehoods about our Church and beliefs often were promulgated in our community. He readily acknowledged that such things occurred. I then asked for his help. He responded that he gladly would be of assistance. I gave him a copy of Elder M. Russell Ballard's book entitled *Our Search for Happiness: An Invitation to Understand The Church of Jesus Christ of Latter-day Saints* (Salt Lake City: Deseret Book, 2001) and requested that he read it. I explained to him that since I would no longer be in a position to explain our beliefs and defend our Church, I needed him to do so. I asked him to become a defender of our faith in a community where Latter-day Saints often were maligned and mocked.

He scanned the table of contents of the book I had given him, paused for a moment, and said sincerely, "Dave, I will." And then he said, "We have been watching the LDS kids in the schools over the years, and we all know that you Latter-day Saints have something we do not have. I will do my best to help stop the falsehoods."

Such a dramatic change of perspective in just a few short years—from an elementary school playground and the taunting of a little LDS boy because he allegedly was not a Christian to an acknowledgment by prominent parents in our community that "you Latter-day Saints have something we do not have."

In this example we again witness the power of a profound spiritual pattern—small and simple things bringing great things to pass. A relative handful of young men and women lived the gospel in small and simple and ordinary ways. On countless occasions when other youth used coarse and inappropriate language, these young disciples did not. On countless occasions when other youth engaged in improper or immoral behavior, these young disciples did not. On countless occasions when other youth turned inward through self-centeredness and selfishness, these young disciples often turned outward with compassion and in service. No big results occurred quickly or all at once. Rather, by small and simple things great things were brought to pass.

WHY DO SMALL AND SIMPLE THINGS BRING GREAT THINGS TO PASS?

I now invite you to reflect on two important questions related to the principles you have learned from this conference:

1. Why do small and simple things bring great things to pass?

2. Why is the spiritual pattern of small and simple things bringing great things to pass so central to living the gospel of Jesus Christ with faith and diligence?

We can learn much about the nature and importance of this spiritual pattern from the technique of drip irrigation that is used in many gardens and in agricultural areas throughout the world. Drip irrigation is sometimes called trickle irrigation and involves dripping water onto the soil at very low rates from a system of small plastic pipes fitted with outlets called emitters or drippers. Unlike surface and sprinkler irrigation that involves flooding or gushing or spraying large quantities of water where it may not be needed, drip irrigation applies water close to a plant so that only part of the soil in which the roots grow is wetted.

With drip irrigation, applications of water are more focused and more frequent than with the other methods. The steady drips of water sink deep into the ground and provide a high moisture level in the soil, wherein plants can flourish. In like manner, if you and I are focused and frequent in receiving consistent drops of spiritual nourishment, then gospel roots can sink deep into our souls, can become firmly established and grounded, and can produce extraordinary and delicious fruit.

The spiritual pattern of small and simple things bringing forth great things produces firmness and steadfastness, deepening devotion, and more complete conversion to the Lord Jesus Christ and His gospel. As you and I become increasingly steadfast and immovable, we are less prone to zealous and exaggerated spurts of spirituality followed by extended periods of slackness. A spiritual "spurter" is one who is given to short bursts of spectacular effort followed by frequent and lengthy periods of rest.

A big spurt may appear to be impressive in the short run, but steadiness in small things over time is far more effective, far less dangerous, and produces far better results. Three consecutive days of fasting ultimately may not be as spiritually efficacious as three successive months of appropriate fasting and worship on the designated fast Sunday—of many small and simple things done consistently well. A great attempt to pray one time for five hours likely will not produce the spiritual results of meaningful morning and evening prayer offered consistently over five weeks—of many small and simple things done consistently well. And a single, great scripture-reading marathon cannot produce the spiritual impact of steady scripture study across many months.

President Spencer W. Kimball taught about the importance of small and simple things in our spiritual development and progress. In explicating the parable of the ten virgins he stated:

"The foolish [virgins] asked the others to share their oil, but spiritual preparedness cannot be shared in an instant. The wise had to go, else the bridegroom would have gone unwelcomed. They needed all their oil for themselves; they could not save the foolish. The responsibility was each for himself.

"This was not selfishness or unkindness. The kind of oil that is needed to illuminate the way and light up the darkness is not shareable. How can one share obedience to the principle of tithing; a mind at peace from righteous living; an accumulation of knowledge? How can one share faith or testimony? How can one share attitudes or chastity, or the experience of a mission? How can one share temple privileges? Each must obtain that kind of oil for himself.

"The foolish virgins were not averse to buying oil. They knew they should have oil. They merely procrastinated, not knowing when the bridegroom would come.

"In the parable, oil can be purchased at the market. In our lives the oil of preparedness is accumulated drop by drop in righteous living. Attendance at sacrament meetings adds oil to our lamps, drop by drop over the years. Fasting, family prayer, home teaching, control of bodily appetites, preaching the gospel, studying the scriptures—each act of dedication and obedience is a drop added to our store. Deeds of kindness, payment of offerings and tithes, chaste thoughts and actions, marriage in the covenant for eternity—these, too, contribute importantly to the oil with which we can at midnight refuel our exhausted lamps."[4]

The key lesson for us to learn from the parable of the ten virgins is that deliberate and consistent preparation and performance provide essential oil for our lamps. By small and simple things are great things brought to pass.

Elder Neal A. Maxwell explained: "Measured steadiness is more efficient than spurts and then a slackening. Further, we are less apt to 'wear away' in prudent persistence than in a combination of breathlessness and ease. Sometimes we may reward our breathlessness with a respite that turns into a permanent repose; we do this by reflecting on all that we have done up to now and how it is surely now someone else's turn."[5]

In a gospel sense, brothers and sisters, you and I need to become intelligent drip irrigators and avoid sporadic and shallow spiritual spurting. We can avoid or overcome unsustainable spiritual spurting as we employ the Lord's pattern of small and simple things and become truly intelligent irrigators.

I conclude now where we began. The Lord declared in the early days of this dispensation, "I will give unto you a pattern in all things, that ye may not be deceived; for Satan is abroad in the land, and he goeth forth deceiving the nations" (D&C 52:14). In a world of increasing wickedness, in a world where good is called evil and evil is called good, in a world "that put[s] darkness for light, and light for darkness" (2 Nephi 15:20), you can be blessed with "the hope of righteousness" (Galatians 5:5), "the light of the Lord" (Isaiah 2:5), and protection against deception (see 1 Nephi 15:24; Helaman 5:12).

As the Savior declared, "Wherefore, be not weary in well-doing, for ye are laying the foundation of a great work. And out of *small things* proceedeth that which is great" (D&C 64:33; emphasis added).

May we all remember the imagery suggested in Doctrine and Covenants 123: "You know, brethren, that a very large ship is benefited very much by a *very small helm* in the time of a storm, by being kept workways with the wind and the waves. Therefore, dearly beloved brethren, let us cheerfully do all things that lie in our power; and then may we stand still, with the utmost assurance, to see the salvation of God, and for his arm to be revealed" (D&C 123:16–17; emphasis added).

I declare my apostolic witness that Jesus the Christ is the light and the life of the world. He lives; I know He lives. I testify that the fulness of His gospel has been restored to the earth in these latter days. And I witness that He speaks and directs the affairs of His living and restored Church through His appointed and anointed servants.

NOTES

1. See L. Tom Perry, "The Value of a Good Name," in *Brigham Young University 1996–97 Speeches* (Provo, Utah: BYU Press, 1997), 179–80.

2. See "Luke Syphus & Christina Long," 167–203, available at http://www.whitneyhistory.com/06_lukesyphus.pdf; accessed 7 September 2011; see also "Pioneer Organ Builder's Story," *Deseret Evening News*, February 16, 1901, 9.
3. See David A. Bednar, "More Diligent and Concerned at Home," *Ensign*, November 2009, 17–20.
4. Spencer W. Kimball, *Faith Precedes the Miracle* (Salt Lake City: Deseret Book, 1972), 255–56.
5. Neal A. Maxwell, *Wherefore, Ye Must Press Forward* (Salt Lake City: Deseret Book, 1977), 74.

"BY SMALL AND SIMPLE THINGS"

Susan K. Bednar

I have been thinking about the lessons, both simple and great, that I learned while I was a student at Brigham Young University—lessons about leaving home, the influence of family and wonderful friends, and the importance of education. I have remembered significant lessons etched in my soul about life and death, love and marriage, covenants and testimony, and parenthood.

In fact, I can tell you where I was in Provo on April 29, 1975, exactly thirty-five years ago. Elder Bednar and I were at the hospital holding our newborn son. You should have seen the big, blue sign Elder Bednar made to hang in our window at married student housing announcing in huge letters, "It's a boy!" I recall my feelings of inadequacy that set in as I thought seriously about the prospects of being a mother and realized that I wasn't totally prepared or sure what to do or how to do it. I just knew that being a parent was part of God's plan, and I knew my mother would arrive soon to help me.

I have also been thinking about the day sixteen months later when my husband and I packed all of our belongings in a Ryder truck and headed to

Susan K. Bednar graduated with a degree in education from Brigham Young University, majoring in elementary education and minoring in music and French. She has served as a ward Primary president, Young Women president, gospel doctrine teacher, ward organist, and Primary chorister. She and her husband, Elder David A. Bednar, are the parents of three sons.

Indiana so he could attend graduate school. Feelings of sadness tugged at our hearts, but we each had the distinct impression and assurance that we would be back in Provo someday. It is a good thing we didn't know then what the phrase "be back in Provo" would mean for us more than three decades later.

I feel that I should share a simple yet great lesson learned during our time spent in Indiana that has continued to bless my life in countless ways. Come with me to my busy life as a young wife and mother. Elder Bednar was enrolled in a demanding doctoral program at Purdue University far away from our families. We had an energetic two-year-old and a young baby, very little money, and hardly any time to spend together as a family. As we struggled to balance family responsibilities, the rigors of school, and Church callings, I became more and more overwhelmed with my duties as a wife and a stay-at-home mother. Many of you may have experienced some of these same emotions and frustrations.

After considerable pondering about my situation, I asked my husband for a priesthood blessing. I was promised in the blessing that if I would exercise, get more sleep, eat regular meals, have meaningful prayer morning and night, and engage in more purposeful and consistent scripture study, I would receive the physical and spiritual tools to better cope with my circumstances and the discouragement I was feeling. The reason I remember the blessing so clearly is because I thought afterward: "Doing this is going to solve my problems? These are typical 'Sunday School' answers."

In my prideful state of mind, I rationalized why I didn't need any more exercise because chasing little boys around all day was exercise enough, why I couldn't get more sleep because of their young ages, and why I couldn't eat properly every single day because I was just too busy taking care of their needs, and, frankly, I sometimes forgot to eat breakfast. Since I was already saying my prayers and reading my scriptures most of the time, that part of the blessing was not even applicable to me.

I suppose you could say I was like Naaman in the Old Testament, who was sent to the king of Israel to be healed of his leprosy but instead was told by a messenger sent by the prophet Elisha to wash in Jordan seven times. Naaman refused to comply with the simple, prophetic injunction until his servants questioned his motives. "And his servants came near, and spake unto him, and said, My father, if the prophet had bid thee do some great thing, wouldest thou not have done it?" (2 Kings 5:13).

I am sure if I had been directed to do some great thing like go on a relaxing Hawaiian cruise, or enroll in an evening art or music class, or pamper myself with a new hairdo and a pedicure, I would have seen the wisdom in responding to that kind of inspiration. But the small and simple steps that were required to receive the promised blessings seemed so mundane to me.

Thankfully, humility took root. Over time I had to decide if I would continue on the path of just going through the motions, or if I would accept and incorporate this guidance in a more steadfast and heartfelt way, having faith that doing these things really could make a difference.

Over the years, I have found that retiring earlier at night and rising earlier in the morning invigorates the mind and body (see D&C 88:124). Regular exercise lifts my spirit, clears my mind, and gives me added energy to meet the demands of my busy schedule. I can "run and not be weary, and . . . walk and not faint" (D&C 89:20). Proper physical nourishment is an important key to unlocking spiritual "treasures of knowledge, even hidden treasures" (D&C 89:19).

I am grateful for the lessons I have learned about asking in faith through meaningful prayer, not just saying prayers. "Be thou humble; and the Lord thy God shall lead thee by the hand, and give thee answer to thy prayers" (D&C 112:10).

I know and testify that I have heard the voice of the Lord speaking to me through the scriptures as I have paid the price of more diligent, meaningful, and consistent gospel study (see D&C 18:34–36). I have felt the power and strength of Christ's word in me as I have faced the challenges and vicissitudes of life (see Alma 26:12–13).

I know by sad experience how easy it is to nudge off our plate of daily responsibilities these small and simple things that can make such a great difference. I know as we apply these powerful principles, the blessings come. "By small and simple things are great things brought to pass" (Alma 37:6).

It was a small yet grand desire in the heart of a young boy, the courage to ask in faith an inspired question, and the resolve to do what God instructed him to do that has brought about this great gathering of faithful women. I know that Joseph Smith saw the Father and the Son in the Sacred Grove. I know that through him the true gospel of Jesus Christ has been restored. I witness that God continues to speak today to living prophets and apostles. And lastly, I testify that Elder Bednar has been called of God, by prophecy, and has been ordained to be a special witness of the name of Jesus Christ in all the world.

Our Goals and Our Weaknesses

Cecil O. Samuelson

Two "one-liner" quotes from wonderful leaders of the past no longer with us will be familiar to most of us but deserve repeating often and especially today. The first, from Sister Barbara Smith, a former Relief Society general president, is perfectly positioned as a key reminder to all of us in our daily strivings: "Ideals are stars to steer by; they are not a stick to beat ourselves with."[1] The second is the wonderful observation of Elder Neal A. Maxwell, who said that "the Church . . . is not a well-provisioned rest home for the already perfected."[2] Both of these statements introduce and affirm the counsel and considerations I would like to share with you.

Our clear doctrinal aspiration for eternal progression and ultimate perfection must not be confused with the reality of daily living. This involves not only the external challenges and difficulties we all face but also our current personal limitations and weaknesses that affect our abilities to deal with our lives in an optimal way. The good news is that this is the way it is supposed to be!

Cecil O. Samuelson is the president of Brigham Young University and an emeritus member of the First Quorum of the Seventy. He received his MD from the University of Utah, and fulfilled his residency and held a fellowship at Duke University Medical Center. He taught medicine at the University of Utah, where he served as dean of the medical school, and as vice president of health sciences. At the time of his call to the First Quorum of the Seventy in 1994, he was a senior vice president at Intermountain Health Care. He and his wife, Sharon G. Samuelson, have five children and twelve grandchildren.

Our Heavenly Father did not send us into our current situations to punish us. He did send us here to gain the experiences, knowledge, and personal characteristics essential for eternal life. He also recognized the need for us to be tested and challenged and wants us to understand this essential dynamic of our personal development as well.

While perhaps understandable in the abstract, dealing with the realities surrounding our circumstances and our own limitations still is not easy when we consider what the expectations of Heaven are for us and what we would like to achieve and accomplish. Over the years, I have come to better understand and more closely relate to the feelings that Nephi expressed during the early days of his family's sojourn in the Western Hemisphere.

After their arrival, Father Lehi in his aged condition counseled and blessed his growing posterity and then he died. Laman and Lemuel and the sons of Ishmael were not pleased with the role of leadership that Nephi was charged by the Lord to assume (see 1 Nephi 2:22) and there was tremendous conflict in the large family. Notwithstanding these troubles, Nephi took comfort in the scriptures and what he had learned from the ministrations of the Lord and His angels. Let me share his words. This is a long passage but worth our very careful consideration. I believe his lament and reconciliation were very significant components of the less than "hundredth part" (Words of Mormon 1:5) that Mormon could include in our current text of the Book of Mormon. Therefore, we should carefully ponder the words and "liken" or apply them (1 Nephi 19:23) to ourselves. These are Nephi's feelings:

"Nevertheless, notwithstanding the great goodness of the Lord, in showing me his great and marvelous works, my heart exclaimeth: O wretched man that I am! Yea, my heart sorroweth because of my flesh; my soul grieveth because of mine iniquities.

"I am encompassed about, because of the temptations and the sins which do so easily beset me.

"And when I desire to rejoice, my heart groaneth because of my sins; nevertheless, I know in whom I have trusted.

"My God hath been my support; he hath led me through mine afflictions in the wilderness; and he hath preserved me upon the waters of the great deep.

"He hath filled me with his love, even unto the consuming of my flesh.

"He hath confounded mine enemies, unto the causing of them to quake before me.

"Behold, he hath heard my cry by day, and he hath given me knowledge by visions in the night-time.

"And by day have I waxed bold in mighty prayer before him; yea, my voice have I sent up on high; and angels came down and ministered unto me.

"And upon the wings of his Spirit hath my body been carried away upon exceedingly high mountains. And mine eyes have beheld great things, yea, even too great for man; therefore I was bidden that I should not write them.

"O then, if I have seen so great things, if the Lord in his condescension unto the children of men hath visited men in so much mercy, why should my heart weep and my soul linger in the valley of sorrow, and my flesh waste away, and my strength slacken, because of mine afflictions?

"And why should I yield to sin, because of my flesh? Yea, why should I give way to temptations, that the evil one have place in my heart to destroy my peace and afflict my soul? Why am I angry because of mine enemy?

"Awake, my soul! No longer droop in sin. Rejoice, O my heart, and give place no more for the enemy of my soul.

"Do not anger again because of mine enemies. Do not slacken my strength because of mine afflictions.

"Rejoice, O my heart, and cry unto the Lord, and say: O Lord, I will praise thee forever; yea, my soul will rejoice in thee, my God, and the rock of my salvation.

"O Lord, wilt thou redeem my soul? Wilt thou deliver me out of the hands of mine enemies? Wilt thou make me that I may shake at the appearance of sin?

"May the gates of hell be shut continually before me, because that my heart is broken and my spirit is contrite! O Lord, wilt thou not shut the gates of thy righteousness before me, that I may walk in the path of the low valley, that I may be strict in the plain road!

"O Lord, wilt thou encircle me around in the robe of thy

righteousness! O Lord, wilt thou make a way for mine escape before mine enemies! Wilt thou make my path straight before me! Wilt thou not place a stumbling block in my way—but that thou wouldst clear my way before me, and hedge not up my way, but the ways of mine enemy.

"O Lord, I have trusted in thee, and I will trust in thee forever. I will not put my trust in the arm of flesh; for I know that cursed is he that putteth his trust in the arm of flesh. Yea, cursed is he that putteth his trust in man or maketh flesh his arm.

"Yea, I know that God will give liberally to him that asketh. Yea, my God will give me, if I ask not amiss; therefore I will lift up my voice unto thee; yea, I will cry unto thee, my God, the rock of my righteousness. Behold, my voice shall forever ascend up unto thee, my rock and mine everlasting God. Amen" (2 Nephi 4:17–35).

Happily, none of us finds ourselves in the exact situation or with the same difficulties as Nephi. It is sobering, however, that each of us has her or his own "thorn in the flesh" (2 Corinthians 12:7) and sometimes multiple thorns that are more than a little prickly! Nevertheless, the expressions of Nephi are ones with which we can and should relate. Like all of us, the scriptural record suggests that Nephi came to his understanding and maturation gradually, "line upon line, precept upon precept" (D&C 98:12), and it was never a completely direct or finished journey. He faced disappointments, sadness, surprises, and occasionally great joy. Likely, in reflection on our own circumstances, we can relate to this very wide spectrum of experiences, expectations, and finally clarity that in spite of our shortcomings, we are known and loved by Heavenly Father and the Savior, who never give up on us.

Having made these observations, we must also acknowledge that our own goals or the expectations of the Father and the Son are not modest but are very stretching and even considered by some to be impossible to accomplish for real people like ourselves and those we know and love. After all, it was Jesus Himself who summarized the first part of His Sermon on the Mount with the injunction, "Be ye therefore perfect, even as your Father which is in heaven is perfect" (Matthew 5:48). Gratefully, through modern revelation and prophetic insights, we are able to understand that the goal, while completely clear, has dimensions and timing that we may not fully understand. For example, the footnote to our Latter-day Saint scriptures points out that this perfection should be viewed in terms of being complete, finished, or fully developed (see Matthew 5:48b).

In a November 1831 conference of the Church, the Prophet Joseph Smith received clarifying revelation for a group of early Saints which likely describes and should enlighten most of us today as well:

"Ye are not able to abide the presence of God now, neither the ministering of angels; wherefore, continue in patience until ye are perfected" (D&C 67:13).

Some of you have already experienced the blessing of ministering angels and are acquainted with the instructions and inspiration of the Holy Ghost, but even for those so blessed, the instruction to "continue in patience" is most appropriate because as of yet, none of us is fully perfected.

The scriptures have dealt with the ideas and notions of perfection in various ways. Most deal with the ideal of eventual perfection through living the gospel and experiencing the blessings of the Savior's atonement. In addition, references are made to certain stalwarts and prophets as being perfect. Captain Moroni is described as "a man of a perfect understanding" (Alma 48:11). Adam and his son Seth (D&C 107:42–43), Noah (Moses 8:27), and even Job (Job 1:1) are described in various ways as being perfect men in their own times and places. While we understand that the Savior Jesus Christ is the only mortal ever born who was completely without sin or blemish, others, including ourselves, can rightly aspire and become perfect—at least in some things.

Because the law of tithing, for example, is clear and the standard is well understood, all of us can be perfect in living this commandment. It may not be easy and requires sacrifice and often adjustment in our attitudes and priorities, but it is possible. The Word of Wisdom, fulfilling certain assignments, and the like are areas where it is reasonable for us to expect achieving perfection even while we continue to struggle with what Jesus described as the "weightier matters of the law" (Matthew 23:23). However, and this is a critical point, we must also acknowledge that for various reasons it is not at all likely we will achieve full and actual perfection in every area of our lives no matter how long we live in mortality. Thank goodness for the atonement of Jesus Christ that provides the rescue we all will need and welcome to reach our eventual goals.

It is part of the human condition and Heavenly Father's plan of salvation for us to be required to make decisions constantly. Many of them are not easy, especially at the outset. Most of our choices, in fact, are not between absolute rights and wrongs, but between various shades of options that have multiple positive and negative components and implications. What should we make of all of this? Should we just give up? Should we just acknowledge our imperfections and go with the flow, as so many in society seem to be doing? The answer to each of these queries is obviously no, but then what are we to do?

The answer is deceptively simple: we must do the best we can and then depend upon the Lord to help us make up the difference. While this statement is intellectually and even spiritually acceptable, for many of us it creates some practical problems or issues. Let me raise one that perhaps does not receive adequate attention. We often discuss the challenge of dealing with those who have low expectations for themselves, who seem to strive to just get by or are casual in keeping their commitments and covenants. These are real problems and deserve attention and consideration. I am not an advocate for mediocrity, nor do I think that our Heavenly Father and the Savior are happy when they see us as satisfied with less than our best efforts.

The matter that I do wish to raise is what mental health professionals describe as "perfectionism." In most ways, perfectionism is the opposite of carelessness, casualness, or any form of low expectations. In fact, it is a condition where anything less than perfect is unacceptable to the person so disposed. For those so oriented or afflicted, life is mostly miserable because people and the world are usually imperfect even in the face of being largely good.

One of the tragedies of perfectionism is that those so oriented are often among the most accomplished and talented among us. Frequently they were precocious children, superior students, and model young adults who have done everything asked of them very well and yet sadly are not satisfied because they have developed unrealistic and even extreme views of what is expected or even required of them. Some become obsessed with their every thought, behavior, action, or perceived mistake and so make their lives miserable and distressing for those who love them and wish to help them.

A characteristic of those trying to deal with perfectionism is common to all people. That is, self-perceptions frequently differ from those of others. Many of the casually focused folk mentioned before seem to feel whatever they do or do not do is just fine. Those suffering from perfectionism tend to be wonderful, contributing, and effective people, and yet may feel that no matter what they do it is never enough. Although very good people, they often suffer from exaggerating their minor errors or mistakes, weaknesses, shortcomings, or perceived failures to the point that they are not only very miserable but may become dysfunctional and unable to cope with the activities of daily living.

One of the unintended consequences of our efforts to help or challenge those whose standards for themselves may be too low, is that it is possible to exacerbate the distress of those suffering with perfectionism. When they hear or observe the admonitions given to those who need the encouragement to do better, they often feel they are the intended audience. They are not!

Those dealing with perfectionism need encouragement to be realistic and to find joy in their earnest but imperfect efforts. In our desires to encourage and motivate, we must understand that people are unique—one size never fits all.

For many dealing with perfectionism issues, there may be sincere confusion about the relationship between the notions of worthiness on one hand and perfection on the other. These are not synonyms! One does not need to be perfect in every dimension to be worthy of a temple recommend, for example. All of us, including the best among us—those we hold up as wonderful models and examples—are "works in process." Even when we are fully worthy, we can still improve. We must strive to be completely worthy now but must be realistically patient in recognizing that full perfection in every dimension of our lives and aspirations is yet to come for every one of us.

The scriptures describe the straight and narrow path. (See 2 Nephi 31:9.) This should help us remember that we are on a journey and the correctness of our direction is most fundamental, wherever we find ourselves positioned on the road of life today. While we must not disregard the Savior's expectations for us or the standards of the commandments, we also must not dishonor them by establishing requirements or obligations that reach "beyond the mark" (Jacob 4:14). Just as Jesus demonstrated approval of the early progress of newly repentant imperfect sinners (see John 8:3–11), we need to be sure that we find satisfaction in the progress of tiny positive steps while acknowledging that perfection may still be quite distant.

As I have discussed this topic on other occasions, I have tried to be clear that we should not be against humility, modesty, or honest recognition of our shortcomings. These are cardinal and important virtues. Jesus taught that we should be meek, but never suggested we should be masochistic. The problem with becoming obsessed with our deficiencies and weaknesses is that of necessity we neglect virtually everything else. Our lives lose balance and our quest toward eventual perfection is thwarted. We must never let the bad or the imperfect overwhelm the good we do and the places where we are on track.

The Lord has a pattern of success for us and it is that we follow Him with devotion and also understanding. Think of this inspiring counsel and promise:

"And if men come unto me I will show unto them their weakness. I give unto men weakness that they may be humble; and my grace is sufficient for all men that humble themselves before me; for if they humble themselves before me, and have faith in me, then will I make weak things become strong unto them" (Ether 12:27).

While we need to recognize our weaknesses, we must not glory in them, magnify them, or find excuse for less than our best because of them. And for some of our challenges, including perfectionism, we may need to get early help from both priesthood leaders and skilled professionals.

King Benjamin, in his great benedictory address (see Mosiah 2–4), was clear and direct in his high expectations for his people and in his explanations of the requirements of the Lord to achieve the full benefits of the Atonement. Recognizing this relationship, we must also gratefully appreciate the concluding comments of this very wise and loyal servant of the Lord.

"And see that all these things are done in wisdom and order; for it is not requisite that a man should run faster than he has strength" (Mosiah 4:27).

Likewise, the Prophet Joseph Smith was not perfect by his own admission, but may have had some perfectionist tendencies in his absolute desire and commitment to fulfill his prophetic calling with excellence.

You will recall the sad saga that occurred in the summer of 1828. One hundred sixteen pages of the early translation manuscript of the "Book of Lehi" had been lost by Martin Harris and the Lord had severely chastised Joseph for this lapse in care and judgment. In fact, the gift of translation was temporarily removed from him. After very serious repentance, the gift and charge to translate the Book of Mormon were restored and Joseph was extremely anxious to move forward. Now, in this context, contemplate the Lord's counsel:

"Do not run faster or labor more than you have strength and means . . . but be diligent unto the end" (D&C 10:4).

We can and must always be diligent but we also must be realistic about our strength and our resources. I also take comfort and find instructive insight in the words of the Lord when He was teaching the Saints of this hemisphere shortly after His resurrection. In speaking to the people, He described them as "weak" (3 Nephi 17:2) and yet he also said to them, "I see that your faith is sufficient that I should heal you" (3 Nephi 17:8). He didn't say because you are weak you cannot be healed. He also did not say that their faith was perfect so that they could be healed. He described their faith as "sufficient" and such faith is attainable by all of us. The scripture then goes on to offer this description of the Savior's actions:

"And it came to pass that when he had thus spoken, all the multitude, with one accord, did go forth with their sick and their afflicted, and their lame, and with their blind, and with their dumb, and with all them that were afflicted *in any manner*; and he did heal them every one as they were brought forth unto him" (3 Nephi 17:9; emphasis added).

Jesus healed all of them without restriction to their condition or their difficulty. The same blessings can be available to us. We need to recognize that the timing and the manner will be in the Lord's way and not dictated by our wishes. Our sufficient faith appears to be an important prerequisite that everyone can achieve.

Thus I return to where we began. We must have ideals to guide us and lead us but not to distract or punish ourselves. Likewise, the Savior's Church which we represent is not a repository of perfect people but is His organization, designed to help us along the road to continuous improvement and qualification for every blessing possible, including eventual perfection, through the perfect atonement of Jesus Christ and the perfect graciousness of our loving Heavenly Father.

That we all might be wise, thoughtful, careful, patient, and realistic in all that we do and try to do is my prayer.

NOTES

1. "A Conversation with Sister Barbara B. Smith, Relief Society General President," *Ensign*, March 1976, 8.
2. Neal A. Maxwell, "'A Brother Offended,'" *Ensign*, May 1982, 38.

SCRIPTURAL HEROINES

S. Michael Wilcox

I particularly love discussing the women of the scriptures. There are so very many stories, in the Bible especially, that lift and edify us whether we are men or women. There are so many lovely examples. They can be particularly edifying for women.

OUT OF SMALL THINGS

The theme for the 2011 BYU Women's Conference is "by small and simple things are great things brought to pass" (Alma 37:6–7). It brings to mind also the scripture "out of small things proceedeth that which is great" (D&C 64:33). Usually when the Lord uses that phrase he is commenting on people, not events. In a sense, a woman or a man *is* a small thing. We are all small things. I am a small thing. You are a small thing. But out of small things—individual lives—out of mothers, sisters, daughters, grandmothers, out of the women of the scriptures, great things have happened and God has worked wonders with individuals who, under

S. Michael Wilcox received his Ph.D. from the University of Colorado and taught for many years at the Institute of Religion adjacent to the University of Utah. He has spoken to packed crowds at BYU Education Week and has hosted tours to the Holy Land and to Church history sites. He has served in a variety of callings, including as bishop and counselor in a stake presidency. He has written many articles and books, including Walking on Water and Other Messages, What the Scriptures Teach Us about Adversity, *and* House of Glory. *He and his late wife, Laurie, are the parents of five children.*

normal circumstances, would be considered perhaps unimportant. I decided that I would read through Genesis, just the first book in the Bible, and choose some of the tales of the women who lived during those early days to see what they have to teach us. Taken as a whole, it seems as if they teach us truths about the value and the worth of women so that both men and women know something about how important they are.

EVE—FIRST HELPMEET

Eve is introduced with these words, "And the Lord God said, It is not good that the man should be alone" (Genesis 2:18). That is a doctrinal statement. In the April 2011 general conference, President Thomas S. Monson, Elder Richard G. Scott, and others taught that principle fairly forcefully to the young unmarried men. It is not good that the man should be alone. We, as males, need help. The book of Moses renders the next sentence slightly differently than does Genesis. The word "wherefore" is added (Moses 3:18). I think the wording is very critical: "Wherefore, I will make . . ." Let me pause here before finishing the sentence and ask you a question. Does the Lord say, "I will make an help *mate* for him," "an *help-meet* for him," or does he say, "an help *meet* for him"? Most of the time we do not separate the two words, but it is always two words in the scriptural accounts. Woman is not an helpmate, or an helpmeet, she is an help meet. We should always pause a little between the two words when we read this description of Eve.

Help in the Hebrew means a number of things—to aid to be sure, but also "to surround and to protect." She provides help that is surrounding and protecting in nature which corresponds so perfectly with the natural qualities of women. Think about that influence in the life of a child or a husband. The word translated in the Bible as *meet* has about fifteen different English words which can be used as synonyms. It suggests "equal to"—meaning equal to the man, but also equal to the task, sufficient, suitable, becoming, right, fit, proper, worthy, sufficient, competent, necessary, satisfying, complementary, and to make whole. Woman—Eve in this case—was a help, a surrounding, protecting help that fit all of those synonyms.

DEEP SLEEP

We are taught about the value and importance of womanhood in the environment in which Eve is brought to Adam. That setting is described in the words "deep sleep." Eve is brought to Adam while he is in a deep sleep. Here is the critical phrase: "And the Lord God caused a deep sleep to fall upon Adam" (Genesis 2:21). I think far too often we read the scriptures so literally that we miss the greater power that can be found in them when we allow the figurative meanings to have equal time. We have the idea that Adam is asleep in the same way that we sleep each night, and he wakes up and there she is. We might obtain additional insight by looking at the other times in the Bible that this phrase is used. Each time the phrase "deep sleep" is used in other scriptures, the individual described is fully awake—they are not asleep, but in a revelatory state. It is used of Abraham when he receives a very important revelation about his posterity (see Genesis 15:12). It is used twice in Daniel when he is receiving knowledge and visions and communication. During this exchange he is speaking and God is speaking to him (see Daniel 8:18; 10:9). That is the truer meaning of deep sleep. I don't like the word *trance,* but there are similarities. I like the expression "deep sleep" much more, but we need to be careful of a too-literal reading. Perhaps two other experiences may provide additional insight.

Joseph Smith used an interesting phrase to describe his state after the First Vision: "When I came to myself" (JS–H 1:20). That is a telling phrase worth pondering. He had been in communication with the Father and the Son and the surroundings faded away, in a manner of speaking. The environment was different for this critical revelation. What was important was what was being communicated to Joseph Smith and the normal setting was enhanced or changed by the Spirit. "When I came to myself," Joseph wrote—or we might say, putting that phrase into Old Testament words, "When I came out of a deep sleep."

Notice Paul's words when he described a vision he received of the celestial kingdom: "I knew a man in Christ above fourteen years ago, (whether in the body, I cannot tell; or whether out of the body, I cannot tell: God knoweth;)" (2 Corinthians 12:2). When we read the phrase "deep sleep" we must think of these types of experiences. Eve is brought to Adam when he is in a revelatory, removed-from-this-world state. If you think about it, the holiest, most sacred spot on earth is a sealing room in a temple, where men and women are bound and united. They're united in an environment of "deep sleep." What a powerful statement about the nature of women and of marriage.

EVE OR EDEN

When Eve was brought to Adam, he said, "This is now bone of my bones, and flesh of my flesh: she shall be called Woman, because she was taken out of Man" (Genesis 2:23).

She is my kind—my species, if you like—Adam is saying, as well as a part of me. And then a conclusion, "Therefore shall a man leave his father and his mother, and shall cleave unto his wife: and they shall be one flesh" (Genesis 2:24).

I don't want to push this too far, but if you think about it, the first great decision made on earth was Adam's decision to leave the Garden of Eden. In doing so he essentially left his Father to cleave to his wife. Given the choice of Eden or Eve, the paradise or the person, he chose Eve. He chose the person. I have a feeling—at least I have felt so more recently— that it wasn't so much Adam leaving his paradisiacal situation so that "men might be" (2 Nephi 2:25) that was so critical in Adam's mind as it was leaving this woman whom he loved. He left his paradisiacal situation, with its fuller communion with God, so that he would not be "a lone man" in the Garden of Eden without Eve. He wanted to remain with her. If we think about it, and ponder the reason Adam gives the Father for partaking of the fruit, we find insight. The reason that he left, the one he stated to the Lord at any rate, is not, "I partook of the fruit so man might be," as true doctrinally as that is. Rather he said, "I took of the fruit because you commanded me to remain with Eve." We might add him saying, "I wanted to remain with Eve." The value and the importance of womanhood are surely being shown to us in this first story of all scripture.

REBEKAH—A GIRL TO BE WONDERED AT

If I had to pick my favorite of all the women in the scriptures it would be a hard choice, but I think it would come down to two women of Genesis—Rebekah and Rachel. Can I have two favorites, or is that a contradiction in terms? I waver between those two. I love the story of Rebekah and the ten camels because the story of Rebekah—as well as the story of Rachel—suggests the tremendous worth and value of little things, in this case of shepherd girls, out of whom great things will come.

Abraham needs a wife for his son Isaac—a matriarch for this great generational line that is going to be a major channel through which God will reveal His words to mankind, to His children. Abraham sends his servant about 500 miles across fairly dangerous and difficult terrain to find a proper wife. Just the distance with its dangers, alone, is a strong suggestion of how important these women are. The servant takes ten camels for his journey and departs at Abraham's instruction. We read in Genesis 24:11, "And he made his camels to kneel down without the city by a well of water at the time of the evening, even the time that women go out to draw water." The critical moment has arrived and the servant prays, "O Lord God of my master Abraham, I pray thee, send me good speed this day." I love the next few words, "and *shew kindness* unto my master Abraham" (Genesis 24:12; emphasis added).

Of what kindness does he speak? I think we can all understand it. I have prayed since the day my boys were born that God would show kindness to me and let them marry righteous women. I've been picking daughters-in-law for thirty-five years, and when you teach college you see a lot of really wonderful ones. For some reason my sons want to pick their own, but I have thought more times than I can recount, "Here is a really fine girl! How I would love to have her in my family."

The servant continues his prayer: "I stand here by the well of water; and the daughters of the men of the city come out to draw water: And let it come to pass, that the damsel [this word indicates she is young; Rebekah is probably in her mid-teens] to whom I shall say, Let down thy pitcher, I pray thee, that I may drink; and she shall say, Drink, and I will give thy camels drink also: let the same be she that thou hast appointed for thy servant Isaac; and thereby shall I know that thou hast shewed kindness unto my master" (Genesis 24:13–14).

He is not asking for a sign as much as a show of character. He's going to ask for a drink of water, which is a very common thing to happen in the Middle East. It's a hot, dry climate. But the proper girl needs to volunteer to water ten camels. Camels can drink a lot of water, gallons of it. At a zoo one day, I read a sign in front of the camel enclosure that stated a camel can drink up to thirty-five gallons. Just for argument's sake, let's say they're not terribly thirsty. They only have a ten-gallon thirst. Rebekah is going to draw a lot of water—and she has to volunteer to do it.

"It came to pass, [as he was] speaking, that, behold, Rebekah came out. . . . And the damsel was very fair to look upon" (Genesis 24:15–16). Notice carefully the wording now: "She went down to the well." Down! Do you picture the well at the bottom of stairs or at the bottom of a hill? It's always good to picture the stories of the scriptures. "She went down to the well, and filled her pitcher, and came up" (Genesis 24:16). So it appears that the well is at a lower level than where the camels and everybody are sitting. "Down to the well . . . and came up." I picture stairs.

"And the servant ran to meet her, and said, Let me, I pray thee, drink a little water of thy pitcher. And she said, Drink, my lord: and she hasted" (Genesis 24:17–18). I love that word *hasted*. It shows eagerness in Rebekah. It isn't the fact that Rebekah served so willingly that draws our attention and our soul to her. It is the eagerness, the "hasted" aspect that is so wonderful. "And when she had done giving him drink, she said, I will draw water for thy camels also, until they have done drinking. And she hasted"—picture this now—"and emptied her pitcher into the trough, and ran again unto the well" (Genesis 24:19–20). If you're running to the well from the trough there has to be a distance between the trough and the well. "And ran again unto the well to draw water, and drew for all his camels" (Genesis 24:20). Can you see that? Down, up, over, empty, down, up, over, empty. It's a wonderful image of womanhood. It is simply splendid! Such a simple action—the watering of camels! It is one of those little things out of which comes greatness. This is one of the most remarkable images in scripture, and we are invited to respond to that image of eager service which makes this one woman great, even though she's young, probably fifteen or sixteen. As a representative of her gender, she stands for all women.

"The man wondering at her held his peace, to wit whether the Lord had made his journey prosperous or not" (Genesis 24:21). We know the story; she waters all ten camels. We marvel and wonder at her today. I also wonder if Rebekah had any idea that for four thousand years of history, people would watch her water those ten camels and be inspired by her—that her whole destiny depended on this unrehearsed demonstration of character which she would display as she walked to the well that day.

RACHEL—SEVEN-YEAR BRIDE

A few chapters later the same long journey to obtain a worthy, righteous wife is made by Jacob at the urging of his mother Rebekah. Esau had married with the local Canaanite population, much to the distress of his mother. She could not bear the thought of a repeat alliance in Jacob's life. As she says, "I am weary of my life because of the daughters of Heth: if Jacob take a wife . . . such as these which are of the daughters of the land, what good shall my life do me?" (Genesis 27:46). Rebekah carries the story forward through Genesis. With all due respect to Isaac, it is really Rebekah who moves the family's commitment forward in Genesis. Her fervor is passed on to Jacob. Let us turn to the story of Jacob and his beloved Rachel.

We are introduced to Rachel in Genesis 29. Jacob has duplicated the journey Abraham's servant took in finding Rebekah. He also stops at a well. It seems there are many great women in the Bible in the vicinity of a well. Rebekah, Rachel, Zipporah, others—they are all at the well. I used to tell the young men at the institute, "You need to hang around the drinking fountain because that's where you'll find the really good wives." While Jacob is resting at the well from his long journey, Rachel arrives with her father's sheep. "And Jacob kissed Rachel, and lifted up his voice, and wept. And Jacob told Rachel that he was her father's brother, and that he was Rebekah's son: and she ran and told her father" (Genesis 29:11–12). Laban then greets Jacob and soon the true goal of Jacob's journey is revealed. We are introduced to a marvelous story of love. This is, I believe, the most beautiful love story in all literature, and as an English major and lover of history, I have read many of them. With all due respect to *Romeo and Juliet,* or Robert and Elizabeth Browning, this is a remarkably beautiful one.

"And Laban said to him, Surely thou art my bone and my flesh. And he abode with him the space of a month" (Genesis 29:14). It only took a month of Jacob looking at Rachel to understand who he wanted. Just a month! And his desire, I am confident, did not only have to do with her beauty and his mother's instructions. "And Laban said unto Jacob, Because thou art my brother, shouldest thou therefore serve me for nought? tell me, what shall thy wages be? And Laban had two daughters: the name of the elder was Leah, and the name of the younger was Rachel. . . . Rachel was beautiful and well favoured. And Jacob loved Rachel; and said, I will serve thee seven years for Rachel thy younger daughter" (Genesis 29:15–18).

Now just think about that for a little while—seven years! Later in Genesis, as Jacob defends himself against Laban, he helps us understand in a small way what that labor was like. It was difficult labor, demanding, hard. "In the day the drought consumed me," he said, "and the frost by night; and my sleep departed from mine eyes" (Genesis 31:40). How do you think Rachel felt watching Jacob going out every day to take care of the flocks, knowing that every minute he was laboring for her?

When I was a boy we watched the first great Mormon movie, the classic of Mormon movie classics. Do you remember what it was? *Johnny Lingo.* Eight-cow wife! What a marvelous message it conveyed. As boys, our favorite line was, "Mahana, you ugly." I was ten or eleven, I think. Johnny Lingo gives eight cows to Mahana's father because he more than anyone else knew her worth. Well, true stories are generally more powerful than made-up ones. I love *Johnny Lingo.*[1] It teaches a tremendous lesson, but I leave it to you: Would you rather be eight-cow wives or seven-year wives? Seven years—seven long difficult years of earnest labor!

We return to Genesis: "And Laban said, It is better that I give her to thee, than that I should give her to another man: abide with me" (Genesis 29:19). Remain with me, Jacob, labor for me, and the desire of your heart will be yours. Though technically Jacob was laboring for Laban, we know what his central motivation was and for whom his efforts were extended. "And Jacob served seven years for Rachel" (Genesis 29:20). I pause here because I want to give proper emphasis to the next phrase. I think it is the most romantic—if I can use that word in this context—phrase in all literature. Here it is: "and they seemed unto him but a few days, for the love he had to her." That verse never fails to move me, even though I have read it probably over a thousand times. So Jacob gives Laban his seven years as Rachel waits and watches. In time the years are accomplished, "and Jacob said unto Laban, Give me my wife, for my days are fulfilled"

(Genesis 29:20–21). What a beautiful story! I have pondered those tender words, "and they seemed unto him but a few days, for the love he had to her," a great deal. Do they mean that the time seemed short? Perhaps. Probably. Do they mean that the required labor did not seem like such a long time to serve because the wages were well worth the effort? I like that thought—not so much that the time was short for him, which it apparently was, but that he received something so great for seven short years. Almost as if somebody came to Jacob and said to him, "Jacob, how did you ever get such a wonderful wife? How did you ever win Rachel? What did you have to do?"

He would reply, "I only had to work seven years."

"That little for Rachel! Only seven years? A bargain!"

Perhaps I can illustrate with a statement by Wilford Woodruff. He once, when addressing the priesthood, explained the value of a covenant-worthy woman: "Bless your souls, if you lived here in the flesh a thousand years, as long as Father Adam, and lived and labored all your life in poverty, and when you got through, if, by your acts, you could secure your wives and children in the morning of the first resurrection, to dwell with you in the presence of God, that one thing would amply pay you for the labors of a thousand years."[2]

MY OWN RACHEL

I have loved this story for as long as I can remember. I have called my own wife "my Rachel" since the first time I met her. Laurie passed away on December 28, 2010, and since then this story has come to mean a great deal more to me. It is my lifeline, tethered to my survival, to all my happiness and hope. There are many emotions that I have gone through over the last months: sorrow, grief, fear, doubt, questions, hopes, certainly deeper love, but among them all there is one stable, solid thing that I have hung on to. It is a prayer that I offer daily to the Lord: "Father in Heaven, let me be a Jacob to your Laban and labor for my Rachel that she might be mine forever. It matters not how long I must be separated from her, how long I labor, as long as one day I can say to thee as Jacob said to Laban, 'Give me my wife, for my days are fulfilled' (Genesis 29:21)."

Now people will say to me, "You were sealed in the temple. She is already your Rachel for eternity."

And I will reply, "Yes, I understand that. The happiest day of my life, the climax, the pinnacle of my eternal journey was that day. However, grief does unexpected things to the soul. It can create fears and doubts and hungers. For me in my present situation the story in Genesis, the desire to labor for Laurie and the link to her in my mind with Rachel is deeper in my soul than faith in temple covenants—and I have a powerful faith in temple covenants. Yet there is something consoling in my belief in this story and how it applies to my own life. If I live another four decades, and I may, it will be a small price to pay for my Rachel."

You are all Rachels! That is the core of my testimony today. You are all worth the seven years. This is one of the great lessons of Genesis, a central theme given early in the scriptural canon because of its extreme importance. This truth I personally bear witness to, and that out of the deepest sorrows and desires of my heart. Laurie's passing has taught me a great deal about those seven years.

I visited Rachel's Tomb in Israel recently and read the words of Jeremiah which are written thereon. They were God's answer to my deepest hopes, his balm to my questioning, fearing heart. "Refrain thy voice from weeping, and thine eyes from tears: for thy work shall be rewarded, saith the Lord. . . . And there is hope in thine end, saith the Lord" (Jeremiah 31:16–17).

Hagar—"God Hears"

A little earlier in Genesis we learn something else about the value of women from the account of a woman named Hagar, found in Genesis 21. For Christians and Jews, Hagar is one of the women who are not always understood or valued as well as others. If you are Muslim—and there are one and a half billion of them in the world—she is the mother, the great mother of the Muslim people. She occupies a central position in Islam, and she teaches a great lesson that we receive in the naming of her son Ishmael. Hagar has a little tiff with Sarah, she presumes too much, and Sarah deals a little too harshly with her. In consequence, Hagar runs out into the wilderness. She's pregnant, and an angel comes to her and asks (I'm paraphrasing), "Hagar, how did you get here, and where are you going?"

Hagar responds, "I flee from my master Sarah."

The angel instructs, "Return and submit to Sarah. You're going to have a son and you are to call him Ishmael."

Almost all the names in Genesis have the theme of the story attached to the name. Ishmael means *God hears*. God hears! Can you begin to perceive the message of Hagar's life and how important that is for us all?

"Name your boy: 'God hears.'"

When her son is born, Hagar gives him that name. Later, when he is a boy, twelve or thirteen years of age, Isaac is born. Sarah worries about the two boys being together, the conflict that might happen, and the consequences for her younger son. She tells Abraham to separate them. Abraham, hesitant to send a woman alone into the very violent world we see depicted in the book of Genesis, is grieved by Sarah's request, but he approaches the Lord in prayer for confirmation. The Lord says, "Listen to Sarah; she is right. The boys must be separated. And don't worry about Hagar and Ishmael. I will raise up a great nation out of him. He too will fulfill the Abrahamic covenant that all the nations of the earth will be blessed through your descendants." Islam and the Qur'an, has been a blessing for almost 1,500 years to billions of people on the face of the earth.

Abraham gives Hagar water and a little food and sends her out into the desert. Very soon she is in desperate straits. She is out of water. "The water was spent in the bottle" (Genesis 21:15). She puts Ishmael under a little shade tree so she can't see him die and removes herself so she can't hear his cries.

What was the name of that boy? God hears! So it is not surprising that we read, "And *God heard* the voice of the lad; and the angel of God called to Hagar out of heaven, and said unto her, What aileth thee, Hagar? fear not; for *God hath heard* the voice of the lad where he is. Arise, lift up the lad, and hold him in thine hand; for I will make him a great nation. And God opened her eyes, and she saw a well of water; and she went, and filled the bottle with water, and gave the lad drink. And God was with the lad" (Genesis 21:17–20; emphasis added).

The great message of Hagar's life is that God hears all of us. He hears because we are important to Him. He hears because we are beings of tremendous value. He certainly hears the Sarahs and the Isaacs of the world—the story we might say is the main story, the main generational line that will be followed throughout the Bible—but he also hears the Hagars and the Ishmaels.

Through no fault of her own, Hagar finds herself raising a child alone. My mother found herself in that situation many years ago. She was the Hagar; I was the Ishmael. We were not the standard Mormon family—husband, wife, children, a loving nuclear family, the ideal. Everybody wants that, but we may not find ourselves in a Sarah/Isaac situation. We may find ourselves in a Hagar/Ishmael situation, and it's important we realize God hears. On a broad scale, though religions for centuries have failed to fully comprehend this truth, becoming somewhat exclusive in their understanding, God hears the prayers of the Muslims, the Jews, the Christians—Catholic, Baptist, Mormon. Every year millions of people go to Mecca for the Hajj. They reenact the story of Hagar by running back and forth between two mountains looking for water. This is such a powerful story. God hears because we are important—all of us!

LEAD WITH THE QUEEN

Esther was told by Mordecai that she would be God's "enlargement and deliverance" (Esther 4:14) for her people when Haman threatened their extinction. We could spend a lot of time discussing what the Haman of today is that threatens the extinction of God's people. There are tremendous forces arrayed against the family, against morality, decency, and integrity. Tremendous forces! Some of them do so maliciously. Some of them do so foolishly. Some don't know any better and some have lost all sense of shame or propriety in their exhibition of the vulgar and ugly, but there is considerable energy channeled against most of what we stand for as a people. The Lord needs "enlargement and deliverance" for His people. He is going to take a lot of small people, simple things, men and women—but especially women—and enlarge them. They are going to do something great. Let me illustrate with a memory from my youth.

When I was little I loved to play chess. Initially I didn't know how to play chess and I didn't know anybody who could teach me. I went to the community swimming pool and there I watched the teenage boys play.

I studied a new piece every day. How did the pawn move? How did the castle move? How did the knights move? After several days, I knew how every piece moved and I began to play chess. Because I was a boy, I guess, I loved the knights. They were fascinating pieces for me. They had those little horse heads. They moved so uniquely. They move in little "L" shapes and they can jump over things. So every game I played during those early years, I led my attack with the two knights. I jumped those two knights over the pawns in the first two moves of the game and then all my strategy centered on their abilities. I had fun playing and I did win some games.

Anyone who has played chess or knows a little bit about chess realizes that the most important piece on the board, the most powerful piece on the playing field is the queen. She has the most moves. She can cover the greatest distance. The queen is the central player, the best able to win the game for you. The loss of the queen is usually devastating. But I was leading with the knights. How many games was I winning? Not as many as I could have. I was leaving my queen back in home territory to protect the king. When I finally realized that if I was going to win I needed to lead with the queen and let all the other pieces support her, I began to win games consistently.

There is a great chess game going on for the souls of men in the world and God will lead with His queens. You will be God's "enlargement and deliverance" to save His people against the Hamans of the day whether they be shortsighted or hostile.

I am grateful that in my own life God has led with the queen. I can say without equivocation and deep sincerity that all the good things in my life have flowed to me through a woman. May you do great things.

NOTES

1. Available at http://www.youtube.com/watch?v=pfahoLfrddU; accessed 9 December 2011.
2. Wilford Woodruff, "Responsibilities of the Priesthood," *Ensign*, September 1971, 20–21.

RELIEF SOCIETY:
A WAY OF LIFE AND A PATTERN
OF FAITHFUL DISCIPLESHIP

Julie B. Beck

I hope that as I deliver my message you will be able to receive it in the spirit in which it was given to me. Sometimes the messages we are asked to give come as a gift and are poured out upon us without us even asking. The Lord just says, "Say this." So we write it down and we give it. Other times the messages are hard-won. We work hard and get pieces and points a little at a time. This address has been one of those where the message has been on my mind for an entire year. I knew that after the 2010 BYU Women's Conference, the next April would come around sooner or later, and so I started preparing. Perhaps the danger of preparing too soon is that there is always more to say. I have a fat folder of ideas and thoughts that have come at different times and places. Knowing how to put them all together has required much thought and prayer and asking.

As you know, while we're worrying about things of this sort, our mortal experience keeps happening at the same time. Life continues and we get opportunities to learn and grow in other ways. Those create

Julie Bangerter Beck, the general president of the Relief Society, was serving as the first counselor in the Young Women general presidency prior to receiving her call to direct the Church's women's service organization. As a child she learned to speak Portuguese when she lived in Brazil with her parents and brothers and sisters while her father served as mission president. She is a graduate of Dixie College and Brigham Young University and was a full-time homemaker prior to her service in the Young Women general presidency. She and her husband, Ramon, are the parents of three children and have fifteen grandchildren.

interruptions and distractions in our lives. That is normal for me and you. This recent season has been a time of interesting and prolific mortal experience where much has happened, good and sad, difficult and enjoyable.

I have been thinking about this message in the wee hours when the phone wasn't ringing and there wasn't a clamor. That was a blessing because I not only felt the companionship of the Holy Ghost, but also the companionship and sweet presence of helpers. There were times of repentance and pointing out faults and failures and times of approval. I hope that all of you have those kinds of opportunities in your own life to stretch and grow. That is why I am grateful for this opportunity. I hope that something that is conveyed here will bless you more than it has me, but I am grateful that through this experience, the Lord has blessed me. I thank Him for His goodness in doing that.

Over the past year, my counselors and I have visited with thousands of women around the world. I like to take the opportunity in those meetings to listen to their questions. I write down the questions and I write down the answers the Lord gives me when we're visiting together. Those questions and answers are part of the stack I've sifted through in preparing this message. There are hundreds of questions—and they are very good questions. Most of them are inspired questions. They talk about your mortal experiences. There are questions about difficulties in families, sometimes about wayward children. Sometimes there are questions from women who have not found husbands and they want to know about the Lord's plan for them. There are questions about the roles and responsibilities of women, and questions about homemaking, and priorities, and parenting. There are questions from women about whether or not to work outside the home or whether to stay at home or whether or not the work they have will be sufficient to feed them, and how to manage the small resources they have. I have been touched by questions that come from the sisters. It gives me an understanding of the broad spectrum of experience you're having, the difficulties, and the joys in your lives, and the things you are trying to accomplish.

Over the past few years at the BYU Women's Conference, the Relief Society general presidency has concentrated on a few things that we hoped would help bless and strengthen you. We've talked about Relief Society as being about *relief,* defined as lifting up—lifting us to a higher level of achievement and behavior and accomplishment in the Lord's kingdom. We've talked about being strong and immovable. We've delineated the purposes of Relief Society. We've talked about families and what should be happening in families. Last year we mentioned the lioness at the gate and that protective feeling we should have as women over our homes and our hearths.[1] And in the general Relief Society meetings we've echoed some of these same topics and themes. In the 2010 general Relief Society meeting, we talked about the history of Relief Society and, with the approval of the First Presidency, we announced that a history of Relief Society was being prepared for the sisters of the Church. That history will be made available to all the sisters of the Church in 2011.[2]

In this conference, Brother John Tanner spoke about an ancestor of his who was present at the beginnings of Relief Society and was an example of the service that Relief Society aspires to. His wife, Sister Susan Tanner, spoke about the general history of Relief Society. Both bore their testimonies about the importance of Relief Society and how they have come to know and understand what it's about.[3] Other speakers focused on various aspects of Relief Society history. We had the former Relief Society general presidents here. They bore testimony of their service and responsibility. It was a marvelous time to be with those of strength and capacity who are continuing to serve as examples and leaders in their homes, their families, and the Church. I was touched and blessed to be with them.

As we in the Relief Society general presidency have overseen the preparation of this history of the Relief Society for you, we have had many opportunities to learn. In that preparation, some aspects of our history have delineated avenues for further learning. It is important to know our spiritual heritage and responsibility. What are the themes that emerge from studying our spiritual heritage? What does the Lord want us to accomplish?

Our history provides the context for what we as sisters in the Church should learn. Some of what I will discuss are things that I have learned, that others involved in the preparation of this history have learned, and that I hope my granddaughters will learn as they read and study Relief Society history. I hope we will all learn these lessons as our history becomes ever more important to us. History helps us to learn who we are and why we are important to the Lord. It connects us and binds us with the covenants we have made. That's why it's important.

STRENGTHENS AND SUPPORTS OUR UNIQUE IDENTITY AS DAUGHTERS OF GOD

The first thing I have learned from the history of Relief Society is that it strengthens and supports our unique identity as daughters of God. Our Father and His Son, Jesus Christ, value and rely on their daughters. God's daughters, we know, have equal importance in His sight with His sons. They have unique responsibilities and duties in the plan of salvation, and they share some responsibilities in the plan with Heavenly Father's sons. They also have a unifying purpose in our Heavenly Father's plan with His sons.

There is an interesting, exciting, and unique female identity of greatness and richness that is choice beyond comparison. This identity, which the Lord has given us and which we understand through the gospel of Jesus Christ, is in direct contrast to the debased and devalued identity of women that we find in the world today. We find in our history an elevated, strong identity that comes from our Heavenly Father. This identity and purpose can only be fully understood through a spiritual confirmation. There is an intellectual study that can be made, but a spiritual confirmation is what teaches us who we are and what we are to do.

There is much out in the world that is false by way of identity. There are identities of sensuality, of women seeking power and prestige, money, leisure—all these are different identities that the world promotes. But the identity of a daughter of God is precious beyond compare, and rich, and full.

We know that women are the guardians of the hearth and home. And that they have the responsibility for the hearts and souls of men and women and the children of our Heavenly Father. They are given this powerful and influential leadership role. Female responsibilities include being a wife, a mother, a daughter, a sister, an aunt, a friend. This is all about nurturing, teaching, and influencing. These are non-negotiable responsibilities. We can't delegate them. We can accept them and live them, but these are things we understood before we were born. We can't negotiate with the Lord about whether or not these are our responsibilities. They have been part of the plan from the beginning; they are not going to change because of any clamor to the contrary. These are our responsibilities.

Not long ago I visited with a young mother who recently had her eighth child. That's difficult to accomplish in these days. It's always wonderful when you can find a woman who wants eight children and can have them. That combination doesn't happen very often. She said that she was interested and a little disappointed in the comments of some of her friends, who she thought understood the gospel, who have been saying, "You're making an interesting lifestyle choice."

She said, "I didn't ever know this was a lifestyle choice; I thought it was a gospel choice. I thought this was what the gospel taught us to do. I don't do this because my children tell me I'm cute! I don't do this because I get all the help I need. I don't do this because anyone affirms what I'm doing. I do this because the Lord has taught me that it's the right thing to do and He will help me in the difficult, backbreaking days."

I understood what she said. When our daughter had her baby recently, I volunteered to tend for five days. We brought home a number of grandchildren—I promise you, giving this talk is easier than doing that! When I finally got into bed at night, I would say to my husband, "I think I'm going to die! Every bone and muscle in my body hurts. How do they do this?" Then someone would wake up in the night and need something. I didn't get the sleep that I needed. Always it was just feeding, feeding, feeding people! I learned that my mothering skills were a little out of date. My grandmother skills were fine, but I had to enter into mothering mode, and I was a little out of practice. That meant I needed to figure out disciplining, and then stopping a child's crying, and other skills I'd let go dormant. I prayed a lot. I couldn't remember what I used to do in any number of scenarios. I thought the Holy Ghost was supposed to bring all things to our remembrance.

But I combined the mothering role with the grandmothering role, and in times of great stress, I fed them cold cereal. I think they may still be coming down from the sugar high, but it made them happy! It was wonderful to be reminded of what that work is like and what is involved, what it entails, what we need to do as a Church to support the actual labor that needs to happen in a home and a family.

One of the questions I am asked frequently is, "Is it okay that I work outside of my home?" or ". . . that I don't work outside of my home?" You have to know that as the president of an international Relief Society, that question isn't always appropriate in many countries in the world. There are many, many places where if our women don't work, they don't eat. So of course they have to work. The question of whether or not to work is the wrong question. The right question is, "Am I aligned with the Lord's vision of me and what He wants me to become, and the roles and respon-sibilities He gave me in heaven that are not negotiable? Am I aligned with that, or am I trying to escape my duties?" We need to understand what our Heavenly Father wants for us. Our Heavenly Father loves His daughters, and because He loves us and because the reward at the end is so glorious, we do not get a pass from the responsibilities we were given. We cannot give them away. They are our sacred duties and we fulfill them under covenant.

Sometimes I'm asked, "What are some of the things you worry about the most?" Some of the things that worry me the most are best described in 2 Nephi 28, where we read about what's happening in the hearts and souls of our women: "At that day [these latter days], shall [Satan] rage in the hearts of the children of men, and stir them up to anger against that which is good" (2 Nephi 28:20). There is a lot of resentment in the world against things that are holy and important. That should be a concern.

The next verse says that "others will he [Satan] pacify, and lull them away into carnal security, that they will say: All is well" (2 Nephi 28:21). In our day we call that apathy. There's a lot of apathy in the world toward important, God-given roles and responsibilities.

"Others he flattereth away, and telleth them there is no hell," and that there is no devil (2 Nephi 28:22). In our day, we call the flattery "entitle-ment." There are many who feel entitled, and that the world owes them something. This even happens in families. Sometimes I hear a wife say, "My husband owes me," either time or help. Sometimes I hear people say, "The Lord owes me this," or "I'm entitled to something." We ought to re-member the Savior Jesus Christ's sacrifice for us, and that no one owes us anything. We owe everything to the Lord for His sacrifice.

What is happening in our day needs to be guarded against, and watched over so that it doesn't happen to us. The Lord says in the same chapter of 2 Nephi that "[He] will be merciful unto [us]," and "if [we] will repent and come unto [Him], . . . [His] arm is lengthened out all the day long" (2 Nephi 28:32).

We cannot put our trust in the arm of flesh or in the messages from the world that are being broadcast to women in our day. Relief Society strengthens and supports the unique identity of daughters of God. How grateful we are for that.

RELIEF SOCIETY IS A RESTORATION OF A PATTERN THAT EXISTED ANCIENTLY

The second thing I've learned from studying Relief Society history is that Relief Society is a restoration of a pattern that existed anciently. There is evidence of this in the scriptures. I call these bread crumbs. You can find links or nuggets in the scriptures that show that pattern. There is evidence of this in the testimony of living prophets. There is evidence of this in the Spirit confirming that this is so. Understanding the heritage we have, that this organization is a restoration of something that existed anciently, helps us understand that we are not a footnote in history, or a sidebar in the Lord's work. We are an essential part in building the kingdom and we've been organized to do such.

One of the first places in scripture where we find the Lord inviting sisters to be part of His work is in the gospel of Luke, in chapter 10. I invite you to read this and get the spirit of it for yourself, but I'll review it here.

The Apostles were called, given their responsibilities, and sent out to do the Lord's work. Off they went. And then the Seventy were called, instructed, and were told they would be able to cast out devils and perform miracles in the Lord's name. They went and came back and reported their ministry to the Savior.

Then in the same chapter, the Lord has this question asked of Him, "What shall I do to inherit eternal life?" (Luke 10:25). He teaches that if we serve and love the Lord with all our heart, with all our soul, and all our strength, and love our neighbors as ourselves, then we are qualifying for eternal life (see Luke 10:27–28). And following that, as an example, He tells the story of the Good Samaritan, where we learn about taking care of someone who has both immediate and long-term needs (see Luke 10:29–37).

Immediately following that is the great and misunderstood story of Mary and Martha. We like to talk about Martha as the bad example and Mary as the good example, but we know that Martha is the one who invited the Savior into her home—it was her home. Aren't we encouraged to do that? Isn't that a good thing? Some of you may have plaques that say, "Christ is the center of our home." That was Martha. She served Him. Isn't that a good thing? That was what women were expected to do and what we're expected to do. But the Savior took this opportunity to invite both Mary and Martha to be official participants in His work of discipleship. He emphasized that discipleship was "that good part" (Luke 10:42). It was the needful part that would never be taken away from them. When you read that with spiritual understanding, when you learn about Mary and Martha and then what happened to them later—that Martha was a woman who bore fervent testimony of the Christ—and when you see the work that they participated in, you learn that this experience was when the Savior officially invited them to be a part of His work, not to be bystanders, but to be included in what He wanted to accomplish (see Luke 10:38–42).

The restored pattern of discipleship we have in Relief Society provides for God's daughters to be aligned with His purpose, and helps us learn our unique duties and responsibilities. It also unifies us in the Lord's work with men who hold the priesthood.

I am asked sometimes, "Why do we have a Relief Society president on both the general level and locally?" The reason we have a president is so we can have an organization. We have an organization because we have a purpose. When we have a purpose there is an expected outcome. Relief Society isn't just a feel good, get together, let's enjoy each other, do anything, anytime, anyplace for any reason kind of organization. Relief Society is part of the Lord's work. It has a president at every level, and a purpose that was delineated by the Lord and His holy prophets. This work needs a specific outcome. As a worldwide organization, it can grow exponentially, country by country. It provides a system of watchcare, sisterhood, discipleship, and education that is growing every day.

The purposes of Relief Society, as determined by the Lord, are to help us increase faith and personal righteousness, strengthen families and homes, and seek out and help those who are in need. That's why Relief Society exists. The outcome is that we will improve women individually and as a whole and thus prepare for eternal life. We will build homes and wards—the Lord's kingdom.

We're not entertainers. This is the Lord's business of salvation. That's the business we're in. We teach as the Savior taught. We teach, and we teach, and we teach, and we build the Lord's kingdom. This isn't about causes or advocacy groups, because we have an advocate. Our Savior, Jesus Christ, is our advocate with the Father. We stand with Him doing His work, working for His great cause.

We're here to provide relief and to rise above life and to live the gospel more fully. We know how essential we are; the expectation is that when a woman joins the Church, or when she enters Relief Society by the age of eighteen, that she has been prepared to be organized under priesthood keys and under priesthood direction, working alongside quorums to move the Lord's work forward. This is not a passé, worn-out organization. It is in ascendancy. It is growing, it is developing, it is becoming a world-class unmatched system. When we come to understand what Relief Society is, and the watchcare responsibility we have, in terms of visiting teaching specifically—if we really understood what it can accomplish, there would be no more shoulder shrugging, no eye-rolling, no excuses. We would come to understand that the results the Lord wants are sisters understanding that they're loved, that they're cared for, that they're watched over, that they're strengthened and supported in living His gospel. If we understand that, then we will do anything to get on our knees and know what the Lord would have us do. Relief Society is a great system, organized after an ancient pattern, that is in its ascendancy and is world-class. We will increasingly provide an example to the world of how the Lord's people should be organized and live.

A MANIFESTATION OF CHARITY

The third thing I learned from studying the history of Relief Society is that Relief Society, when functioning properly, is a manifestation of charity. Charity is much more than a feeling of benevolence. It is more than virtuous living. It is living as Christ lived and being as He is. It is more than niceness. It is what we are to become. We learn from the scriptures— in Alma and Moroni—that if we have not charity, we are as dross before the Lord (see Alma 34:29; Moroni 7:44). If we don't have charity we cannot achieve eternal life. We should pray with all of our hearts to be filled with charity. It is a great goal for us. It is a Christ-like quality. President Spencer W. Kimball said, "The cultivation of Christlike qualities is a demanding and relentless task—it is not for the seasonal worker or for those who will not stretch themselves, again and again."[4] This wonderful charity is what we in Relief Society do, and who we are, and what we're becoming, because we know that two or three of us gathered together in an organized way is more than one of us working in a disorganized way. Charity is a purifier. It is the Atonement working in us, purifying us, changing us. It is covenant keeping at its purest. It requires repentance and change.

A hundred years ago the Relief Society general presidency selected the motto for Relief Society as "Charity Never Faileth." They knew what they were doing. The Relief Society motto was distilled by women who had been taught by Joseph Smith and understood the purpose of Relief Society. Joseph taught (and taught and taught) this more excellent way to the sisters. He taught them about becoming holy and using this organization to learn how to become like the Savior. Relief Society is more than benevolence. It is becoming like the Savior, utilizing the atonement of Jesus Christ.

The history of Relief Society is a history of women of strong faith. We've heard in this conference about some of those. Earthly trials and tears and opposition and difficulties are part of the Lord's plan for us. Through those difficulties, we learn and make progress. We will always have opposition. We learn in the Book of Mormon that if we don't have opposition then we are nothing. We are compounded in one (see 2 Nephi 2:11) and will always feel this opposition. Eve knew this and she chose mortality and experienced opposition. She led her family and rejoiced in knowing that her trials would perfect her.

Life is difficult. I have a friend who said to me recently that for years she had a plaque that said, "I can do hard things," and she said, "I've changed that. I now say I *do* hard things!" We actually do hard things. We have learned that trials can be endured and overcome only through strong faith—faith in the Savior, Jesus Christ, and in His atoning power, in His capacity to heal and strengthen us, faith in the Father's plan and in His mission, and faith that He will fulfill every promise. With strong faith we can triumph over life's adversities; without it we become fearful, confused, discouraged, depressed, distracted, and lost. Faith is how the Lord heals us and strengthens us.

I love the teaching in Matthew 9 when the two blind men approached the Savior and said, "Thou Son of David, have mercy on us." How many times have you gone to the Lord and said, "Have mercy"? The Lord said, "Believe ye that I am able to do this? They said unto Him, Yea, Lord. Then touched he their eyes, saying, According to your faith be it unto you" (Matthew 9:27–29).

With strong faith, the Lord can heal us, strengthen us, and help us accomplish this mortal experience. We will have happy days and we will have difficult days and the Lord can heal us. He can heal us from our faults and our failings and change us. What I've learned from studying Relief Society history is that faith is possible. With the strength of the Holy Ghost and the companionship of that faith, we become stronger, and our difficulties become our opportunities and our blessings.

WE HAVE AN INSEPARABLE CONNECTION TO THE PRIESTHOOD

I've learned through the study of the history of Relief Society that we have an inseparable connection to the priesthood. The Prophet Joseph Smith put the sisters in the position to receive all the gifts, blessings, and privileges of the priesthood. We need never confuse the idea of the priesthood with those who hold the priesthood and that trust.

The priesthood is God's power. It is His power to create, to bless, to lead, to serve as He does. The priesthood duty of every righteous man is to qualify for the blessing of holding that priesthood and trust from the Lord so that he can bless his family and those around him. I would say that the priesthood duty of sisters is to create life, to nurture it, to prepare it for the covenants of the Lord. Don't confuse the power with the keys and the offices of the priesthood. God's power is limitless and it is shared with those who make and keep covenants.

Too much is said and misunderstood about what the brothers have and the sisters don't have. This is Satan's way of confusing both men and women so neither understands what they really have. Whether a sister or brother, each has every ordinance, every gift, and every blessing available to get back to our Father in Heaven. No one, male or female, is left outside of those blessings to qualify for exaltation. There is a unity in the council and the covenant that is required us to get there. Neither the man nor the woman can ascend without the other. We are inseparably connected in that way. I understand how special women are. I understand how special men are. And together we're more special; we can become what the Lord wants us to become.

Home is where the Lord expects the priesthood to work best. When brothers and sisters are mutually responsible to protect and maintain and value the power of the priesthood, the keys of the priesthood, and priesthood covenants and blessings, then we will be truly achieving something.

The first priesthood covenants we make are baptism and receiving the gift of the Holy Ghost. We teach the importance of those covenants to children and they are honored and kept in our youth, looking forward always to the covenants found in the temple. I hope that when you go to the temple that you pay attention and listen and look and learn and feel and understand what is happening, and find the blessings and the gifts of the priesthood that come through the covenants and ordinances of the gospel.

Young women are prepared to receive the priesthood temple covenants in Young Women. Relief Society was given the responsibility to firm up that maturity and get women prepared for the temple. Joseph Smith gave that assignment to the Relief Society and it has never been taken away from them. It is one of the major responsibilities of the Relief Society—preparing women for temple covenants.

Recently I reviewed what the Church handbook says about young women and other members preparing for the temple. It says, "Single members in their late teens or early twenties who have not received a mission call or are not engaged to be married in the temple, should not be recommended to receive their own endowment; however, they may receive limited use recommends." (This is something we should encourage in all of our youth.) "Worthy single members, who have not received their endowment in connection with a marriage or mission, may become eligible to receive their endowment when the bishop and stake president determine they are sufficiently mature to understand and keep the sacred covenants made in the temple. Such eligibility is determined individually per each person, not by using a routine criteria, such as reaching a certain age or leaving home for college." That's what our handbook teaches. When I read that, I said to myself, "So the goal of every woman, every Relief Society member, is to become sufficiently mature to understand and keep the sacred covenants made in the temple. That is our goal for every woman."

We learn from reading the Doctrine and Covenants that in the ordinances of the gospel, the power of Godliness is manifest (see D&C 84:20). We have those ordinances: baptism, the gift of the Holy Ghost, conferring the priesthood upon men, the temple ordinances of endowment and sealing. There is a power of Godliness that comes to us in each of those ordinances. That power of Godliness is our goal. The Lord has promised that the Holy Ghost is a precious revelator that is given to all faithful women and men. This teaches us to know and to do what we need to do.

I recently reviewed a Primary song with which you're probably familiar. It says, "Mine is a home where ev'ry hour is blessed by the strength of priesthood pow'r, / With father and mother leading the way, / Teaching me how to trust and obey."[5] That is your responsibility—to help your home be a home that is blessed every hour by priesthood power. It isn't just when Dad is there. It's not just when Mom is there. It's not just when a priesthood ordinance or blessing is being performed—it's in every hour as ordinances and covenants are made and kept.

I've reviewed here some of what I have learned from studying the history of Relief Society. My hope is, as you read that history, that the power and strength of these things will settle upon your hearts and that other lessons the Lord has to teach you personally will emerge in your study. We've learned about our female identity and duty in the Lord's plan. It is larger than knowing I am a child of God. It's an expectation to live and choose and make progress into God's life—not only to accept His plan, but to fulfill it.

Relief Society is a restoration or a bringing back of an ancient practice of discipleship. Relief Society on a general and local level has a president, and a president is the spiritual leader of an organization that has set purposes and work to do. We are to increase our faith and personal righteousness, strengthen families and homes, and seek out and help those in need. The Lord can't build His kingdom without Relief Society. It's in its ascendancy in importance and value. The Lord's kingdom is going forward. In the future it is going to require strong leadership from all women.

We've learned that the motto for Relief Society, "Charity Never Faileth," is our motto for good reason. It is the Atonement of Jesus Christ in action in our lives. It is becoming as He is. It is a life-changing and life-saving quality that is the aim of every Latter-day Saint.

We learn through Relief Society history about faith: deep, strong faith. We learn from those who have faced trials in the past how to overcome our mortal experiences. The scriptures are replete with examples and testimonies of this also.

There is an inseparable connection to the priesthood with all righteous women individually and with this organization. When we operate under that authority in an authorized manner to do the Lord's work, every sister can fully possess the blessings, the gifts, and the covenants of the priesthood. God's power should be in, around, and through our lives in every moment. The companionship of the Holy Ghost is our strength and our goal. We are not at liberty to choose contrary to the Lord's plan without consequence.

We are a tremendously blessed people. Relief Society brings value and importance to God's daughters and it is as strong as the weakest sister among us. Our responsibility is to reach out and help strengthen each other and create a sisterhood of watchcare that is so powerful no one will be lost. No one can do it alone.

I'm grateful for Relief Society, not only for its beginnings, but for what it is today. I'm just beginning to have a glimpse of what the Lord has in mind for his daughters. The vision that comes to me sometimes is so glorious and staggering and humbling and thrilling. It is difficult to contemplate. It is part of Daniel's vision of the stone rolling forth to bless the earth (see Daniel 2). The Lord expects and requires that His daughters participate in building His kingdom in bringing to pass what He calls His strange act (see Isaiah 28:21; D&C 95:4; D&C 101:95).

Until the history of who you are is in your hearts, you won't be as strong as you could be. Rather than prepare for a product, I would suggest that you prepare yourself to receive the Lord's message for you. Go to the temple, pray, and live, and become what the Lord would have us all become. The answer to anger, to entitlement, to resentment, to apathy is in the Relief Society of this Church. It is the response and the defense and the offense going forward.

President Henry B. Eyring taught an important lesson in the priesthood session of the April 2010 general conference. What he said then about priesthood duties also applies to your Relief Society duties—receiving a vision of the expanse of what that means as daughters of God. He said, "[When] I am tempted to feel that I have finished some hard task in the Lord's service and deserve a rest[,] the Savior's example gives me courage to press on. . . . Whenever we remember Him, it becomes easier to resist the temptation to want a rest from our priesthood labors. We must have remembered Him today, and so we're here to learn our duties, determined to do what we are covenanted to do, in all diligence. And because of His example we will endure to the end of the tasks He gives us in this life and be committed to do the will of His Father forever, as He was and is.

"This is the Lord's Church. He called us and trusted us even in the weaknesses He knew we had. He knew the trials we would face. . . . We can become ever more like Him."[6] When I read that, I want to say, "Thank you, President Eyring." He described how to go forward, even when we are tired and when it seems difficult.

I am so grateful for the blessing I have had in my life to connect with and get to know and be lifted up by strong, faithful, purposeful women who knew their identity in the kingdom of God and helped move this gospel forward. I'm grateful for those who have exemplified charity and have become as the Savior is. I am thankful for this wonderful association and sisterhood which unites us in the Lord's work. I am grateful for the association that I have with the Young Women presidency, the Primary presidency, and also the Sunday School and Young Men presidencies of this Church. I am grateful to our priesthood advisors and the counsel offered to think about and work on how to bless and build families and individuals of this Church. It's all the Lord's work.

I leave you my testimony that this is the true, restored gospel of Jesus Christ on the earth. He is directing it today through prophets, seers, and revelators, who seek to know His mind and will and carry it out. I see that on an ongoing basis. I bear testimony of the goodness of sons and daughters of our Heavenly Father who understand their lives' mission and move it forward. I leave my love and confidence with you and express my great appreciation for your fine lives and for your continuing attempts to exemplify charity that never fails.

NOTES

1. See Julie B. Beck, "What Is Your Mission?" *Choose Ye This Day to Serve the Lord: Talks from the 2010 BYU Women's Conference* (Salt Lake City: Deseret Book, 2011), 1–13.
2. Beck, "Daughters in My Kingdom: The History and Work of Relief Society," *Ensign,* November 2010, 114; see also *Daughters in My Kingdom: The History and Work of Relief Society* (Salt Lake City: The Church of Jesus Christ of Latter-day Saints, 2011); available at http://lds.org/relief-society/daughters-in-my-kingdom?lang=eng; accessed 14 September 2011.
3. See John S. Tanner, "In Praise of Eve's Faithful Daughters: The Legacy of Relief Society through the Life of a Great-Grandmother" and Susan W. Tanner, "The Legacy of Relief Society" in this volume, 66–76 and 55–65, respectively.
4. Spencer W. Kimball, "Privileges and Responsibilities of Sisters," *Ensign,* November 1978, 105.
5. Janice Kapp Perry, "Love Is Spoken Here," *Children's Songbook* (Salt Lake City: The Church of Jesus Christ of Latter-day Saints, 1989), 190–91.
6. Henry B. Eyring, "Act in All Diligence," *Ensign,* May 2010, 62–63.

THE LEGACY OF RELIEF SOCIETY

Susan W. Tanner

You may have noticed recently much emphasis on the history of Relief Society. Why has there been such an interest in this? What are we supposed to be learning as we study our history? Over the past months, I have been given the opportunity to study and write about our great Relief Society legacy. It has been a wonderful, challenging, miraculous journey. I am so grateful for all I've learned about the divinity of the Relief Society organization and also for the ordinary yet extraordinary women I have met from our past. These are noble examples of faith, testimony, sacrifice, and charity. I've come to love and admire them. I will share some of what I have learned about Relief Society's inspiring legacy.

As I immersed myself in this history, I felt again powerfully of Heavenly Father's great love for His daughters and of their crucial place and important purposes in His plan. He knows us. He needs us. There are things we need to do, people we need to bless, virtues we need to develop, and ways we need to behave.

You may have a vague idea about the beginning of Relief Society

Susan W. Tanner served as the twelfth general president of the Young Women organization from 2002 to 2008. She graduated from Brigham Young University with a humanities degree, and is the author of Daughters in My Kingdom, *the history of the Relief Society recently published by The Church of Jesus Christ of Latter-day Saints and distributed to all adult female members of the Church. She is serving with her husband, John, who is president of the Brazil São Paulo South Mission. They have five children and fifteen grandchildren.*

in Nauvoo in 1842. You may think that it began with a few sisters who wanted to create a sewing society to make shirts for the men who were building the temple. In the mid–1800s it was popular for women to create such benevolent societies. When the Prophet Joseph Smith heard of these stirrings among the women, he invited them to meet him above the Red Brick Store on March 17 where he would share, as he said, "something better" for them.[1]

As the gospel and the church organization were gradually revealed to him, Joseph Smith had learned of the exalted station of women in our Father's plan. He taught the sisters that "the Church was never perfectly organized until the women were thus organized."[2] In that first meeting he organized them "under the priesthood after the pattern of the priesthood,"[3] and with the opportunity to receive all of the blessings of the priesthood. He told them that this "charitable society . . . is according to your natures—it is natural for females to have feelings of charity—you are now plac'd in a situation where you can act according to those sympathies which God has planted in your bosoms."[4] Latter-day Saint women would now have greater scope, opportunity, and authorization to be participants in God's work.

Joseph Smith taught the sisters on numerous occasions in their Relief Society meetings during that inaugural summer of 1842. We have minutes of those choice discourses, carefully recorded by Eliza R. Snow and safely guarded in her keeping as she journeyed across the plains to the Salt Lake Valley. He taught the sisters that the purpose of Relief Society was "not only to relieve the poor, but to save souls."[5] They were taught to become holy, to "repent and get the love of God."[6] "Meekness, love, purity, these are the things that should magnify us," he said.[7] One specific way he encouraged the sisters to be better is to hold their tongues. He said, "Put a double watch over the tongue. . . . The tongue is an unruly member—hold your tongues about things of no moment,—a little tale will set the world on fire."[8] I feel certain that this meaningful advice could well be taught to women in Relief Societies today.

Our Nauvoo sisters were qualifying themselves to receive all of the priesthood blessings of the temple. Their intentions in the beginning were to help prepare a temple for the people. Under the guidance of a prophet, they also participated in preparing a people for the temple. In short, the sisters were taught to serve others, to save families, to sanctify themselves. Not surprisingly, these foundational principles continue today as our guiding purposes in Relief Society. You have often heard Sister Julie B. Beck say, "the Lord has commissioned each Relief Society sister and the organization as a whole to: 1. Increase in faith and personal righteousness. 2. Strengthen families and homes. 3. Serve the Lord and His children."[9]

How are we doing as women today in fulfilling these purposes? Let me tell you about an experience I had as I worked on this project. I had written to a certain point, and then I wasn't sure how to proceed. I was stumped. After one particularly frustrating day where I couldn't figure out what to do next, I had a very vivid dream, which I am not prone to have. I was hiking and following a man up ahead of me who seemed to know where he was going. He turned a corner, and I lost sight of him. No longer could I find my way. Suddenly I found myself lost within the four walls of an amusement park with no way out. I could see over the walls to where I needed to be, but I couldn't figure out how to get there. Then I woke up. It occurred to me that this was an allegory of my situation. I was lost in an amusement park, and the things of the world were crowding out the spiritual influences I needed to help me in this project. Then I thought, "Maybe this is also an allegory about many of the sisters of the Church around me. They might be stuck in an amusement park too, allowing themselves to get distracted and diverted from their noble responsibilities." Emma Smith was told to "lay aside the things of this world, and seek for the things of a better" (D&C 25:10). We know Section 25 was not for Emma alone, but was His "voice unto *all*" (D&C 25:16; emphasis added).

My husband asked me how I got out of the amusement park. I didn't in the dream. But several days later, President Henry B. Eyring gave a talk at the general Relief Society meeting about the history of Relief Society. I was thrilled by his words and filled with the Spirit. Our history carries a strong spirit about it. As I studied every word, I was inspired to know how to continue with my project. I was also inspired by Eliza R. Snow, the great poetess of the early Church who described how the Spirit guides and comforts us and protects us from worldly trials. She said:

"To be sure we have trials; but what are they? I want to ask my sisters now a serious question. When you are filled with the Spirit of God, and the Holy Ghost rests upon you—that comforter which Jesus promised, and which takes of the things of God and gives them to us, and shows us things to come and brings all things to our remembrance—when you are filled with this spirit, do you have any trials? I do not think you do. For that [spirit] satisfies and fills up every longing of the human heart, and fills up every vacuum. When I am filled with that spirit my soul is satisfied; and I can say in good earnest, that the trifling things of the day do not seem to stand in my way at all. But just let me loose my hold of that spirit and power of the Gospel, and partake of the spirit of the world, in the slightest degree, and trouble comes; there is something wrong. I am tried; and what will comfort me? You cannot impart comfort to me . . . but [it is] that which comes from the fountain above. And is it not our privilege to so live that we can have this constantly flowing into our souls."[10]

That spirit which flows to us from the fountain above will comfort us and help us to rise above the trials, distractions, and amusements of the world. The truth of Eliza R. Snow's words reached my heart. President Henry B. Eyring said, "The history of Relief Society is recorded in words and numbers, but the heritage is passed heart to heart."[11] I have loved how the sisters from the past have touched my heart. They have taught me by their examples of faith, sacrifice, testimony, wisdom, charitable acts; by their ability to live by the Spirit and personal revelation; and by their stories of everyday righteous living.

I can't wait to meet Zina Diantha Huntington Young some day. I feel as if we are kindred spirits. She was asked to help Eliza R. Snow rees-tablish Relief Societies in the Salt Lake Valley. Eliza was known as the "head" because of her articulate leadership style, and Zina was known as the "heart" because of her tender nature. In her patriarchal blessing, Zina was blessed with nurturing, healing gifts, which she used in her home and as a midwife.

Brigham Young called Zina to be in charge of the silk industry, which was established as part of the Church's great efforts at becoming self-sufficient. She abhorred the silkworms, even having nightmares about them, but she did what she was asked to do.

After her mother's death, Zina was inconsolable. Finally one night she heard her mother's voice say to her: "Zina, any sailor can steer on a smooth sea; when rocks appear, sail around them." In answer Zina cried, "O Father in heaven, help me to be a good sailor, that my heart shall not break on the rocks of grief."[12] I love this story. It makes me want to be a good sailor too.

The widowed Mary Fielding Smith had nothing but her strong testimony and the guidance of the Spirit as she left Nauvoo in extreme poverty. She walked by faith with her fellow Saints to Winter Quarters, across the Missouri River, and into the valleys of the mountains without sufficient wagons or teams. She said, "'The Lord will open the way,' but how He would open the way no one knew."[13] Later her son, President Joseph F. Smith remembered how his mother's unwavering devotion to God served as a protecting shield for him. He said:

"Would not her children be unworthy of such a mother did they not hearken to and follow her example?"[14] "Whenever . . . temptations became most alluring and most tempting to me, the first thought that arose in my soul was this: Remember the love of your mother. . . . Remember how willing she was to sacrifice her life for your good. . . . This feeling toward my mother became a defense, a barrier between me and temptation."[15]

Mary Fielding Smith instills in me the desire to have my children see me live with faith in every act as she did.

Lucy Meserve Smith, a little-known pioneer woman from Provo, was present in the Salt Lake Tabernacle in October 1856 when Brigham Young announced there were stranded and destitute handcart companies caught in early snowstorms that needed immediate help. She, along with others, stripped off her petticoat and stockings right there in the Tabernacle and began loading wagons with these personal donations. As a local Relief Society president, she said, "We did all we could . . . to comfort the needy as they came in with Hand-carts late in the Fall. . . . [The] Bishops could hardly carry the bedding and other clothing we got together. . . . We did not cease our exersions til all were made comfortable. . . . I never took more satisfaction and I might say pleasure in any labour I ever performed in my life. . . . [We] wallowed through the snow until our clothes were wet a foot high to get things together." And then, my favorite line from her journal entry comes last. After her extensive labor of love she says, "What comes next for willing hands to do?"[16] This simple statement typifies Relief Society sisters past and present, who willingly, lovingly, tirelessly reach out to those who are in need. It's become a motto for me: "What comes next for willing hands to do?"

In my studies, I met another extraordinary ordinary woman: Louise Yates Robison. Sister Robison grew up on a farm in Scipio, Utah, where she learned all the pioneer skills of self-sufficiency—raising animals, growing a garden, weaving cloth, sewing, and cooking. When the sixth general Relief Society president, Clarissa Williams, was called, it was announced over the pulpit that Louise Robison would be her second counselor. Louise raised her hand in support of the new counselor, surprised that she had a name so similar to hers. When she realized that she was the one who had been called Louise was upset. She did not think she had the qualifications to fulfill this assignment. When she went to President Heber J. Grant's office to be set apart, she told him that she was willing to serve, but that she felt sure he had been misinformed about her abilities. She told him that she had a limited education and very little money or social position, and she was afraid that she wouldn't be the example that the women of the Relief Society would expect in a leader. She said, "I'm just a humble woman." President Grant responded, "Louise, 85 percent of the women of our church are humble women. We are calling you to be the leader of them."[17] Later she was called as the seventh general Relief Society president, and served during the years of the Great Depression. She was perfectly suited to preside in hard times. She lived by the motto, "Welcome the task that takes you beyond yourself."[18]

Sister Louise Robison initiated "Singing Mothers Choruses," for she believed that a "singing mother makes a happy home."[19] This is a personally important legacy to me, because my mother was a "Singing Mother." One of my earliest memories of Relief Society was going with her to song practices. And yes, she did bring happiness into our home with her constant singing. My mother was a Relief Society woman in every way—devoted to strengthening her family, reaching out to others in need, and always striving to grow in personal righteousness. Her all-consuming service as the eleventh general Relief Society president reduced her to tears one night when she returned home after a very long day. "What's wrong?" my dad asked. She said, "I just wish I had time to give some service." He almost laughed. "But that is all you do, all day every day," he said. "But my friend just had surgery, and there are new babies in the ward, and I would like to be taking food to them and helping them." She wanted to provide the same kind of loving care for her close neighbors as she had always done.

My mom, Barbara W. Winder, left a lasting legacy of unity for the Church. She was called at a time when the auxiliaries were quite independent from each other. She was asked to unify the auxiliaries under the priesthood umbrella. She said, "I want so, and desire so, that we be unified, one together with the priesthood, serving and building the kingdom of God."[20] This unity with the priesthood and the auxiliaries continues to be the pattern today as we work closely together in families and in councils, for we know that if we are not one, we are not His (see D&C 38:27).

After learning about the lives of these women and a host of other women with great faith, I felt like the Apostle Paul, who said, "Seeing we also are compassed about with so great a cloud of witnesses, let us lay aside every weight, and the sin which doth so easily beset us, and let us run with patience the race that is set before us, looking unto Jesus the author and finisher of our faith" (Hebrews 12:1–2). We the women of the Church are surrounded by a great cloud of witnesses who have laid aside the problems and temptations that beset them to run the race the Lord has set before them.

Every generation has noble, charitable, faithful, holy women. Although few of these women are well-known to history, they are all well-known to God, which is all that ultimately matters. As Eliza R. Snow put it: "There are many of the sisters whose labors are not known beyond their own dwellings and perhaps not appreciated there, but what difference does that make? If your labors are acceptable to God, however simple the duties, if faithfully performed, you should never be discouraged."[21]

Each of us in our own small or large spheres has the opportunity to add our stories to the pages of the history of Relief Society. It is now our turn, as Joseph Smith urged, "to live up to [our] privileges."[22]

A sister from my stake told how she was blessed by the Relief Society and then gave back in return. Lynne was in her late teens when her stepfather, who was on a military training mission, was senselessly shot. She and her mother quickly got on a military plane to go to him, but partway through their journey, they learned that he had died. Grief-stricken and confused, they returned to the base. She recalled, "As my mother and I, exhausted and heartsick, walked down the steps from the plane, [a] man and woman standing on the airstrip walked over and put their arms around us. It was the branch president and the Relief Society president, neither of whom we had met before."

In the week that followed, "sisters we had never met floated in and out of the kitchen of our quarters like soft shadows, bringing food to serve the officers and families who came to call, then cleaning up. Then staying, serving food again, and cleaning up. Those days were confusing as we struggled to deal with the fact that Stew was dead, a victim of a senseless shooting. But there was always a sister there, waiting quietly in the background—to take messages, to answer the door, to hold our hands as we made phone calls to our families and friends. . . . Through it all, I developed such a sense of gratitude that I couldn't imagine how I could repay those dear sisters."

Several years later, when Lynne was married with three small children, she was called to serve in a Relief Society presidency. At times she wondered if she could meet the demands of her calling. "But then the memory came back," and she said to herself: "Now . . . it's my turn."

"A woman in the ward had lost her fourteen-year-old daughter. The mother asked me to buy a beautiful gown and to dress her daughter's body in it in preparation for the burial. I was able to do it—and found it a very tender experience. It was my turn to serve, as those sisters in North Carolina had served me.

"An elderly woman in the ward who lived alone overdosed on her medications and was in a helpless condition for three days. The other counselor and I found her still alive in her apartment and cleaned her up before the ambulance arrived. We then stayed to scrub the apartment—walls and floors—with disinfectant. My turn again.

"A young mother in the ward, one of my friends, suddenly lost her only child, a beautiful three-year-old daughter, to an infection that took her life before the doctors were even aware of how serious her illness was. The other counselor and I went to the house as soon as we heard of little Robin's death. As we approached the screened patio door, we heard the father (who was not a member of the Church) sobbing as he talked long distance to his mother. Looking up, he saw us and, still sobbing, spoke into the phone: 'It will be all right, Mother. The Mormon women are here.' My turn once more."

Lynne says that when people ask her what she thinks of Relief Society, she tells them her story. She says, "That's how I feel about Relief Society way down deep."[23]

We as women resonate to Lynne's "way down deep" feelings about Relief Society. Because we too have been surrounded by "so great a cloud of witnesses," we are ready to "run the race that is set before us."

President Joseph F. Smith urged Latter-day Saint women to "lead the world and to lead especially the women of the world, in everything that is praise-worthy, everything that is God-like, everything that is uplifting and that is purifying." He said, "You are called by the voice of the Prophet of God to do it, to be uppermost, to be the greatest and the best, the purest and the most devoted to the right."[24]

My daughters are here today. They are also examples to me. They, like the noble women of the past, stand as witnesses of everything that is pure and right. They know that they are daughters of God with responsibilities to bless and serve His children. They know that they belong to a divinely inspired organization which prepares them to receive all the blessings the Father has for them and gives them vision and direction to serve others and strengthen their families. Like Zina Young, they are nurturers and healers. Like Mary Fielding Smith, they live with faith and testimony. Like Lucy Meserve Smith, they provide relief for those in need. Like Louise Yates Robison, no matter how humble they feel, they do whatever they are called to do. Like their grandmother, Barbara Winder, they cheerfully sing in their homes and work unitedly with priesthood brethren in their families and in their callings.

I want my granddaughters—Jane, Claire, Susie, Eliza, Emma, Hannah, Abby, Annie, Gracie, Natalie, and Meg—to know of the legacy that is theirs through the great organization of Relief Society. I want them to know their mothers' stories of faith, testimony, and charity—and their mothers' mothers, and their mothers. Because then they will know who they are and what their purpose is. They will do as the Prophet Joseph urged: "To act according to those sympathies which God has planted in [their] bosoms. . . . To live up to [their] privileges." And they, like each of us, will be worthy to receive the blessing he promised, that "the angels cannot be restrain'd from being your associates."[25]

Notes

1. Joseph Smith, quoted in Sarah M. Kimball, "Auto-Biography," *Women's Exponent*, September 1, 1883, 51.

2. Ibid.

3. Ibid.

4. Joseph Smith, in Relief Society Minute Book, Nauvoo, Illinois, April 28, 1842, 38; available at http://josephsmithpapers.org/paperSummary/nauvoo-relief-society-minute-book#35.

5. Joseph Smith, in Relief Society Minute Book, Nauvoo, Illinois, June 9, 1842, 63; available at http://josephsmithpapers.org/paperSummary/nauvoo-relief-society-minute-book#60.

6. Ibid.

7. Joseph Smith, in Relief Society Minute Book, Nauvoo, Illinois, April 28, 1842, 38.

8. Joseph Smith, in Relief Society Minute Book, Nauvoo, Illinois, May 26, 1842, 52; available at http://josephsmithpapers.org/paperSummary/nauvoo-relief-society-minute-book#49.

9. Julie B. Beck, "Fulfilling the Purpose of Relief Society," *Ensign*, November 2008, 109; paragraphing altered.

10. Eliza R. Snow, in *Woman's Exponent*, September 15, 1873, 62; available at http://contentdm.lib.byu.edu/cgi-bin/showfile.exe?CISOROOT=/Womans Exp&CISOPTR=15696&filename=15697.pdf.

11. Henry B. Eyring, "The Enduring Legacy of Relief Society," *Ensign*, November 2009, 125.

12. "Mother," *The Young Woman's Journal* 22 (January 1911): 45; available at http://contentdm.lib.byu.edu/cgi-bin/showfile.exe?CISOROOT=/YWJ& CISOPTR=16345&filename=1312524.pdf. See also Mary Brown Firmage, "Great-Grandmother Zina: A More Personal Portrait," *Ensign*, March 1984, 34–38.

13. Cited in Joseph F. Smith, *Joseph F. Smith* [manual], in Teachings of Presidents of the Church series (Salt Lake City: The Church of Jesus Christ of Latter-day Saints, 1998), 31.

14. Joseph F. Smith, *Joseph F. Smith*, 32.

15. Ibid., 35.

16. Lucy Meserve Smith, in Kenneth W. Godfrey, Audrey M. Godfrey, and Jill Mulvay Derr, *Women's Voices: An Untold History of the Latter-day Saints, 1830–1900* (Salt Lake City: Deseret Book, 1982, 268–69; paragraphing altered.

17. Gladys Robison Winter, in *The Life and Family of Louise Yates Robison*, comp. Gladys Robison Winter, Church History Library.

18. Janet Peterson and LaRene Gaunt, *Elect Ladies: Presidents of the Relief Society* (Salt Lake City: Deseret Book, 1990), 124.

19. Ibid., 122.

20. Barbara W. Winder, "'I Love the Sisters of the Church,'" *Ensign*, May 1984, 59.

21. Peterson and Gaunt, *Elect Ladies*, 37.

22. Joseph Smith, in Relief Society Minute Book, Nauvoo, Illinois, April 28, 1842, 38.

23. Lynne Christy, "Now It's My Turn," *Ensign*, March 1992, 25–27.

24. Joseph F. Smith, *Joseph F. Smith*, 184.

25. Joseph Smith, in Relief Society Minute Book, Nauvoo, Illinois, April 28, 1842, 38.

IN PRAISE OF EVE'S FAITHFUL DAUGHTERS: THE LEGACY OF RELIEF SOCIETY THROUGH THE LIFE OF A GREAT-GRANDMOTHER

John S. Tanner

I believe that many, if not most, of the greatest spirits to have ever lived on earth have been women. There is scriptural warrant for this assertion in President Joseph F. Smith's vision of "the hosts of the dead," in which he saw "an innumerable company of the spirits of the just" (D&C 138: 11–12). He wrote that "among the great and mighty ones who were assembled in this vast congregation of the righteous were Father Adam . . . and our glorious Mother Eve, with *many* of her faithful daughters who had lived through the ages and worshiped the true and living God" (D&C 138:38–39; emphasis added). I love this verse. It confirms the presence of faithful women "among the great and mighty ones" who have walked the earth, and many of them. Although he mentions none of their names, I imagine that President Smith beheld at least as many women as men in that "vast congregation of the righteous"—and likely more, for women have played a disproportionate, if often unrecorded, role in promoting righteousness upon the earth. I am confident that when Heaven writes the history of the world out of the Lord's Book of Life, it will be replete with

---

John S. Tanner graduated magna cum laude with a BA in English from Brigham Young University in 1974, and received his PhD from the University of California at Berkeley in 1980. He has been a Senior Fulbright Lecturer in Brazil. He taught for several years in the English department at BYU, serving as chair of that department and in other leadership capacities at BYU, most recently academic vice president. He serves as the president of the Brazil São Paulo South Mission with his wife, Susan W. Tanner. They have five children and fifteen grandchildren.

stories of Eve's faithful daughters. It will tell of women whose lives may have seemed unremarkable in the grand sweep of history to some, but who will be remembered and celebrated long after many more famous figures pass into oblivion or infamy. The praises of Eve's faithful daughters will be sung by the hosts of heaven, their fame will echo across the eternities, and they will be crowned with unspeakable glory.

I praise all Eve's faithful daughters who have "worshiped the true and living God," especially the women who first burnished Relief Society's glorious legacy. To do this I shall focus on the life of one such woman, a faithful foremother who joined Relief Society in Nauvoo and who lived to celebrate its jubilee fifty years later. Her name is Elizabeth Haven Barlow. She is the first of seven generations of Relief Society presidents, and counting, in my mother's matrilineal line.[1] I focus on Elizabeth in order to put a name and face on the many relatively unknown rank-and-file women who established Relief Society. In doing so, however, let me stress that Elizabeth Haven Barlow stands for thousands upon thousands of Eve's faithful Latter-day Saint daughters in our day. These women are to be found in every era and every nation. They are new converts and multigenerational Mormons. They are married and single, rich and poor, tall and short, educated and unlearned. And they are legion. I am confident that Eve's faithful daughters are well represented in this conference. We truly "are compassed about with so great a cloud of witnesses" (Hebrews 12:1)—women witnesses, including women like Elizabeth Haven Barlow who formed the first Relief Societies.

These faithful daughters of Eve came in all shapes and sizes, as they do now. According to her daughter, Elizabeth Haven had dark eyes and hair (like her mother before her), a large frame, fine figure, and intensely rosy cheeks that turned so pink during periods of merriment that some accused her of painting them. Her daughter goes on to say that her mother had a "natural queenly appearance," was "charmingly proportioned," and "weighed over 200 pounds."[2] Alas, how ideas of beauty have changed!

The first women to join Relief Society also came with a variety of gifts and abilities, as they do today. Elizabeth's gifts included nimble fingers that could braid bonnets and straw hats "fifteen strands at a time,"[3] a bright mind, an independent spirit, a college education, and a deeply religious nature. She described herself as "a great lover of the Scriptures" even as a girl.[4] She used her practical skills as a milliner to earn money to attend Amherst and Bradford colleges, where she obtained a teacher's diploma and often led her friends in lively, lengthy discussions about religion.[5]

Like all the original members of Relief Society, Elizabeth had a conversion story to tell. Elizabeth's conversion occurred when she was twenty-six, still single and living at home. Her second cousins Brigham Young and Willard Richards visited her home in Holliston, Massachusetts, with a message about angels, revelation, and the Book of Mormon, which she said, "I read very attentively. The Spirit of God rested on me and I felt to say in my heart, 'This is the way I have long sought.'"[6] Conversion came at a cost for Elizabeth, as it often has for Eve's faithful daughters. Against the strenuous objections of her father,[7] a deacon in the Congregational Church, Elizabeth was baptized by Parley P. Pratt. She soon emigrated to Far West, Missouri. Happily, she eventually convinced her parents to join the Church and migrate to Nauvoo. Elizabeth taught school in Far West and in Nauvoo. Her students included the children of Joseph Smith, Hyrum Smith, and Brigham Young. When the mob came for the Prophet in Far West, Helen Mar Whitney writes that Elizabeth Haven, "a sweet lady, beloved by her scholars and all who became acquainted with her . . . allowed the children to go to the windows and look out."[8]

We often think of the Nauvoo Relief Society sisters as genteel, and many were. But they were not fragile. These women were made of stern stuff. Their resilient faith was forged in the fires of persecution, as was Elizabeth's. We can get a sense of Elizabeth's tenacious testimony from long letters she wrote in 1839 from Quincy, Illinois, to a Latter-day Saint cousin named Elizabeth Howe Bullard back in comfortable Holliston. Following are a few snippets that speak of her testimony amid trial. Such trial-tested testimony is among the most priceless legacies left by the faithful women who formed the Female Relief Society of Nauvoo.

Having been driven out of Missouri in the bitter winter of 1838–39, Elizabeth Haven writes her cousin on February 24, 1839:

"O! how Zion mourns, her sons have fallen in the streets by the cruel hand of the enemies and her daughters weep in silence. It is impossible for my pen to tell you of our situation, *only those who feel it, know.* . . .

"About 12 families cross the river into Quincy every day and about 30 are constantly at the other side waiting to cross; it is slow and grimy; there is only one ferry boat to cross in. . . .

"By the River of babylon we can sit down, yes, dear E[lizabeth], *we weep when we remember Zion.*"[9]

Yet despite her tears, Elizabeth's faith in the cause of Zion remained unshakable. Her letter continues: "To look at our situation at this present time it would seem that Zion is all destroyed, but it is not so, the work of the Lord is on the march."[10] Where others saw failure, Elizabeth saw the fulfillment of prophecy; she saw the gospel being spread at a quickening pace because of persecution. Although she recognized that things would get worse, having been warned by Heber C. Kimball to be prepared for trials ten times more severe,[11] she faced this prospect with courage and expected others to do so as well. She wrote to her cousin back home: "Let all who desire to live with the Saints, count the cost, before they set out on their pilgrimage to Zion. Come prepared to suffer with the Church in all their afflictions, not to flee as many have. . . . This church 'Wants no more cowards.'"[12] As I said, these women were made of stern stuff.

By the time Elizabeth Haven wrote her cousin again about six months later, the situation had become even more desperate. Fevers had broken out among Elizabeth's family in Quincy as well as among the Saints in swampy Commerce. In a letter composed while "sitting by herb tea close to the fire," Elizabeth admitted to being "wore out with fatigued [body] and loss of sleep" from tending those suffering from burning fevers and shaking ague. Yet she saw in the suffering not purposeless pain but purposeful sanctification. She wrote her cousin:

"Sister, we will rejoice for these trials are for our sanctification and will purify us to receive a bright crown of glory in the Celestial Kingdom with our crucified Christ. . . . The Spirit of the Lord has rested upon me within a few months as it never did before and although I have laboured hard, over the sick, night and day, yet communion with my Heavenly Father has sweetened many hours of toil."[13]

Women then and now have learned to find communion with God in the extremities of sickness, storm, sorrow, and suffering. Such robust faith is a priceless legacy from Eve's faithful daughters.

So is the legacy of loyalty to the Church and its leaders. Elizabeth concluded this letter by telling about a wealthy non-LDS neighbor in Quincy named Mr. Wells who "asked me one day if I would give up Mormonism if he would pay my passage back to Holliston." Mr. Wells and his family expected this educated, genteel young lady from the East to accept the invitation. "But in this," Elizabeth writes, "they were mistaken. I know in whom I have believed." Rebuffed, Mr. Wells told others that Elizabeth Haven would be sorry that she had followed "Joe Smith," but she remained, as she wrote, "undaunted." Her letter to her cousin concludes: "Pray for our Prophet, for it is a great blessing to us to hear a Prophet's voice again in the land. . . . Your sister in the gospel. Elizabeth Haven."[14]

These letters from Quincy give a sense of the character of the women who sat at Joseph's feet in the early meetings of Relief Society in Nauvoo. These meetings with Joseph were extremely important. They functioned as a sort of School of the Prophets for the sisters. Joseph's teachings inspired and guided Elizabeth and other Latter-day Saint women for generations. Thankfully, the minutes of these meetings were carefully recorded and preserved by Eliza R. Snow. Eliza brought them west, where they were used to reestablish Relief Society. They constitute an inestimable treasure for Latter-day Saint women and for the entire Church.[15]

One of the most remarkable of these meetings was held on April 28, 1842, the day Elizabeth Haven Barlow was admitted to the Society. At this meeting, the Prophet promised the sisters that "if you live up to your privileges, the angels cannot be restrain'd from being your associates—females, if they are pure and innocent can come into the presence of God." He told the sisters: "Iniquity must be purged out—then the vail [sic] will be rent and the blessings of heaven will flow down—they will roll down like the Mississippi river. This Society shall have power to command Queens in their midst."[16]

Joseph then instructed the Sisters in the principles of charity from 1 Corinthians 13, from which Relief Society would later draw its motto. He told them, "Let your hearts expand—let them be enlarged towards others—you must be longsuff'ring and bear with the faults and errors of mankind. How precious are the souls of men! . . . You must not be contracted, but you must be liberal in your feelings."[17]

" . . . I now turn the key to you in the name of God and this Society shall rejoice and knowledge and intelligence shall flow down from this time—this is the beginning of better days, to this Society."[18]

After recording Joseph's teachings in the Minutes for April 28, 1842, Eliza R. Snow wrote, "The spirit of the Lord was pour'd out in a very powerful manner, never to be forgotten by those present on that interesting occasion."[19]

Elizabeth Haven Barlow certainly never forgot what she learned in the Female Relief Society of Nauvoo. She understood that Relief Society was organized "under the priesthood after the pattern of the Priesthood,"[20] with a duly called and set apart president, assisted by two counselors. She knew that it was much more than a class and more than a benevolent society, for she heard the Prophet Joseph teach that "the Society is not only to relieve the poor, but to save souls."[21] And she realized, with keen anticipation, that Relief Society was preparing the sisters to be sanctified through temple ordinances. Before she left Nauvoo, Elizabeth was endowed with power and sealed to her husband Israel Barlow, whom she had married in 1840. She and Israel were privileged to serve as ordinance workers in the Nauvoo Temple.[22]

All her days, Elizabeth cherished her experiences in the Female Relief Society of Nauvoo. She carried a deep love for Relief Society across the plains to Utah. Her daughter Pamela wrote that "Mother had the privilege of associating with many noble women including Emma Smith, Eliza R. Snow, Zina D. Young, Mary Richards, Mary Fielding, Alvira Holmes, and many others who managed the affairs for the women in Nauvoo and gave such wonderful instruction. Many and many a time have I heard mother bear testimony of their greatness."[23]

Elizabeth enjoyed a special sisterhood with Relief Society sisters in Nauvoo. Pamela describes her mother and the other sisters taking crackers, cookies, and babies and gathering "to some home to discuss conditions" and to seek safety together when the mobs threatened and "no person could guess what was going to happen next."[24] Such sisterhood was precious to Elizabeth. It provided refuge for her, as Relief Society has for other Latter-day Saint women in these days.

By the time Elizabeth left Nauvoo, she had given birth to four children. Her first child died at birth in 1841. Her fourth was born in May 1846, just after the main body of Saints had left Nauvoo. She bore another baby while crossing the plains in 1848 and three more in Utah. Her last two children, twin boys, were born three months after her husband arrived in England on a mission. The twin named Willard died as a toddler. His father never saw him. The death of little Willard broke Elizabeth's heart. She wrote to Israel in England that people had often remarked, "'What a beautiful little boy Willard is!' Beautiful as he was the cruel hand of death marked him for his prey and snatched him from our sight. His lovely face and playful tricks are fondly intwined [sic] about my heart."[25]

Many years later the pain of Willard's death was still fresh. When Elizabeth received news that her daughter Pamela in faraway Panaca, Nevada, had "lost [her] lovely babe, sweet boy . . . I felt for a while I could hardly believe what I read." The news brought back memories of the death of "my little Willard" still "so fresh in my memory . . . I could never forget it." We do pioneer women a great injustice to suppose that, because infant mortality was common, it was not as trying for them as it is for us. Elizabeth wrote Pamela: "There are but few mothers but are called to part with their little ones. But O! how keen is the anguish of a fond mother's heart."[26]

Yet, in true Relief Society fashion, her own sharp sorrows engendered in Elizabeth's heart a readiness to reach out in compassionate service to others. Elizabeth's letter to Pamela continues: "Tuesday went to the Relief Society. . . . That night Sister Ashby gave birth to a pair of twin boys. The oldest lived 2 days, the other's alive yet. I have been down several times."[27] Eve's faithful daughters have always gone down to help the Sister Ashbys. Such is the glorious legacy of Relief Society.

Eventually, the Barlows settled in Bountiful. There, Elizabeth served as the first president of her ward Relief Society—twice. Such faithful service in Relief Society callings is also part of the legacy. Elizabeth was first called as Relief Society president in 1857. Her daughter records that the Bountiful society "soon had seventy-five active members holding meetings and doing wonderful work for the needy. The records show that during summer they gave sixty dollars in cash to help a poor widow in South Bountiful who had a sick son."[28] Sixty dollars! Out of pioneer poverty, when money was scarce, these Relief Society sisters somehow scraped together sixty dollars cash for a needy widow. It's amazing, yet typical. Such charity has been the hallmark of Relief Society from its inception.

With the coming of Johnston's army, the Bountiful Relief Society was disbanded less than a year after it was organized. It was not reestablished until 1868. Once again Elizabeth was called to serve as president—or in the language of the time, "presidentess"—with Lucinda Sessions and Mary Jane Crosby as her counselors.[29] Elizabeth served in this capacity for almost twenty years.

The local minutes of the Society's meetings provide a detailed record of her activities. Her most conspicuous accomplishment was to raise money to build a Relief Society hall. The fund-raising took many forms. In June 1875, she "moved that the ladies save their Sunday eggs and donate them for the building of the hall."[30] She also organized what were called "Fancy Fairs," at which were sold homemade rugs, mats, carpets, quilts, hats, bonnets, stockings, artificial flowers, many fine specimens of needle work, and "a thousand and one other things."[31] Eventually, the sisters in Bountiful raised $3,332.54 for a Society Hall. I love the exactness of this figure. It bespeaks hardworking, honest, frugal women on the frontier for whom every penny counted.

Elizabeth often hosted distinguished visitors to Relief Society, like Eliza R. Snow, Emmeline B. Wells, and Brigham Young, whom she delighted with her famous peach pies. She along with them instructed the sisters in their duties. On January 12, 1875, for example, she encouraged sisters to share more freely the things of the Spirit "which often burns in our bosoms." Then she admonished the visiting teachers to be "more alive to their duties and callings." Finally, she addressed the "young sisters who are present." After complimenting them for being there and encouraging them to "love virtue," she expressed concern that she often saw many of them on the Sabbath whispering and chewing gum while the elders were preaching. "My young sisters, refrain from such. . . ."[32]

At seventy-seven years old, Elizabeth was released as Bountiful's first Relief Society president, but she continued to champion Relief Society until the end of her days. In 1892, the year she died, Bountiful celebrated the fifty-year anniversary (or jubilee) of Relief Society. Elizabeth was invited to speak. The *Davis County Clipper* reported that this aging matriarch, "Not withstanding her feeble condition . . . *spoke at some length.* Aided, one would think, by some power higher than that of man."[33] She bore powerful testimony. Elizabeth was known for her ardent testimony. Her grandson observed that "Grandmother Barlow always had a deep burning testimony of the Gospel . . . the kind that came from her very soul, that is borne by one having the Holy Ghost."[34] But her testimony that day was particularly extraordinary. That day at the jubilee, a person who heard her speak reported that he "saw a halo of light . . . surrounding Sister Elizabeth H. Barlow, and [saw] the Prophet Joseph Smith come and stand by her side while she was talking."

I hope it is true that the Prophet Joseph came to the jubilee to provide his benediction upon the life and testimony of Grandma Barlow. For she had been true to the teachings and testimony that she absorbed at his feet and to the Female Society he organized in Nauvoo. She had lived as one of Eve's faithful daughters, burnishing the bright, beautiful legacy of Relief Society.

These faithful daughters of Eve are now, like Elizabeth Haven Barlow, often little-remembered except, perhaps, by their posterity. Yet the good they did is incalculable. They are like Dorothea, the heroine of George Eliot's novel *Middlemarch,* of whom Eliot wrote:

"Her full nature, like [a] river . . . spent itself in channels which had no great name on the earth. But the effect of her being on those around her was incalculably diffusive: for the growing good of the world is partly dependent on unhistoric acts; and that things are not so ill with you and me as they might have been, is half owing to the numbers who lived faithfully a hidden life, and rest in unvisited tombs."[35]

Eve's faithful daughters have often lived "a hidden life" in mortality, but I am persuaded that in eternity their lives will not be hidden. They will be well-known to heaven. They will be queens and priestesses who will assume an honored place among the mighty and great ones of heaven.

This same possibility holds for all those found possessed of charity at the last day. If charity never faileth in us—if it indeed flourishes—then it will be well with us. We too shall take our place among the noble and great ones. And our posterity may write of us what Elizabeth's daughter Pamela wrote of her mother in the tender, moving conclusion of her biography, with which I shall conclude this tribute to all Eve's faithful daughters: "To mother the gospel meant everything. No sacrifice was too great. . . . She dug sego roots and thistles and went to the canyon for wood while her husband was on his mission and she would have done it again had it been necessary. Nothing stirred her soul more than repeating the events she had passed through in Missouri and Nauvoo. The Gospel, coupled with seeing her family live righteously, was the joy of her life.

"She bore eight children, six sons and two daughters. . . . Let me close this biography by quoting from Revelation, 7th Chapter, ' . . . What are these which are arrayed in white robes? . . . And he said to me, These are they which came out of great tribulation, and have washed their robes, and made them white in the blood of the Lamb. . . . They shall hunger no more, neither [shall they] thirst . . . and God shall wipe away all tears from their eyes.'"[36]

May we too be numbered among the faithful sons of Adam and daughters of Eve who have washed their robes and made them white in the blood of the Lamb.

NOTES

1. See Athelia T. Woolley and Athelia S. Tanner, "Our Five-Generation Love Affair with Relief Society," *Ensign*, June 1978, 37–39.
2. "Biography of Elizabeth Haven Barlow: As Told by Pamela E. Barlow Thompson," typescript, prepared by Pamela Emeline Smith Grant, published by Israel Barlow Family Association, 1958, 1–2.
3. "Biography," 2.
4. Quoted in Ora H. Barlow, *The Israel Barlow Story and Mormon Mores* (The Israel Barlow Family Association and Publishers Press, 1968), 139.
5. "Biography," 2.
6. Barlow, *Israel Barlow Story*, 141.
7. See letter from John Haven to Elizabeth in Church History Library, MS 16271 in Elizabeth Haven Barlow Collection.
8. Barlow, *Israel Barlow Story*, 153.
9. Ibid., 142–43; This letter is also reprinted, in part, in Kenneth W. Godfrey, Audrey M. Godfrey, and Jill Mulvay Derr, *Women's Voices: An Untold History of the Latter-day Saints, 1830–1900* (Salt Lake City: Deseret Book, 1982): 106–15. The original letter of 24 February 1839 is held by the Church History Library, Barlow Family Collection, MS 941.
10. Barlow, *Israel Barlow Story*, 143.
11. Ibid., 145.
12. Ibid., 146–47.
13. Ibid., 159–61.
14. Ibid., 163–64.
15. The Nauvoo Relief Society Minute Book has recently been made available

online by the Church History Office as part of the Joseph Smith Papers Project. All citations from the Minutes are from this source. See http://beta.josephsmithpapers.org/paperSummary/nauvoo-relief-society-minute-book; accessed 29 September 2011.

16. Minutes, 35–36.
17. Ibid., 36–37.
18. Ibid., 40.
19. Ibid., 41.
20. Sarah M. Kimball, "Auto-biography," *Women's Exponent*, September 1, 1883, 51.
21. Minutes, 63.
22. Barlow, *Israel Barlow Story*, 222.
23. "Biography," 5.
24. Ibid.
25. Barlow, *Israel Barlow Story*, 369.
26. Ibid., 488.
27. Ibid., 489.
28. "Biography," 9. Also in Barlow, *Israel Barlow Story*, 420.
29. Barlow, *Israel Barlow Story*, 451.
30. Ibid., 478.
31. Ibid., 484–85.
32. Ibid., 493–94.
33. Ibid., 532.
34. Ibid.
35. George Eliot, *Middlemarch*, 4 vols. (London: William Blackwood and Sons, 1873), 4:371; available at http://books.google.com/books?id=bbYNAAAA QAAJ&printsec=frontcover&dq=middlemarch; accessed 24 August 2011.
36. "Biography," 10.

"DIVINELY ORDAINED OF GOD"

Heidi S. Swinton

On Wednesday, October 5, 1904, the fourth general president of the Relief Society, Bathsheba W. Smith, stood before the annual conference of sisters and admonished, "May we increase in love and have patience with each other, and may we have strength to do all that is required of us."[1]

Love, patience, and strength. Are not these the expressions of charity for which the Relief Society is known?

Bathsheba knew of what she spoke. She had been about the work of Relief Society for a very long time. She was among the twenty women who were invited to sit down with the Prophet Joseph Smith as he organized the Female Relief Society of Nauvoo by the power of the holy priesthood of God. At age nineteen, she was the youngest in the small congregation in the Red Brick Store. She began in the Lord's service at the same place in life that our young women join Relief Society today.

I have stood in that restored room, what is clearly sacred space, and reflected on the life and example of my third great-grandmother Bathsheba W. Smith. She counted herself so blessed to have been a sister of Relief Society, to have been schooled by the Prophet in the ways of the Lord,

Heidi S. Swinton *is the author of* To the Rescue: The Biography of Thomas S. Monson *and the screenwriter of several PBS documentaries, including* American Prophet. *She served with her husband, Jeffrey, who presided over the England London South Mission. They are the parents of five children and grandparents of nine grandchildren.*

to have been blessed by the power of the priesthood, to have been in the company of such remarkable women. So do I.

President Joseph F. Smith described Relief Society as "divinely made, divinely authorized, divinely instituted, divinely ordained of God."[2] It is the only such society commissioned of God within the framework of the restoration of all things.

The sisters' contributions to the Restoration could be chronicled by speaking of wheat and granaries, Relief Society halls in remote pioneer outposts, or the gracious office building facing the Salt Lake Temple. The historical records are filled with accounts of canning assignments, statistics of those visited, weekly meetings, curriculums, manuals, and work days. Many of us remember glass grapes and stuffed sock monkeys offered for sale at bazaars. But my focus of Relief Society is on the sisters. Indeed, the history of Relief Society is a stirring and continuously engaging account of women who have turned their lives over to God.

The Prophet Joseph charged the sisters in their June 9, 1842, meeting to "[search] after objects of charity"[3] and in the process to "not only relieve the poor but to save souls."[4] That is the essence of our heritage and our legacy. The history of Relief Society is found in these concise words, "Charity never faileth" (1 Corinthians 13:8). It has always been so.

Speaking of the early sisters, President Henry B. Eyring has explained, "Charity meant to them far more than a feeling of benevolence. Charity is born of faith in the Lord Jesus Christ and is an effect of His Atonement working in the hearts of the members. There are many benevolent groups of women who do great good. . . . This society," he said, "is composed of women whose feelings of charity spring from hearts changed by qualifying for and by keeping covenants offered only in the Lord's true Church. Their feelings of charity come from Him through His Atonement. Their acts of charity are guided by His example—and come out of gratitude for His infinite gift of mercy—and by the Holy Spirit, which He sends to accompany His servants on their missions of mercy. Because of that, they [the sisters of Relief Society] have done and are able to do uncommon things for others and to find joy even when their own unmet needs are great."[5]

I love that President Eyring ties Relief Society to the Atonement. The most significant act of charity in all dispensations of time was signaled by the Lord's declaration, "It is finished" (John 19:30). That we, as sisters of

Relief Society, have been blessed with the assignment of charity and mercy says much about the Lord's faith in us, His reliance on us to be His disciples and His desire for us to learn holiness from serving others. Amaleki spoke of offering "your whole souls" to Jesus Christ (Omni 1:26). We do that by putting on the altar our time, our gifts and blessings, our willingness and desires that we might in the process become "more Savior like thee."[6]

No question, Relief Society—its glorious past, present, and future—is inextricably tied to the testimonies the sisters have borne and today bear in words and deeds that Jesus Christ lives and that He atoned for us. Each one.

The Lord made it clear how we were to fulfill our singular assignments in this mortal world in Doctrine and Covenants 25: "Lay aside the things of this world, and seek for the things of a better" (D&C 25:10).

The early sisters did just that. They came together with "the fire of Israel's God"[7] burning in their hearts. Their faith gathered them together from different countries. They spoke different languages until it came to the language of the heart. They shared faith in God, and love He placed in their hearts, and charity that helped sustain them through terrible hardships and heartaches. Emma Smith described in their first meeting that they would face "extraordinary occasions and pressing calls."[8] Could there be a better description of "charity never faileth"?

Think for a moment when you have been part of an extraordinary occasion or pressing call. My thoughts go to Betty Walton. She is ninety-four. Betty was my first friend in my new ward. When I sat down next to her she beamed as she asked, "How are you, dear?" And she patted my hand. It reminded me of those days when I would pat the back of my son when he faced something new, something hard, as if to say, "Don't worry, I'm right here." The Savior has done that for each one of us for He has promised, "Be of good cheer, and do not fear, for I the Lord am with you, and will stand by you" (D&C 68:6). There is no question that He is standing by and placing a sister by our side.

So for me there was Betty, smartly dressed, her lovely white hair topped up generously in a bun. She is the matriarch of our ward, the weekly provider of flowers for the Relief Society and the chapel, the one quick to answer questions in Sunday School, the sister who makes you feel welcome. She's been at this work that Joseph Smith described as "caring for the poor and needy and saving souls" for a very long time. Betty is remarkably adept at ministering to anyone and everyone with great charity. Clearly, she has taken the Savior for her guide, knowing that He "went about doing good, . . . for God was with him" (Acts 10:38).

She is always leaving little things at my door as if I were a Beehive needing encouragement to press on in middle school. Just recently, she left me an Easter basket filled with chocolates, homemade cookies, and a little note expressing her love—and the statement, "No returns."

Betty is looking for nothing from me in return. President Thomas S. Monson calls it reaching out "to rescue." That is relief at its best. Indeed, the work of Relief Society is, as former Relief Society general president Elaine Jack has reminded us, "the power and strength of the fruits of the Spirit described in Galatians: love, joy, *peace,* longsuffering, gentleness, goodness, faith [Galatians 5:22; emphasis added]."[9]

President Joseph F. Smith said at a Relief Society conference in 1914, "It is for you to lead the world and to lead especially the women of the world, in everything that is praise-worthy, everything that is God-like, everything that is uplifting and that is purifying to the children of men."[10] Is there any question that our world—feeding on anger and placards in the streets, lawsuits in the courtrooms, demands for self-fulfillment, and the need for more power and position—desperately needs us!

Our offerings embrace both the work we do and the heart with which we do it. Through our efforts, small and simple though they may be, we are changed. Relief Society spurs us to be better, to do as the Lord asked: "Take my yoke upon you, and learn of me; for I am meek and lowly in heart" (Matthew 11:29). The prophet Alma puts it this way: "Have ye spiritually been born of God? Have ye received his image in your countenances?" (Alma 5:14). We all know sisters who are both Christlike and Christ-centered. My question today is, "Are *we?*"

Alma continues, "If ye have felt to sing the song of redeeming love, . . . can ye feel so now?" (Alma 5:26). What does that feel like? When has your heart been so full of the love of God that your expressions were far beyond just acts? They were filled with a chorus of angels singing, "Glory to God in the highest" (Luke 2:14). We are those angels.

President Joseph F. Smith held up the early sisters of Relief Society as an example to those who have followed. He said: "Think of Aunt Em [Emmeline B. Wells, the fourth general Relief Society president, who followed Bathsheba Smith] . . . coming into the Church when she was a little girl, passing through the trials and tribulations and disappointments and all the causes of anxiety and care incident to the early life of the Latter-day Saints, their exodus from Missouri and from Nauvoo to the Valleys of the mountains, over the deserts with nowhere to plant their feet and nowhere to lay their head. Was she discouraged? Was my mother discouraged? Was Aunt Vilate Kimball discouraged? No; they counted all these things dross and refuse to the light that they bore in their souls for God and His truth. Could you turn one of these women away from their convictions in the Church of Jesus Christ of Latter-day Saints? Could you darken their minds as to the mission of the Prophet Joseph Smith? Could you blind them with reference to the divine mission of Jesus Christ, the Son of God? No, never in the world could you do it. Why? Because they knew it. God revealed it to them, and they understood it, and no power on earth could turn them from what they knew to be that truth. Death was nothing to them. Hardship was nothing. Cold or rain, or heat, was nothing to them. All they felt and knew and desired was the triumph of the kingdom of God and the truth that the Lord had given to them."

And then he asked this sobering question, "My soul, where are these women now?"[11]

Are we such women, who press on, not demanding our own path be cleared but rather clearing the path for others? That was the divine mission of the Savior and He asks us to follow. Will we hear the voice of the Lord saying at that triumphant day, "Come unto me ye blessed, for behold, your works have been the works of righteousness upon the face of the earth" (Alma 5:16)?

Bonnie Parkin, when called as the Relief Society general president in 2002, said in her remarks at general conference, "If I could have one thing happen for every woman in this Church, it would be that they would feel the love of the Lord in their lives daily."[12] Sometimes that love pours down from heaven when we are on our knees, or standing with the wind in our face. But most often it comes from a sister sharing the love the Lord placed in her heart to fill our need.

We have come to expect that rescue efforts must be accompanied by cameras and media such as we have seen for the recent mine disasters and tsunami. We may define service as a project that calls for us to sign up for several hours on a Saturday, or travel to foreign soil, or other grand heroics. Certainly Relief Society is tied to welfare efforts around the world, from wheelchair deliveries to flood cleanup to measles campaigns. But I think that when the Lord promised "angels round about to bear you up," he was thinking of Relief Society sisters who serve those who live next door, down the street, or in a neighboring ward. We sing, "The errand of angels is given to women,"[13] because that is what we shoulder in this great Restoration.

Genevieve Allen is one of my angels. I was sitting in stake conference twenty-five years ago when my husband was called to serve as a counselor in the newly organized stake presidency. I had four young boys lined up on the row by me and to all appearances this was a wonderful moment for our family. Except it meant leaving the young single adult ward in which we had served for eight years; my husband had been the bishop. I loved that ward. I loved that the sisters so loved the Lord. For them, living away from home and often alone, the Lord was their companion. That reverence and reliance on Jesus Christ was not lost on me.

But now we would go back to our resident ward. It was a highly transient ward; I was sure I wouldn't know anyone. My eyes were spilling tears as I contemplated starting over in essentially a new ward—alone—when a hand from behind me touched my shoulder. I turned and there was Genevieve Allen, sitting with the other widows on the bench behind. She said softly, "Oh, what a blessing to have you back. I will save you a seat on Sunday in Relief Society."

And she did.

It is curious that those who have blessed me in Relief Society are widows. It is supposed to be the other way around!

President Monson, our prophet, seer, and revelator on the earth today, has described charity, the pure love of Christ, this way:

"I have in mind the charity that manifests itself when we are tolerant of others and lenient toward their actions, the kind of charity that forgives, the kind of charity that is patient.

"I have in mind the charity that impels us to be sympathetic, compassionate, and merciful, not only in times of sickness and affliction and distress but also in times of weakness or error on the part of others.

"There is a serious need for the charity that gives attention to those who are unnoticed, hope to those who are discouraged, aid to those who are afflicted. True charity is love in action. The need for charity is everywhere.

"Needed is the charity which refuses to find satisfaction in hearing or in repeating the reports of misfortunes that come to others, unless by so doing, the unfortunate one may be benefited. . . .

"Charity is having patience with someone who has let us down. It is resisting the impulse to become offended easily. It is accepting weaknesses and shortcomings. It is accepting people as they truly are. It is looking beyond physical appearances to attributes that will not dim through time. It is resisting the impulse to categorize others."[14]

President Monson often speaks of the Relief Society in his days as a bishop more than fifty years ago. He was twenty-two when he was called to serve a ward that was enormous by today's standards: 1,080 members. A man with a great eye for detail, he discovered that the record for subscriptions to the *Relief Society Magazine* had hit what he called "a low ebb." Prayerfully, he called Elizabeth Keachie to the task of increasing the influence of Relief Society in every home by increasing the number subscribing to the magazine. She responded in her thick Scottish accent, "I'll do it."

She and her sister-in-law, Helen Ivory, both of them barely five feet tall, canvassed the ward street by street, alley by alley, and home by home. They were unbelievably successful bringing in subscriptions—their efforts equaled all the other wards in the stake combined. When Bishop Monson congratulated the two sisters for a job well done, Elizabeth spoke up, "We still have two square blocks to cover."

"Oh, Sister Keachie," he responded, "no one lives on those blocks. They are totally industrial."

She was not to be diverted. "I will feel better if Nell and I go and check them ourselves."

It was raining the day Elizabeth and Helen covered the final area. They had found no homes until they paused to cross the puddles in the street and noticed down the alley a solitary and uninviting garage. But it was not totally dark or deserted. A door, not easily seen from the street, had been cut into the side and a light shone through a small window.

You can almost hear their exchange: "There's a light in that window of that garage down at the end. Do we know who lives there? Do you think we should see if they are interested in subscribing to the magazine?" The two sisters made their way to the door. An older man, William Ringwood, answered and they launched into their pitch to have every home in the ward receive the *Relief Society Magazine*. William, age sixty-eight, replied, "You'd better ask my father."

Charles Ringwood, age ninety-two, came to the door and listened to their presentation. There was no woman living in that house, but he subscribed.

Their visit had little to do with magazine circulation. Those two women that night rescued two lost souls. When Bishop Monson requested their records from Church headquarters, he learned they had been in the "lost and unknown" file for sixteen years.

President Monson is quick to say that the saving work performed by Relief Society sisters is not about programs or assignments. It's about people. He has described gazing upon those two faithful sisters sitting on the back bench at the funeral of Charles Ringwood. "I have contemplated their personal influence for good," he has said, and "the promise of the Lord filled my very soul: 'I the Lord am merciful and gracious unto those who fear me, and delight to honor those who serve me in righteousness and truth unto the end. Great shall be their reward and eternal shall be their glory' [D&C 76:5–6]."[15]

President Monson has described Charles Ringwood as the oldest deacon he had ever met. Those two sisters, with the help of young Bishop Monson, got him to the temple. They prepared him to go to his heavenly home. Brother Ringwood died just weeks after receiving his endowment.

For Brother Ringwood, charity never faileth.

When we are tempted to question the significance of an assignment President Monson would point us to these words:

> *"Father, where shall I work today?"*
> *And my love flowed warm and free.*
> *Then he pointed out a tiny spot*

And said, "Tend that for me."
I answered quickly, "Oh no, not that!
Why, no one would ever see,
No matter how well my work was done.
Not that little place for me."
And the word he spoke, it was not stern;
He answered me tenderly:
"Ah, little one, search that heart of thine;
Art thou working for them or for me?
Nazareth was a little place,
And so was Galilee."[16]

In 2010, our bishop called a new Relief Society presidency. I received a phone call a few weeks later and the new Relief Society president asked if she and her counselors could come and visit me. I was trying feverishly, night and day, to complete President Monson's biography. I didn't have time to eat, sleep, or talk to the new presidency. But I found myself saying yes. They arrived and we chatted. I didn't know them well, but I could feel that the Lord had called them to serve. And they had come to serve me. The president said after a few minutes, "How can we help you?"

I started to cry. You see, I knew I was safe with these sisters, my sisters in Relief Society. They were on the Lord's errand. I said, as I wiped my eyes, "Just support me, have faith I can get this done, that I can get it right. Please pray for me." On Sunday, the Relief Society president asked the sisters in the ward to keep me in their prayers. I was so grateful. From that experience we formed a bond, my sisters and I, that renews every time I see them. That's what we do for each other.

The history of Relief Society abounds with illustrations of such charity. When Bathsheba Smith visited the homes of sisters—for both social and compassionate purposes—she left with these words, "Peace be unto thee, peace to this house." We can all offer such prayers for one another.

When Alma admonished at the waters of Mormon that we "bear one another's burdens, that they may be light" (Mosiah 18:8), he must have been thinking of Relief Society sisters. Such charity never faileth. It has always been so.

To those of us who think of Relief Society as a meeting on Sunday, or an obligation to visit one another, but take it no further, think again. It was Lucy Mack Smith who, in one of the first meetings of Relief Society, spoke with vision for our time: "We must cherish one another, watch over one another, comfort one another and gain instruction that we may all sit down in heaven together."

In her closing remarks at a 1905 general Relief Society meeting, Sister Bathsheba (that's what they lovingly called her) said, "I feel to . . . ask the Lord to bless you . . . and give you faith in the Gospel and in each other . . . may you be united in all things you undertake to do, and the Lord will bless you and prosper you in your labors and give you faith for the sick and the afflicted, and give you means for the poor and the needy, that you may fill up your days in righteousness and in doing good."[17]

This work is not about mortality. It is about applying God's principles to how we live here that we may be exalted hereafter. The Lord has gone before us and shown the way. May we add to the pages of the history of this great Relief Society our own witness that "Charity Never Faileth."

NOTES

1. "General Relief Society Conference," *Woman's Exponent*, 1 January 1905 (vol. 33, no. 7): 53.
2. Joseph F. Smith, *Joseph F. Smith* [manual], Teachings of Presidents of the Church series (Salt Lake City: The Church of Jesus Christ of Latter-day Saints, 1998), 183.
3. Nauvoo Relief Society Minute Book, March 17, 1842–March 16, 1844, 7; available at http://josephsmithpapers.org/paperSummary/nauvoo-relief-society-minute-book#4; accessed 25 August 2011.
4. Ibid., 63; available at http://josephsmithpapers.org/paperSummary/nauvoo-relief-society-minute-book#60; accessed 25 August 2011.
5. Henry B. Eyring, "The Enduring Legacy of Relief Society," *Ensign*, November 2009, 121.
6. Philip Paul Bliss, "More Holiness Give Me," *Hymns of The Church of Jesus Christ of Latter-day Saints* (Salt Lake City: The Church of Jesus Christ of Latter-day Saints, 1985), no. 131.
7. Jane Charters Robinson Hindley, cited in Fred E. Woods, "'We Wanted to Come to Zion,'" *Ensign*, March 2005, 30.
8. Emma Smith, Nauvoo Relief Society Minute Book, March 17, 1842–March

16, 1844, 12; available at http://josephsmithpapers.org/paperSummary/ nauvoo-relief-society-minute-book#9; accessed 25 August 2011.

9. Elaine L. Jack, "Relief Society: A Balm in Gilead," *Ensign*, November 1995, 91.

10. Joseph F. Smith, *Joseph F. Smith*, 184.

11. Ibid., 188–89.

12. Bonnie Parkin, "Feel the Love of the Lord," *Ensign*, May 2002, 84.

13. Emily H. Woodmansee, "As Sisters in Zion," *Hymns*, no. 309.

14. Thomas S. Monson, "Charity Never Faileth," *Ensign*, November 2010, 124.

15. Monson, "Your Personal Influence," *Ensign*, May 2004, 22–23.

16. Meade MacGuire, "'Father, Where Shall I Work Today?'" in *Best-Loved Poems of the LDS People*, comp. Jack M. Lyon et al. (Salt Lake City: Deseret Book, 1996), 152.

17. Bathsheba Smith, in *Women's Exponent*, June 1905 (vol. 34, no. 1): 5.

THE LEGACY OF A WOMAN OF GOD

Ann M. Dibb

My theme comes from a powerful talk given by Sister Margaret D. Nadauld, former Young Women general president, at the October 2000 general conference. I recommend that you read and study her talk, "The Joy of Womanhood." It is a classic for all women. I still remember the spiritual confirmation that came over me when I heard Sister Nadauld express:

"Women of God can never be like the women of the world. The world has enough women who are tough; we need women who are tender. There are enough women who are coarse; we need women who are kind. There are enough women who are rude; we need women who are refined. We have enough women of fame and fortune; we need more women of faith. We have enough greed; we need more goodness. We have enough vanity; we need more virtue. We have enough popularity; we need more purity."[1]

Sister Nadauld's life is a testimonial of her personal conviction. She models each of these attributes in everything she says and does. I believe one of the ways she became such a woman of God is that she had a mother who modeled and taught these virtues to Sister Nadauld and many others

---

Ann M. Dibb is the second counselor in the Young Women general presidency. She graduated from Brigham Young University with a bachelor's degree in elementary education and has served in each of the Church auxiliaries. At the time of her call to the Young Women general board, she was serving in the Relief Society presidency of her home ward. She is married to Roger Dibb, and they are the parents of one daughter and three sons.

for eighty-nine years. Sister Nadauld observed and applied her mother's teachings in her own life and in turn taught others.

How do I know these things? I read Sister Nadauld's mother's obituary, which began, "Our dearly beloved Helen Bailey Dyreng . . ." It continued by stating, "She was revered for her deep beauty, artistic touch, elegant entertaining, handmade quilts, beautiful writing, rolls and canning the abundance of [her husband] Morgan's garden."[2]

I like to read the obituaries found in my daily newspaper. I've been reading them for years. I believe there are good and important lessons to be learned by reading these brief abridgments of an individual's life. My testimony and my desire to live a righteous life have been strengthened by doing so.

The chorus of a gospel pop song I enjoy begins with the words, "I want to leave a legacy / How will they remember me? Will it be for _____?"[3] I'm omitting the last word because this is the question each of us should be asking ourselves continually. Interestingly enough, we are the ones who determine, by the individual choices we make and the relationships we nurture, the legacy we leave behind and how we are remembered. Will we be remembered for our tenderness, kindness, refinement, faith, goodness, virtue, and purity, as taught by Sister Nadauld? Will we be known as women of the world or women of God?

Many times, while reading obituaries, I learn "the good, the bad, and the ugly" about an individual's life.

There are those like Sister Dyreng, who have lived a full and memorable life. Then there are those which are quite sad, and it is evident the deceased lived their life distant from the teachings of the gospel. There is a fascinating variety.

Today I'd like to share with you just a few interesting tidbits taken from my "obituary file" and what I have learned from them. I didn't know any of these individuals in mortality, but because of what I've read, I wish I had. I share these words with you because they make me reflect upon the refrain of that song, "I want to leave a legacy / How will they remember me?"

"'Doris' [not her real name] danced to her own drummer." This brief phrase is usually a red flag that tells me this individual's life may be different than my own. "She built hot rods and loved telling a dirty joke to good friends." Personally I would not choose to be remembered in such a way. However, the same obituary continues: "If your path was hard and muddy, 'Doris' would put you on her shoulders and carry you through. She will be dearly missed."

After reading such an obituary, I ask myself, Would others express the same sentiment about my willingness to serve others? I'm not sure. Would I want them to? Absolutely. What am I going to do about this discovery? I guess I should become more sensitive to others' needs and strive to be more compassionate. I need to be less judgmental. These are needful lessons I'm reminded of and want to implement in my life.

A surprising number of obituaries state, "She was an avid Utah Jazz fan." I didn't like the worldly comment expressed by daughters about their mother: "We loved to go tanning and get manicures with our mother." Unfortunately, I didn't have time to attend the funeral of one woman I didn't know. I wanted to because her obituary stated that her secret cookie recipe would be shared with all who attended the funeral.

Leland Wright's family "will cherish fondly the memories of his personal attention."[4] This compliment is in keeping with a man who had served as a bishop, a counselor in two stake presidencies, a patriarch, and a temple worker. Obviously his children, in spite of his continual Church service, were the recipients of their father's personal attention.

I liked Arthur's happy picture and the comment, "He was a most gentle and honest man."[5]

Alice Hafen accomplished many great things in her ninety-seven years. Her obituary reads: "Always service oriented, her hands were never idle as she sought to do good each day. Skilled at the art of homemaking, she used her heart and hands to bless the lives of others, nourishing our bodies as well as our souls. Alice exhibited extraordinary yet simple faith and grit in challenging times. She maintained a joyful and positive perspective. She was without guile. . . . She touched the lives of all within her family circle, and considered family her most prized possession. . . . She helped us unlock the knowledge of who we really are by teaching us about our forebears and showing us what it means to truly be Christ-like."[6]

Sometimes we are tested in mortality in ways that we may not have chosen for ourselves. Wanda Roberts's obituary reads: "These past few years she agonized over her memory loss, but she never forgot her testimony of Jesus Christ. She never forgot to keep His commandments and express gratitude. . . . Proverbs is true. ' . . . for her price is far above rubies.'"[7]

I don't know if Mr. Young was a member of the Church or not. Latter-day Saints are not the only ones who are admirable for their Christian adherence and devotion. They are not the only ones who qualify for my file of favorite obituaries. I certainly was touched by what I read and want to be more like him and his wife. The obituary told of his final illness and how his loving wife "battled alongside him, caring for him 'in sickness,' true to the vows they made sixty-six years ago. [He] was a man of exemplary character and remarkable achievement, but most importantly he was a strong and loving husband, father, grandfather and great-grandfather. He inspired us with his dedication to family and his strong work ethic; his honesty and his willingness to speak the truth in love; and his optimistic approach to life. . . . He was frugal, but generous of spirit, willingly sharing the fruits of his labor with family, friends, and charitable causes." He inspired through his example. He was patient, encouraging, kind, fair, and loyal. This is my favorite statement concerning Mr. Young: "We know that he is now with God who loves him even more than we do."[8]

Being a Young Women leader, I identified with Betty Lee Taggart's obituary. It said, "Through . . . challenges [she] learned the virtues of industry and thrift, lessons that served her well throughout her life." She married her husband in the temple, and together they raised eleven children. "Her family was her life's work and joy." Betty passed away one day before her eighty-third birthday, surrounded by her family. "Mom was released the Sunday before her death as the secretary in her ward Young Women's organization and was presented with her Young Womanhood Recognition medallion the day before she died."[9]

"I want to leave a legacy / How will they remember me?" Betty will be remembered as being resilient, hardworking, a noble mother, faithful, and as having endured to the end.

There are other commendations that at times bear a resemblance to the accolades listed in obituaries. These tributes are found in our scriptures. Let me list just a few:

- The brother of Jared was given a miraculous vision because of his great faith (see Ether 12:20).
- Noah, Nephi, King Benjamin, and many other prophets were known as being just men (see Moses 8:27; Alma 3:6; Omni 1:25).
- David was a courageous boy. He became a mighty king, but he lost eternal blessings because he failed to keep God's commandments and endure to the end.[10]
- The prophet Ammaron recognized greatness in the young boy and future prophet Mormon, saying he was "a sober child, and . . . quick to observe" (Mormon 1:2).
- Naaman was "mighty . . . in valour" (2 Kings 5:1).
- Moroni was "a strong and a mighty man . . . of a perfect understanding" (Alma 48:11).
- Ruth was greatly blessed and eventually married Boaz because "all the city . . . doth know" that Ruth was "a virtuous woman" (Ruth 3:11).
- A very noble expression of approval is found in D&C 124:20: "And again, verily I say unto you, my servant George Miller is without guile; he may be trusted because of the integrity of his heart; and for the love which he has to my testimony I, the Lord, love him."
- A singular tribute and honor was given to Abraham. Abraham is referred to by the Lord as being "my friend" (Isaiah 41:8).
- It was prophesied of Mary, the Savior's mother, in 1 Nephi 11:15 that she would be "a virgin, most beautiful and fair above all other[s]." Mary described herself as "the handmaid of the Lord" (see Luke 1:38).
- There is no finer example of one who exemplified every noble attribute than our Savior, Jesus Christ, God's Only Begotten Son in the flesh. He was known as the Good Shepherd, Advocate, Servant, Prince of Peace, Teacher, Life and Light of the World. We must do as the Primary song encourages: "Try to be like him, / Try, try, try."[11]

How do *we* become so good? Will people ever write such words about us? In order to leave such a legacy, we must be obedient in keeping all of God's commandments. We must be teachable and practice moral discipline. As parents, we must live faithfully, as we are constant examples to our children. Many times we must master the virtues of patience and long-suffering. We must shun evil; repent; forget self and serve God by serving others, showing charity in all that we do; work; pray; be worthy of and respond to the promptings of the Holy Ghost; "feast upon the words of Christ," because "the words of Christ will tell [us] all things what [we] should do" (2 Nephi 32:3).

Some may say, "All of this is too hard. It is impossible because of the wickedness of the world and our mortal condition." Unfortunately, in weakness, the natural man may fall prey to the temptations of Satan. Satan is very real and wants us to be "miserable like unto himself" (2 Nephi 2:27). We must choose to fortify ourselves. We are admonished to "be strong and of a good courage" (Joshua 1:9).

I remember once lamenting to our son Alan, "Why can't everyone just choose to be good?" He wisely responded, "Everyone is not the same, Mom. The true test comes when you make a mistake and you have to practice humility and then change. You have to have the courage to pick yourself up and repent." One of the greatest prophets in the Book of Mormon was Alma the Younger. In a miraculous manner, he changed his legacy and how he would be remembered. He repented. He picked himself up and went forward in righteousness. After this mighty change of heart, he continually proclaimed the power of Jesus Christ, the Savior's love, His gospel, and His atoning sacrifice for all mankind to all who would listen.

Why should we strive to be remembered for our righteous life? One reason is that we never know when we will leave mortality. "Joe" was not ready to leave this mortal existence. His obituary was written in first-person narrative and read, "On Friday evening I was driving to dinner with my wife and suddenly the plan was changed and I was called home against my wishes." I felt a tinge of bitterness as I read these words. We don't control when we leave mortality. We must strive to live day by day in such a manner that we are prepared for this very real eventuality.

I'd like to close with one final obituary, experience, and lesson. On January 17, 2009, I opened my paper and there was the picture of a beautiful young girl. Her obituary reads: "Megan Sylvie Pysnak, fifteen, passed away . . . after a skiing accident. . . . Megan was nicknamed 'Love,' because she was full of charity." She received her Young Womanhood Recognition award when she was thirteen and was in the process of applying for a presidential scholarship at Brigham Young University because of her extraordinary achievements.[12] It continued by listing many wonderful things. I was so moved by what I'd read, I chose to attend her viewing and her funeral. I didn't know Megan.

I was unprepared for what I saw, learned, and felt. Beautiful childhood pictures and remembrances were displayed. Also included was her Young Womanhood medallion and Megan's ACT scores. I could understand how she could apply for BYU's highest scholarship, even though she was only fifteen. I was teary as I saw Megan's handwritten testimony and her little handmade temple recommend case. There was a poster with Megan's picture and personalized comments written by her teenage friends. These are the sentiments I read: "She was an amazing spirit; she radiated light. She was talented and smart. She was sweet and happy. She was the nicest person. She knew everything about the Book of Mormon. She had a spirit that words can't express. She always smiled at me. She was kind, truly a daughter of God. She was filled with love, and she raised everyone up by showing her love to everyone." One young man wrote, "I can imagine Megan, enclosed in Christ's arms, with Christ saying, 'Well done, my wise and faithful servant.'" Megan was prepared to return home to her Heavenly Father.

Reading and learning of a beautiful young girl, Megan Sylvie Pysnak, in an eight-inch obituary made me want to be better. And that is what this earth life is all about—becoming better, becoming more like our Savior, Jesus Christ.

I'm going to continue to read my obituaries. I'm going to continue to read my scriptures. I believe the truth and importance of the words of a simple song: "I want to leave a legacy / How will they remember me?"

May each of us live our life in such a way so as to be known for being tender, kind, refined, faithful, good, virtuous, and pure. In this way we will have demonstrated that choice to forgo being considered women of the world. We worked diligently in mortality to leave as our personal legacy the remembrance that we were women of God. We were disciples of our Lord and Savior, Jesus Christ. May this be our constant desire and prayer.

NOTES

1. Margaret D. Nadauld, "The Joy of Womanhood," *Ensign*, November 2000, 15.
2. Obituary of Helen Bailey Dyreng, *Deseret News*, 7 July 2010, B5.
3. Nichole Nordeman, "Legacy," *Woven and Spun*, audio CD (Brentwood, Tenn.: Sparrow Records, 2002).
4. Obituary of Leland Heiner Wright Sr., *Deseret News*, 20 January 2010, B6.
5. Obituary of Arthur R. Christensen, *Deseret News*, 20 January 2010, B7.
6. Obituary of Alice Peel Hafen, *Deseret News*, 20 January 2010, B7.
7. Obituary of Wanda Roberts, *Deseret News*, 6 April 2005, B6.
8. Obituary of Robert Paul Young, *Deseret News*, 20 January 2010, B6.
9. Obituary of Betty Lee Howell Taggart, *Deseret News*, 20 January 2010, B6.
10. See "Guide to the Scriptures," s.v. "David"; available at http://lds.org/scriptures/gs/david?lang=eng&letter=d.
11. James R. Murray, "Jesus Once Was a Little Child," *Children's Songbook* (Salt Lake City: The Church of Jesus Christ of Latter-day Saints, 1989), 55.
12. See obituary of Megan Sylvie Pysnak, *Deseret News*, 17 January 2009, B5.

"Charity Never Faileth"

Elaine S. Dalton

In his discourse near the end of the Book of Mormon, Mormon declares that "charity [pure love] never faileth" (Moroni 7:46). The gift of charity comes from the Savior. Charity is there because Christ is there. It endures from the darkest night through difficult trials and on into the sunshine because He does. God so loved us that He gave His Only Begotten Son (see John 3:16). Christ so loved us that His infinite Atonement made it possible for us to return back to our heavenly home and into the presence of God's pure love. Mormon's promise is that such love, the pure love of Christ, is bestowed only upon true followers of Jesus Christ (see Moroni 7:47–48). Christ loved us, and that is how He hoped we would love each other.

I think I will have forever emblazoned in my mind an image of twin girls that was published in a magazine some years ago. These two little girls were born twelve weeks premature. One of the girls weighed two pounds and was struggling with problems ranging from breathing issues

Elaine S. Dalton is the Young Women general president. She was born and raised in Ogden, Utah, and received her bachelor's degree in English from Brigham Young University. Before her calling as the Young Women general president, she served as both first and second counselor in the Young Women general presidency. Prior to this service she served on the Young Women general board for five years. She has served in all the auxiliaries of the Church on both ward and stake levels. She is married to Stephen E. Dalton, and they are the parents of five sons and one daughter and the grandparents of ten grandchildren.

and troubling blood-oxygen levels to heart-rate difficulties. Her sister was two pounds three ounces and was considered the stronger of the two.

When the twins were a little less than a month old, the smaller of the two girls went into critical condition. The article recounted: "She began gasping for breath, and her face and stick-thin arms and legs turned bluish-gray. Her heart rate was way up. . . . Her parents watched, terrified that she might die." The nurse did all she could, and nothing seemed to work. She then remembered a common procedure in parts of Europe that helped struggling premature babies that was called double-bedding. After the parents gave permission, the nurse put the two babies together in one incubator, hoping it would do some good. "No sooner had the door of the incubator closed than [the struggling twin] snuggled up to [her sister]— and calmed right down. Within minutes [her] blood-oxygen readings were the best they had been since she was born. And as she dozed, [her sister] wrapped her tiny arm around her smaller sibling."[1] The rest of the story, as they say, is history.

Do any of you ever feel stressed or overwhelmed or have an especially bad day? Perhaps what we all need is an arm around us, a snuggle, or to feel the warmth and strength of a sister's loving touch.

I love this true story because I think it is what we can do for others. It is what we, as sisters, can do for each other, what wives can do for husbands and children, and what each of us can do for everyone in the world. We are all God's precious children; each is beloved. We are here to become like Him—to follow the example of His Son and to become as He *is* as we do as He *does*. I believe the words of a once popular tune are more true today than ever: "What the world needs now is love, sweet love / It's the only thing that there's just too little of."[2]

In order to possess true charity, each of us must come to know and understand several things. First is our identity—who we are and who we have always been. The Young Women theme is true doctrine: "We are daughters of our Heavenly Father, who loves us, and we love Him."[3] His love is infinite and eternal. He loved us so much that He sent His Son to make it possible for us to return to Him once again. When we understand our identity, then that understanding defines all of our relationships. As C. S. Lewis said, "There are no *ordinary* people. You have never talked to a mere mortal."[4] And Brigham Young taught, "When we look upon the human face we look upon the image of our Father and God; there is a divinity in each person, male and female; there is the heavenly, there is the divine."[5]

Second, we must be pure. Moroni's final words to each of us in these latter days—a generation he literally saw—exhorted us to "come unto Christ, and lay hold upon every good gift, and touch not the evil gift, nor the unclean thing" (Moroni 10:30). His exhortation or warning to us was to be pure and virtuous. He was an eyewitness to what happened to a society who had lost their faith, hope, and charity because they had lost their virtue and purity. Why did he exhort us in this manner? It corresponds to his father's message on charity and gaining eternal life and the need to "lay hold upon every good thing . . . until the coming of Christ" (Moroni 7:25). Why? That "when he shall appear we shall be like him, for we shall see him as he is; . . . that we may be purified even as he is pure" (Moroni 7:48). The principle is never-changing—*purity* cannot come from an *impure* source. Mormon teaches that "a bitter fountain cannot bring forth good water; neither can a good fountain bring forth bitter water" (Moroni 7:11). Thus, pure love cannot come from an impure source. In order to possess pure love, we must *be* pure and virtuous! We are developing patterns of thought and behavior, and they must be based on high moral standards. Our personal purity in thought and action will entitle us to receive the constant companionship of the Holy Ghost.

Third, since charity is a spiritual gift that is *bestowed* upon us, it comes as a result of the reception of the Holy Ghost. And since the gift of the Holy Ghost is given only to members of the Church, it follows that the fruits and gifts of this Spirit are given in their fulness to Church members. Elder Bruce R. McConkie taught this principle: "Men [and women] must receive the gift of the Holy Ghost before that member of the Godhead will take up his abode with them and begin the supernal process of distributing his gifts to them. . . . Thus the gifts of the Spirit are for believing, faithful, righteous people; they are reserved for the saints of God."[6]

Fourth, as we make and keep our covenants, the promises those covenants contain will help us to become as the Savior and—bit by bit, week by week—develop the ability to love as He would love until we will become possessed with charity at the last day. This is a process, not an event.

So we must continually, daily, step by step, keep moving in that direction, always remembering Him and keeping His commandments.

Several years ago, President Gordon B. Hinckley spoke about the women of the Church—you and me—in a worldwide broadcast. I still remember how I felt as I heard him refer to the women of the Church "as the one bright shining hope in a world [that is] marching toward [moral] self-destruction."[7] I still have my dog-eared copy of that speech. It awakened inside of me a sense of who I am and of my eternal identity and possibilities. When imperfect people commit to shining, loving, and serving in our appointed places, as we stretch forth our arms and encircle others, we can know that all the while we are encircled "in the arms of [His] love" (D&C 6:20). I testify that this is true, because I have felt that love here from time to time. As women we must never lose sight of our divine identity and the fact that our influence, our love—our pure love—is powerful and paramount. We set the tone in our homes; we nurture and love. And charity—the pure love of Christ—never faileth.

We often think of charity as an action, but I think of charity as a state of the heart. Since my call to be the Young Women general president, I have felt it come as a gift in my life. It is powerful; it is life changing; and it includes the ability to see with new eyes and feel with a new heart. It includes the gift of seeing others as God sees them. The true charity of which I speak makes it possible, and even easy, to look beyond behavior, outward dress, or appearance to the nobility within. It is a technicolor look into an immortal soul. The gift of charity enables the recipient to discern and to know the heart. Words are inadequate to describe this gift. But this I absolutely know: nearly every young woman can be reached, softened, and brought back to a knowledge of her infinite worth by love—that pure love of which I speak today. Pure love—charity—never faileth.

Charity is a spiritual gift that is bestowed from the Father to all who are true followers of His Son, Jesus Christ. The gift of charity comes because of the Savior's infinite Atonement. It is more than outward actions, more than casseroles and canned-goods donations; it is a condition of the heart. This I also know: it is a gift that is earned, sought after, and does not come easily because it is in direct opposition to the natural man. It is *bestowed*. It doesn't come without patience, practice, repentance, and purity—but it comes. President Ezra Taft Benson described the process this way: "The Lord works from the inside out. The world works from the outside in. The world would take people out of the slums. Christ takes the slums out of people, and then they take themselves out of the slums. The world would mold men by changing their environment. Christ changes men, who then change their environment. The world would shape human behavior, but Christ can change human nature."[8] Charity can not only transform us; it can transform the world. Imagine what it would be like to live in a society that was constantly striving to possess this heavenly gift. It would be a Zion society! And Zion is the pure in heart—pure hearts, pure people, pure love!

I have been tutored about charity by each of you. I have been its recipient. In every country, in every circumstance in which I have traveled in my calling as the Young Women general president, the women I have met have exhibited this gift. And as Elder Quentin L. Cook said in the April 2011 general conference, you are extraordinary![9] It is a daunting task to go to places where you don't know a soul and to walk into a chapel filled with leaders you have never met and then in a second be encircled and enveloped by the love in the room—the love of the Savior for them, the love of the Savior in the eyes of those present, the love of the gospel, and the love of others. It is pure, undiluted, unadulterated love—it is charity. You wear the mantle of charity regally!

Shortly after the heartbreaking stillbirth of our daughter's first child at eight and a half months, I had to leave her and return home to Salt Lake City. I was worried about leaving her to face the ensuing gray Chicago winter days with this grief in her heart. Shortly after I returned home, Emi received a package on her doorstep. When opened, it held the statue of a woman, a pioneer woman, standing straight and erect, perhaps looking beyond present difficulties herself. The note accompanying the gift read simply, "You are strong and courageous." This inspired act of pure love from a woman who was prompted by the Spirit has served as a beacon and a light in the days and even years that have followed for my daughter and for me. That magnificent woman's charity is a beacon in my life to this day.

Charity is not limited to age. I have seen it manifest in the young women of the Church. One young woman told her story about her situation and her feeling toward the Mormon church. Her story is the telling of how pure love changed her life. She relates it as follows:

"I came from a family of four. My mother was LDS, but my father was intolerant toward the Mormon Church. There was great discord, many arguments, and much bitterness in our home. My parents quarreled constantly, both verbally and physically.

"We paid a price. At sixteen my older brother had been convicted on a narcotics charge and had been placed in a detention home. I was fourteen and headed down that same road.

"I had been baptized at eight and had always attended Sunday School with my mother. Now, at fourteen, I went to church only to get out of the house and keep peace with my mom."

Then she said, "I'll never forget the first Sunday some girls from my Mutual class came around to invite me to Mutual. Four girls! Two of them were cheerleaders at . . . school [and the] other two I had . . . seen at church and school and knew were popular and well liked.

"How I hated those girls! I hated them because they were everything I wanted to be and couldn't. I was nothing, I was low-class—I knew it and I knew they knew it, too. I hated them all. I took their crummy little invitation note and smugly lied that I'd be sure to make it out to Mutual. Of course, I never went."

She said, "This story could have ended there. Those four girls had done their duty at the beginning of the year. I had been personally invited out to Mutual and had refused. What more could they do?

"Fortunately for me, the story did not end there. In the months that followed, every Sunday one of those four girls would be at my door with an invitation. But she wouldn't just drop it off and leave. Each girl would stay and talk to me for at least an hour. At first we would talk about the weather and about Sunday School, which were the only two things I had in common with them, and then we would sit through eternal silences.

"Gradually our conversations became closer. The girls always seemed so eager to listen to my ideas and problems. They never yelled at me or called me names. And yet I was still apprehensive and I still disliked them greatly. I never attended Mutual.

"Time went on, yet those same four girls never gave up. They took a special interest in me. They always said 'hi' at school and would stop and talk to me. They sat by me in classes. They found out which subjects I was flunking . . . and would invite themselves over to study with me.

"I could not understand it. Why me? They knew the things I did—my reputation. Surely they felt my resentment toward them. Why did they keep on trying? I knew I was a lost cause. I felt pushed and cornered, my own conscience hurting. Still I fought them."

Then she shares, "December 12 was my birthday. My family never made birthdays special. I got a 'happy birthday' from my mom and nothing from my dad, and I went through the school day not letting anyone know I was a year older. I planned on celebrating that night by sneaking out and going over to see some friends.

"At 8:00 that night the doorbell rang. I answered it and there stood my Mutual class. One girl had a cake in her hands and another a gallon of ice cream. They were all smiling and suddenly broke out singing 'Happy Birthday.' I didn't even know how to react.

"I went to Mutual twice that month and once in January. But that was all. The three times I attended were great, and I felt a strange closeness toward those four girls, but the social pressure from my other friends was too great and after leading the kind of life I led all week, I just couldn't face those Mutual girls. Still they befriended me and never judged.

"March 12 was a very dreary day in my life. I came home from school late. I had flunked an exam that afternoon and was very blue. I came home to find my parents in a very heated argument. Knowing how it would be, I went to my room and sat there, numb, just listening. I don't remember much after that except losing all control.

"A few days later I gained consciousness in the hospital. For three weeks I lay in the hospital, and for three weeks not one of my friends came to see me. Not one! . . . Where were they now when I needed their friendship?

"Instead, every day at 3:30 one of those four Mutual girls would be at my side. They were there every day. They brought me things to read, they sneaked in candy, and they brought in a transistor radio for me to listen to. We would do crossword puzzles together, and they would tell me the latest happenings at school. They never asked what happened and I never offered to tell.

"After I got out of the hospital I began to go to Mutual. I finally realized that those four girls who had taken an interest in me really were sincere. Not only had I grown to like them, but now I felt a bond of love between us. My life seemed to be going so much better. I was happier than I had ever been.

"April 2 was a day I shall never forget. . . . During the final period of school, the principal walked into the room with a note for me. I was to go home immediately. . . .

"What was wrong at home?

"By the time I reached the house I knew something dreadful had happened. I raced through the front door and almost collided head-on with my dad. I looked up into a ghostly white, tear-streaked face. . . . He was trembling all over and could only mutter, 'She's gone, your mother's passed away.'"

She said, "I was stunned. I turned and I began to run. I ran and ran and my tears mixed with the rain. I ran until I was exhausted, but I did not stop. My face was swollen and my head hurt. Still I ran. Then, suddenly, I saw from the opposite direction someone coming toward me. I paused and wiped my eyes. Could it be? One of those four Mutual girls, the girls who truly cared about me? One of those girls was running through the rain for me. I began to run again, and when we met I threw my arms around that girl and we both collapsed to the ground. I sat there crying, and she cried with me."

Then she relates: "In the years that followed, I became one with those four Mutual girls. I learned to care, really care about others and to give of myself. I found that by helping others my own problems diminished.

"When the most important day of my life came, I knelt across the altar from my sweetheart and in the reflection of mirrors were those four Mutual girls, . . . with tears running down their cheeks. They had made this possible for me.

"I'll never know why I had been so important to them. Me, a nobody. I can only thank my Father in heaven for those girls and pray with all my heart that there are many more like them in his Church."[10]

And there are! I know this because I know many of you and I know your daughters. You are not ordinary. You are the Lord's elect daughters. You know what it means to make and keep sacred covenants, and because of that you are striving to "always remember him" in your thoughts and your actions (Moroni 4:3). By your small and simple acts of charity, you are changing the world. Don't get discouraged, and don't give up. Your light, your love makes all the difference. Will each of you commit today to reach out and light up the life of a young woman daily? It doesn't take much, and it doesn't have to be grand—just a smile, a loving touch, an arm around, a compliment. Will you do that with me?

The world teaches us it is all about winning. The Savior teaches us that winners help others succeed. The world teaches that we have no responsibility for another's actions, decisions, or failures. The Savior teaches us that we can change lives, influence choices as we reach out, forget ourselves, and extend a hand of charity. President Thomas S. Monson reminded each of us of this eternal truth when he said: "In a hundred small ways, all of you wear the mantle of charity. Life is perfect for none of us. Rather than being judgmental and critical of each other, may we have the pure love of Christ for our fellow travelers in this journey through life. May we recognize that each one is doing her best to deal with the challenges which come her way, and may we strive to do *our* best to help out."[11]

Now, one more illustration of charity at its finest, this Christlike attribute of pure love. It occurred at the Seattle Special Olympics several years ago. The story was told of "nine contestants, all physically or mentally disabled, assembled at the starting line for the hundred-yard dash.

"At the gun, they all started out, not exactly in a dash, but with a relish for running the race to the finish and winning. All, that is, except one little boy, who stumbled on the asphalt, tumbled over a couple of times, and began to cry.

"The other eight heard the boy cry. They slowed down and looked back. Then they all turned around and went back . . . every one of them.

"One girl with Down's syndrome bent down and kissed him and said, 'This will make it better.' Then all nine linked arms and walked together to the finish line. Everyone in the stadium stood, and the cheering went on for several minutes. People who were there are still telling the story.

"Why? Because deep down we know that what matters in this life is more than winning for ourselves. What matters in this life is helping others win, even if it means slowing down and changing our course. . . . We achieve happiness when we seek the happiness and well-being of others."[12]

I am grateful to know with an absolute certainty that there is One who, when I trip or stumble or fall, will be there to pick me up, dust me off, encircle me in the arms of His love, and walk with me to the finish line. I testify that He lives and that the more we become like Him in understanding our identity, being pure and virtuous in every aspect of our lives, following the voice of the Spirit, and keeping our covenants, the more our personal charity—our pure love—will never fail. "Wherefore . . . let us lay aside every weight," everything that may hold us back, "and let us run with patience the race that is set before us, looking unto Jesus the author and finisher of our faith" (Hebrews 12:1–2).

Life teaches us that "charity never faileth" (Moroni 7:46). In fact, we can be assured "it endureth forever; and whoso is found possessed of it at the last day, it shall be well with him [and her]" (Moroni 7:47).

NOTES

1. Nancy Sheehan, "A Sister's Helping Hand," *Reader's Digest*, May 1996, 155–56.
2. "What the World Needs Now Is Love," lyrics by Hal David, composed by Burt Bacharach, first recorded by Jackie DeShannon on *This Is Jackie DeShannon*, LP record (Los Angeles: Imperial Records, 1965).
3. "Young Women Theme," available at http://lds.org/pa/display/0,17884, 6826-1,00.html; accessed 7 September 2011.
4. C. S. Lewis, *The Weight of Glory: And Other Addresses* (New York: HarperCollins, 2001), 46.
5. Brigham Young, *Discourses of Brigham Young*, sel. John A. Widtsoe (Salt Lake City: Deseret News Press, 1925), 78.
6. Bruce R. McConkie, *A New Witness for the Articles of Faith* (Salt Lake City: Deseret Book, 1985), 370–71.
7. Gordon B. Hinckley, "Standing Strong and Immovable," *Worldwide Leadership Training Meeting: The Priesthood and the Auxiliaries of the Relief Society, Young Women, and Primary*, January 10, 2004 (Salt Lake City: The Church of Jesus Christ of Latter-day Saints, 2004), 20; available at http://lds .org/broadcast/archive/wwlt/WLTM_2004_01___24240_000.pdf.
8. Ezra Taft Benson, "Born of God," *Ensign*, November 1985, 6.
9. See Quentin L. Cook, "LDS Women Are Incredible!" *Ensign*, May 2011, 18–22.
10. Name withheld, "'How I Hated Those Girls!'" in Jay A. Parry, *Everyday Heroes: True Stories of Ordinary People Who Made a Difference* (Salt Lake City: Eagle Gate, 2002), 73–77.
11. Thomas S. Monson, "Charity Never Faileth," *Ensign*, November 2010, 125.
12. Kirk Douglas, *My Stroke of Luck* (New York: HarperCollins, 2002), 162–63.

"IDEALS ARE STARS TO STEER BY; THEY ARE NOT A STICK TO BEAT OURSELVES WITH"

Barbara Thompson

"Ideals are stars to steer by; they are not a stick to beat ourselves with." This quote is from Sister Barbara B. Smith, the tenth general president of the Relief Society. This wise counsel was recorded in an *Ensign* article in 1976.[1] Sister Smith was concerned that some women were judging themselves too critically. She hoped that women would always pursue excellence, but didn't want women to condemn themselves when extremely high expectations weren't met all at once.

When I read this quote, the first thing that came to my mind was a birthday card I received from a friend many years ago. It went something like this: On the front of the card there was a beautiful fairy with a magic wand. The caption said: "For your birthday, the birthday fairy will tap you on the head and you'll become a beautiful princess." Then I opened the card and there is a picture of a beaten down woman and the caption said, "Oh my, she must have beaten the tar out of you."

There is a difference between a gentle tap on the head and being beaten. Often a gentle nudge or some kind advice is very helpful. But too often, either with ourselves or with others, we tend to beat the tar out of

Barbara Thompson is the second counselor in the Relief Society general presidency. Prior to her call, she worked as the executive director of an international charitable organization for abused and neglected children. She has worked in the social services field directing a number of state-level human and family services programs. She holds degrees in social work from Brigham Young University and the University of Utah.

people. Have you ever heard that some people try to get rid of a pesky fly by shooting it with a shotgun?

Too often a sister will look all around her and see other women who seem to be so much better. Some women take the greatest virtues and abilities of others and compare them with their own faults, finding that almost everyone is better than they are. We frequently hear such things as: "My friend is a great cook and I have trouble boiling water without burning down the house." "The woman next door is always dressed so fashionably while I look rather frumpy." "The Sunday School teacher knows her scriptures so well and I have to sing the song I learned in Primary to find where 1 Timothy is in the New Testament." "Her husband makes more money than mine and they have life so much easier." "Her children always get As on their report cards and my children are cute but just get average grades." "She has it all and then there is me."

The comparison list seems to go on and on. The result of making these comparisons is not that we become better—more often we become bitter. It causes us to begin to believe that we can never make it. We begin to believe that eternal life and happiness are something which we can never obtain. Satan loves it when we talk like this—and Heavenly Father is grieved when we talk like this. We are precious children of a loving Heavenly Father. I hope each of you knows that our Heavenly Father and our Savior love us with a pure and holy love. They love us unconditionally. They know us individually and what each one of us needs.

Really, the only person I need to be better than is the person I was yesterday. We are sometimes too busy comparing ourselves that we forget this.

Lately I have been reading many accounts of pioneer women, both in Nauvoo and in the early settlements of Utah. Reading diaries and journals of Latter-day Saint women gives me a much better perspective on life. I learn about the faith, sacrifice, and diligence of these good women. Many of these women were wonderful and strong. They had some challenges that are similar to our challenges today and some that were, of course, very different from our challenges.

One thing I've noticed is that these women always seemed to work hard. I remember reading account after account that said such things as: "This morning I got up, got the fire started, baked ten loaves of bread, churned the butter, fed the animals, washed the clothes and hung them out to dry, and tidied up the house. Then it was time to get the children up for breakfast and off to school." I became exhausted just reading accounts like this, but these women did this work early in the morning, without a washing machine or clothes dryer, or a modern mixer and oven for baking. This is just what they did. I didn't notice much in their journals that said anything about how fabulous all the other women were and how they were much less by comparison. The women just didn't seem to have the time or energy to spend time comparing themselves with others.

Today I want to briefly discuss the three questions I mentioned previously. They are as follows:

1. How do we resist the tendency to beat ourselves up when we fall short?
2. How do we keep a healthy perspective on our weaknesses while striving for the eternal ideal?
3. In what ways can the Atonement help us live a happy life while in our imperfect state?

Number 1: How do we resist the tendency to beat ourselves up when we fall short?

As I listened to the April 2011 general conference, many things came to mind that I could do to improve myself and become a better disciple of Jesus Christ. I was enthusiastic about making changes. However, after I finished compiling my list, I had twenty-seven major things I needed to do quickly in order to be a better person. In the days following conference as I reflected on that long and wonderful list, I realized I would be a complete failure if I tried to give major attention to everything at once. As I looked back over the list I began to prioritize my goals, giving greater attention to some, knowing that I could not do everything at once.

I considered on the theme of this BYU Women's Conference, "By small and simple things are great things brought to pass" (Alma 37:6). Then I began a process of working on my goals and striving to reach my ideals, one or two at a time. Actually, I sometimes try to throw in an easy goal here or there so I will have something I can do quickly and cross off my list. This seems to encourage me and gives me a sense of accomplishment.

If I really were to beat myself up for each time I fell short, I truly would be bruised from head to toe. Instead, I need to realize that generally, most good things come "line upon line, precept upon precept" (D&C 98:12).

Some goals are definitely more important than others and need more attention. Christ made this abundantly clear when He spoke to the people who were gathered to receive His wise counsel. He was displeased with the scribes and Pharisees, who made a big deal out of some smaller matters, but completely ignored the weightier matters of the law. Here is what Christ said as it is recorded in Matthew 23:23: "Woe unto you, scribes and Pharisees, hypocrites! for ye pay tithe of mint and anise and cummin, and have omitted the weightier matters of the law, judgment, mercy, and faith: these ought ye to have done, and not to leave the other undone."

Christ continued His teaching by saying, "Ye blind guides, which strain at a gnat, and swallow a camel" (Matthew 23:24).

Christ felt that judgment, or in other words, justice, mercy and faith, were clearly the weightier matters that needed priority. This is a good standard for us to use in prioritizing our lives.

We seek good judgment or justice in all our dealings. We have been commanded to "judge righteously." In Alma 41:14 we read, "Therefore, my son, see that you are merciful unto your brethren; deal justly, judge righteously, and do good continually; and if ye do all these things then shall ye receive your reward; yea, ye shall have mercy restored unto you again; ye shall have justice restored unto you again; ye shall have a righteous judgment restored unto you again; and ye shall have good rewarded unto you again."

In Doctrine and Covenants 11:12 we read, "And now, verily, verily, I say unto thee, put your trust in that Spirit which leadeth to do good—yea, to do justly, to walk humbly, to judge righteously; and this is my Spirit."

Good judgment and justice in our dealings helps us to truly become Christians. We won't criticize or find fault, either with ourselves or with others. We will be more willing to forgive ourselves and others. This simple act of forgiveness brings a sense of joy and happiness.

For me, *mercy* is a loving and kind word. Mercy is showing compassion or being forgiving. Again, this is a quality that Christ wanted us to obtain. It is one of the weightier matters of the law. I am sure each of us wants to be judged in a merciful way. We should also extend that mercy to ourselves and to others.

The Old Testament stresses how important it is to be merciful. In Proverbs 3:3 we learn, "Let not mercy and truth forsake thee: bind them about thy neck; write them upon the table of thine heart." This scripture suggests that we should have mercy as part of our very being. It should be a way of life. In Matthew 5:7 we read, "Blessed are the merciful: for they shall obtain mercy."

Another weightier matter is faith. As noted in the Bible Dictionary, "Faith is to hope for things which are not seen, but which are true (Heb. 11:1; Alma 32:21), and must be centered in Jesus Christ in order to produce salvation. . . . Faith is a principle of action and of power. . . . By faith one obtains a remission of sins and eventually can stand in the presence of God. . . . Where there is true faith there are miracles, visions, dreams, healings, and all the gifts of God that he gives to his saints."[2]

Remember the tiny mustard seed? It "is the least of all seeds: but when it is grown, it is the greatest among herbs, and becometh a tree" (Matthew 13:32). The Lord Jesus Christ taught, "If ye have faith as a grain of mustard seed, ye shall say unto this mountain, Remove hence to yonder place; and it shall remove; and nothing shall be impossible unto you" (Matthew 17:20).

By following the weightier matters of the law—judgment, mercy, and faith—we will learn how to prioritize our lives because we will be paying attention to the things that matter most. This will help us to resist the temptation to be too hard on ourselves.

Number 2: How do we keep a healthy perspective on our weaknesses while striving for the eternal ideal?

When there is a difference of opinion I have often said that "everyone has a right to my opinion." Further, when things go wrong, as they sometimes will, I have made the statement, "I did not say it was your fault, I said I am going to blame you!" Obviously, I make these statements facetiously, knowing that if these were my true beliefs, they would make it very difficult for me to have a healthy perspective on my own weaknesses.

Many of us are familiar with the scripture found in Ether 12:27: "And if men come unto me I will show unto them their weakness. I give unto men weakness that they may be humble; and my grace is sufficient for all men that humble themselves before me; for if they humble themselves before me, and have faith in me, then will I make weak things become strong unto them."

This is one of the best guides I have found to help put a healthy perspective on our weaknesses while striving for the eternal ideal.

The Doctrine and Covenants reminds us that it is our duty "to expound scriptures, and to exhort the church" (D&C 25:7). This revelation was given through the Prophet Joseph Smith to his wife, Emma, but the Lord made it clear "that this is my voice unto all" (D&C 25:16). Emma taught the sisters in the early Relief Society meetings to be charitable, to be kind, and to follow the prophet.

Her successor, Eliza R. Snow, also expounded the scriptures and exhorted the Church. Eliza was given the charge by President Brigham Young to go throughout Utah and teach the women what it means to be a woman in the kingdom of God. She taught the gospel, the plan of salvation, and helped the various wards to organize their own Relief Societies.

Sometimes women felt discouraged or challenged as they would strive to live righteously and teach their children. They did endure many hardships and difficulties. Eliza R. Snow gave this wonderful counsel in May 1869: "Tell the sisters to go forth and discharge their duties, in humility and faithfulness and the Spirit of God will rest upon them. . . . Let them seek for wisdom instead of power and they will have all the power they have the wisdom to exercise."[3]

Later, on August 14, 1873, Eliza addressed the sisters in the Ogden, Utah tabernacle. Her wise counsel then still rings true for us today. She said: "To be sure we have trials; but what are they? I want to ask my sisters now a serious question. When you are filled with the Spirit of God, and the Holy Ghost rests upon you—that comforter which Jesus promised, and which takes of the things of God and gives them to us, and shows us things to come, and brings all things to our remembrance—when you are filled with this spirit, do you have any trials? I do not think you do. For that satisfies and fills up every longing of the human heart, and fills up every vacuum. When I am filled with that spirit my soul is satisfied; and I can say in good earnest, that the trifling things of the day do not seem to stand in my way at all. But just let me loose my hold of that spirit and power of the Gospel, and partake of the spirit of the world, in the slightest degree, and trouble comes; there is something wrong. I am tried; and what will comfort me? You cannot impart comfort to me that will satisfy the Immortal mind, but that which comes from the fountain above. And is it not our privilege to so live that we can have this constantly flowing into our souls?"[4]

Again, while instructing the sisters, Eliza called upon her niece, Emily Richards, to stand and speak to a body of sisters. Fear overcame young Emily Richards and she could not say anything. Aunt Eliza kindly said, "Never mind, but when you are asked to speak again, try and have something to say."[5] Emily Richards turned her weakness into strength. It was reported later that she spoke at the annual convention of the National Woman Suffrage Association held in Washington, D. C. She was described as being "self-possessed, dignified, and as pure and sweet as an angel. . . . It was not the words themselves but the gentle spirit [that] went with the words and carried winning grace to every heart."[6]

This is how we change our weaknesses into strengths, by using the Holy Spirit to guide and direct our paths. (Having the Holy Spirit with us strengthens us in our trials and weaknesses, helps us to put things in their proper perspective, and helps us learn how we can obtain the eternal life we seek).

Number 3: In what ways can the Atonement help us live a happy life while in our imperfect state?

The Atonement is the greatest event in the history of the world. There is nothing that was more important to the children of God. The Atonement gives me hope. This is sometimes the only thing that keeps me going because I know of the reality of the Atonement. It means that I can repent. I can have another chance at keeping the covenants I have made. I can go forward knowing that I can continue to progress in my quest to qualify for eternal life.

I remember some time ago when I was struggling. Things didn't seem to be going particularly well in my life. I was still dealing with the death of my mother. Work was very difficult; I was going through big changes in my employment. My Church calling was challenging and I felt I could never accomplish the things that needed to be done in order to magnify my calling. I was generally discouraged. I decided a vacation was what I needed. I traveled to my sister's home in Virginia.

One evening I stayed up late, basically feeling sorry for myself. I was reading in the scriptures and came across a few verses that seemed to jump off the page at me. These were the words I read from Revelation 3:19–22: "As many as I love, I rebuke and chasten: be zealous therefore, and repent. Behold, I stand at the door, and knock: if any man hear my voice, and open the door, I will come in to him, and will sup with him, and he with me. To him that overcometh will I grant to sit with me in my throne, even as I also overcame, and am set down with my Father in his throne. He that hath an ear, let him hear what the Spirit saith unto the churches."

These verses were exactly what I needed to hear. Rather than feeling sorry for myself and how badly things were going in my life, I needed to repent, humble myself, and come unto Christ. I needed to invite Him into my life much more than I had been doing. I needed to remember the words of the sacrament prayers and more fully live by those things I had promised to do.

Here are some of the things stated in the sacramental prayers:

- We eat in remembrance of the body and blood of the Savior.
- We witness that we are willing to take upon us the name of the Son and always remember Him.
- We signify that we are willing to keep His commandments.
- Then we can expect that we will "have his Spirit to be with [us]" (D&C 20:77, 79).

President Boyd K. Packer stated, "Nowhere are the generosity and the kindness and mercy of God more manifest than in repentance. Do you understand the consummate cleansing power of the Atonement made by the Son of God, our Savior, our Redeemer? He said, 'I, God, have suffered these things for all, that they might not suffer if they would repent' [D&C 19:16]. In that supernal act of love, the Savior paid the penalties for our sins so that we might not have to pay."[7]

In an inspiring general conference address, President James E. Faust said, "The Atonement and the Resurrection accomplish many things. The Atonement cleanses us of sin on condition of our repentance. Repentance is the condition on which mercy is extended [see Alma 42:22–25]. After all we can do to pay the uttermost farthing and make right our wrongs, the Savior's grace is activated in our lives through the Atonement, which purifies us and can perfect us [see 2 Ne. 25:23; Alma 34:15–16; 42:22–24; Moro. 10:32–33]."[8]

One of my favorite sermons in the Book of Mormon is the sermon of King Benjamin to his people as he was preparing to turn over the leadership of the kingdom to his son Mosiah. He called his people to the temple and they sat in their tents with the doors facing the temple. King Benjamin taught the people about faith, repentance, and baptism, about the value of hard work, and the blessing of serving others.

He taught them that Christ, our Savior, would come and would suffer "temptations, . . . pain, . . . hunger, thirst, . . . fatigue, even more than man can suffer" (Mosiah 3:7). He taught them that Christ is our Redeemer and His was the only name by which salvation is possible (see Mosiah 3:16, 17).

The people listened carefully and were filled with the Holy Spirit as King Benjamin taught them. Then they "cried aloud with one voice, saying: O have mercy, and apply the atoning blood of Christ that we may receive forgiveness of our sins, and our hearts may be purified; for we believe in Jesus Christ, the Son of God" (Mosiah 4:2). As a result, "they were filled with joy, having received a remission of their sins, and having peace of conscience, because of the exceeding faith which they had in Jesus Christ" (Mosiah 4:3).

This is true joy and happiness, receiving a remission of our sins and having peace of conscience. This is how we can be happy while in this imperfect state. This feeling of peace and happiness will enable us to continue striving to improve and reach our righteous goals as outlined in the gospel of Jesus Christ. We will be encouraged to strive for excellence. By our small and simple efforts and actions, great things will be brought to pass. We will have greater power to receive personal revelation, which will enable us as we strive to increase our faith and personal righteousness, strengthen our families and homes, and will encourage us to seek out and care for those in need. By doing these things, our goal of eternal life will be within our reach.

I testify that our Heavenly Father and our Savior Jesus Christ live and love us dearly. I testify that we can enjoy the blessings of eternal life as we keep our covenants.

NOTES

1. "A Conversation with Sister Barbara B. Smith, Relief Society General President," *Ensign*, March 1976, 8.
2. Bible Dictionary, s.v. "Faith," 669–70.
3. Eliza R. Snow, letter to Mary Elizabeth Lightner, May 27, 1869, Church History Library.
4. Snow, in *Woman's Exponent*, September 15, 1873, 62; available at http://contentdm.lib.byu.edu/cgi-bin/showfile.exe?CISOROOT=/WomansExp&CISOPTR=15696&filename=15697.pdf.
5. Jill Mulvay Derr, Janath Russell Cannon, and Maureen Ursenbach Beecher, *Women of Covenant* (Salt Lake City: Deseret Book, 1992), 93.
6. Ibid.
7. Boyd K. Packer, "Cleansing the Inner Vessel," *Ensign*, November 2010, 76.
8. James E. Faust, "The Atonement: Our Greatest Hope," *Ensign*, November 2001, 19.

Becoming Women of God

Mary N. Cook

I would like to explore how we become women of God and specifically how we can influence our young women to become more faithful and virtuous daughters of God.

One of the great principles I learned in the April 2011 general conference was that of "desire," as taught by Elder Dallin H. Oaks. He said:

"Desires dictate our priorities, priorities shape our choices, and choices determine our actions. The desires we act on determine our changing, our achieving, and our becoming. . . . When we have a vision of what we can become, our desire and our power to act increase enormously."[1]

During the past four months, my husband has been through his third recurrence of a serious health problem. Near the end of his treatments, we had a life-and-death scare with his reaction to one of the drugs. Through fasting, prayer, priesthood blessings, temple attendance, and the faith of

Mary N. Cook served as second counselor in the Young Women general presidency and as a member of the Young Women general board before her call as first counselor in the Young Women general presidency. She served with her husband, Elder Richard E. Cook, a former member of the Seventy, when he was called to preside over a newly created Mongolian mission. Later she accompanied her husband to Hong Kong, where he served in the Asia Area presidency. She helped train young women and young women leaders in Mongolia and other parts of Asia. She received bachelor's and master's degrees in speech pathology and audiology and an EdS degree from Brigham Young University. Professionally, she worked as a special education teacher and administrator and as an elementary school principal. She is stepmother to four children and step-grandmother to seventeen grandchildren.

many, his health has been restored. An experience like this gives one a focused look at life and eternity. As a couple, our desires have changed, and as a result, our priorities have shifted. This life-changing experience has forever altered our priorities, our choices, and our actions.

If you desire enough, you have it within you to become a woman of God. I pray that you will come to know of your identity as I have of late—that you are a daughter of God; He knows you; that your testimony can give you fuel for the trials that you face; that through your worthiness you may access the power of the Holy Ghost. As women of God, guardians of virtue, we are the examples who can create a chain reaction of righteousness that can change our world.

"The Family: A Proclamation to the World" verifies that we come to earth with a divine nature and destiny: "All human beings—male and female—are created in the image of God. Each is a beloved spirit son or daughter of heavenly parents, and, as such, each has a divine nature and destiny."[2]

I am encouraged by a video clip I've seen of Lauren, a little girl, reciting the thirteenth Article of Faith—which is the 2011 Mutual theme—from memory. As I watch it, it causes me to reflect on children and how each child comes to earth with an inherent divine nature.

At this early age, Lauren believes! She has confidence, hope, enthusiasm, and yes, maybe just a bit of pride in her accomplishments—after all, this was the last of the thirteen that she recited! But a concern we have for women, and especially our young women, is that the adversary, in subtle but very real ways, is extinguishing this spark of divine nature. Of course Satan would target women, the greatest influencers! How can we resist this pull of the world and realize our divine potential?

I would like us to consider what we can do not only to fan the spark of divinity that is in each of us but also to help others fan the flame of their divine nature.

As you may know, the purpose of the Young Women organization is to help each young woman be worthy to make and keep sacred covenants and receive the ordinances of the temple, that she might return to our Father in Heaven. In order to accomplish this, we have several objectives that we hope each young woman will achieve. Three of these objectives will not only help a young woman prepare for temple blessings, but they are also essential to fulfilling her divine roles and becoming a woman of God:

First, *identity*. She must understand her identity as a daughter of God.

Second, *testimony*. She must strengthen her faith in and testimony of Jesus Christ.

And third, the *Spirit*. She must be worthy to receive, recognize, and rely on the promptings of the Holy Ghost.

I would like to make a comparison of these objectives to the components of fire. Let me talk for a moment about fire in very simple terms. In order to create fire, four elements are required: *oxygen, fuel,* and *heat,* which, when combined, produce a *chain reaction*. This is referred to as the fire tetrahedron. Fires start when a flammable material, or *fuel,* in combination with a sufficient quantity of an oxidizer such as *oxygen,* is exposed to a source of *heat* and is able to sustain a rate of rapid oxidation, producing a *chain reaction*. Now, let me draw these comparisons.

Oxygen is life-giving. Our Heavenly Father is the giver of life. We *are* His spirit daughters, created in His image. In choosing to follow our Heavenly Father's plan, we were permitted to come to earth and experience mortal life. And the gift of eternal life is made possible through the Atonement of Jesus Christ. To know where we came from, why we are here, and where we are going is key to understanding who we are—our *identity*.

Fuel is something that sustains. Our knowledge of the plan of salvation and of the Savior's role in the plan sustains us through mortality. A *testimony* is the fuel that will sustain us through life's challenges.

Heat. One definition of *heat* is "intensity of feeling."[3] We often associate the promptings of the Holy Ghost with feelings. In Galatians 5:22–23 we are taught that the fruits of the Spirit are feelings: "love, joy, peace, longsuffering, gentleness, goodness, faith, meekness, temperance." As women of God, we will need the guidance of the Holy Ghost. We must be worthy to receive, recognize, and rely on the feelings or promptings of the *Spirit*.

A *chain reaction* is a series of events in which each one influences the next. As members of the Church, we have been given the responsibility to build the kingdom of God and help others realize their divine nature and destiny. Example is key to helping others recognize this divine nature, particularly our children. We are the models, the mentors, and the teachers to help them define their identity, strengthen their testimonies, and have experiences with the Spirit.

Just as each of these components is required to ignite a fire, a fire can be extinguished by removing any one of the elements of the fire tetrahedron.

Let's consider identity, testimony, and the Spirit in light of some of the statements in the Young Women theme that is repeated worldwide each week by our young women.

First, "We are daughters of our Heavenly Father, who loves us, and we love Him."[4] This *is* our identity. President Dieter F. Uchtdorf said:

"Much of the confusion we experience in this life comes from simply not understanding who we are. Too many go about their lives thinking they are of little worth when, in reality, they are elegant and eternal creatures of infinite value with potential beyond imagination.

"Discovering who we really are is part of this great adventure called life. . . .

"God has given again in these latter-days the truth about where we came from, why we are here, and where we are going. . . .

"You are something divine—more beautiful and glorious than you can possibly imagine. This knowledge changes everything. It changes your present. It can change your future. And it can change the world."[5]

Knowing our identity does change everything. It gives us perspective; it provides confidence and direction. Like oxygen, it gives us *life!*

However, "the adversary is having a heyday distorting attitudes about gender and roles and about families and individual worth."[6] He is doing his best to distort and suffocate our identity. Elder M. Russell Ballard expressed this concern when he taught us that some are falling victim to false ideas about who we should be. He said: "For that reason I am concerned about what I see happening with some of our young women. Satan would have you dress, talk, and behave in unnatural and destructive ways in your relationships with young men. . . . He is the author of mass confusion about the value, the role, the contribution, and the unique nature of women. Today's popular culture, which is preached by every form of media from the silver screen to the Internet, celebrates the sexy, saucy, socially aggressive woman. These distortions are seeping into the thinking of some of our own women."[7]

Do you really know who you are? Are your desires, priorities, choices, and actions consistent with your identity as a daughter of God, or are Satan's distortions seeping into your life and dousing your spark of divinity? The best way we can influence others to understand their identity is to know we are women of God and live our beliefs with confidence.

Now let's consider another declaration of the Young Women theme: "We will 'stand as witnesses of God at all times and in all things, and in all places' (Mosiah 18:9)."

In order to witness, we must have a testimony. Our testimony will be the fuel that will sustain us through the tests and trials of life.

At Young Women camp, we teach the Beehives the essentials to build a successful fire. Their first assignment is to gather the tinder. It takes time and effort to collect enough tinder to start a fire. Testimonies are like that. Testimonies grow gradually through an accumulation of spiritual experiences—most of them quiet and small. No one receives a complete testimony all at once. And, like a fire, it takes constant rekindling. As President Henry B. Eyring counseled the young women in March 2011:

"Your living testimony will expand as you study, pray, and ponder in the scriptures. . . .

"Frequent and heartfelt prayers of faith are crucial and needed nutrients. Obedience to the truth you have received will keep the testimony alive and strengthen it. Obedience to the commandments is part of the nourishment you must provide for your testimony."

He then warned: "There is danger in neglecting prayer. There is danger to our testimony in only casual study and reading of the scriptures."[8]

To feed the fire of a young woman's testimony, we have asked each young woman to do four small and simple things, 100 percent, every day: (1) pray night and morning; (2) read the Book of Mormon five minutes every day; (3) obey and live the commandments and standards in *For the Strength of Youth;* and (4) smile—because, as 2 Nephi 9:39 reminds us, "to be spiritually-minded is life eternal."

We have asked Young Women leaders to lead out in setting the example in doing these four things daily: pray, read, obey, and smile. Many have witnessed to us regarding the difference it is making not only in their callings but also in their relationships and in their families.

If you want to help a young woman strengthen her testimony, teach her by example how to daily rekindle her testimony to keep it aglow. Help her realize that for the rest of her life, her living and growing testimony will be the fuel that will fortify her and keep her on the path to eternal life.

Vital to becoming women of God is to receive, recognize, and rely on the guidance of the Holy Ghost. A third statement from the Young Women theme that will help us qualify for that guidance is, "We [will] strive to *live* the Young Women values, which are: faith, divine nature, individual worth, knowledge, choice and accountability, good works, integrity, and virtue" (emphasis added). Living these values will demonstrate our desire to remain worthy for the constant companionship of the Holy Ghost. Worthiness will give us the confidence we need to set priorities, make correct choices, and act upon the promptings of the Holy Ghost.

Elder Neil L. Andersen cautioned: "We live in a time when transportation, communication, and access to information all tower in comparison to the past. But moral issues such as honesty, chastity, Sabbath observance, family responsibility, and even the sanctity of life—issues long held in unison by the world and by Latter-day Saints—now find themselves interpreted in every way and open to debate (see D&C 1:16).

"As the developments of technology and communication ever press the modern world upon us, being in the world but not of the world requires that we make constant choices and decisions (see John 17:14). Spiritual discernment is paramount. As disciples of Christ, we must make the gift of the Holy Ghost a conscious, daily, prayerful part of our lives. . . .

"How can we use this heavenly gift as a vital compass for our daily actions? We must believe that even in our weaknesses, the still, small voice we feel comes from our Father. We must pray and ask and seek and then not be afraid when answers come into our heart and mind. Believe they are divine. They are."[9]

Disobedience suffocates these divine promptings of the Holy Ghost. Nephi explains: "Ye are swift to do iniquity but slow to remember the Lord your God. . . . Yea, ye have heard his voice from time to time; and he hath spoken unto you in a still small voice, but ye were *past feeling,* that ye could not *feel* his words" (1 Nephi 17:45; emphasis added).

As women of God, we must constantly strive to be worthy of the Spirit. We must do everything we can to make our lives and our homes a sanctuary for the Spirit. Beware of becoming "past feeling" because of the noise of the world telling you who you aren't or who you need to be, competing for your time, and making your life so complex that you can no longer "feel his words." Make it a priority to be still so that you can hear the promptings of the Holy Ghost, which will help you make correct choices and give you confidence that your actions are consistent with a woman of God.

As you and I know, values and standards are being cast adrift. Values and standards must be taught and exemplified in the home, as women are the great influencers. We are the guardians of virtue. We are the examples. We are the catalysts to start a chain reaction that *can* change the world.

Following the recent earthquake in Japan, I read this response to the question, "Why don't the Japanese loot?":

"In Japan, people are conditioned not to bring shame to themselves or their family. . . . Thomas Lifson describes how people even in large urban areas do not live in anonymity. People associate a person's actions with the family, and everyone is taught a deep respect for property. . . .

"If a child finds even a small coin, a parent will take the child to the police to report the item as lost. . . . The police take this seriously because they see it as a way of passing along moral instruction."[10]

Our examples *do* matter! Women are the catalysts of these chain re-actions in society. Elder Ballard described it this way: "Every sister who stands for truth and righteousness diminishes the influence of evil. Every sister who strengthens and protects her family is doing the work of God. Every sister who lives as a woman of God becomes a beacon for others to follow and plants seeds of righteous influence that will be harvested for decades to come. Every sister who makes and keeps sacred covenants be-comes an instrument in the hands of God."[11]

Identity, testimony, and Spirit—three key factors to become women of God. Guard each of these components, and if one is flickering, access the enabling power of the Atonement to make necessary changes.

Think of young women you know who really are in the embryonic stages of becoming women of God. Should you see one of these components in a young woman dimming, help her by sharing your love, wisdom, and example. Remember Elder Oaks's promise: "When we have a vision of what we can become, our desire and our power to act increase enormously."[12]

Please read the Young Women theme that follows, and as you do, consider the vision of what you can become:

"We are daughters of our Heavenly Father, who loves us, and we love Him. We will 'stand as witnesses of God at all times and in all things, and in all places' (Mosiah 18:9) as we strive to live the Young Women Values, which are:

> *Faith*
> *Divine Nature*
> *Individual Worth*
> *Knowledge*
> *Choice and Accountability*
> *Good Works*
> *Integrity and*
> *Virtue.*

"We believe as we come to accept and act upon these values, we will be prepared to strengthen home and family, make and keep sacred covenants, receive the ordinances of the temple, and enjoy the blessings of exaltation."[13]

In closing, may I remind you of one of my favorite quotes from President Spencer W. Kimball that we hear often: "Much of the major growth that is coming to the Church in the last days will come because many of the good women of the world . . . will be drawn to the Church in large numbers. This will happen to the degree that the women of the Church reflect righteousness and articulateness in their lives and to the degree that the women of the Church are seen as distinct and different— in happy ways—from the women of the world. . . . Thus it will be that female exemplars of the Church will be a significant force in both the numerical and the spiritual growth of the Church in the last days."[14]

I spoke at Relief Society at the Provo Missionary Training Center recently to those beautiful sister missionaries—some of the "female exemplars of the Church." I learned from one of these young sisters, who said something like this: "We don't know and can't really comprehend what our potential is, and we should not deprive our Savior of the opportunity to help us become all that He knows we can become." Our Savior wants us to be women of God, and He will help us. He needs women of God to fulfill His purposes. I testify that if we will desire enough, it is within us to become the women of God who can change the world.

NOTES

1. Dallin H. Oaks, "Desire," *Ensign*, May 2011, 42, 44.
2. "The Family: A Proclamation to the World," *Ensign*, November 1995, 102.
3. *Merriam-Webster's Collegiate Dictionary*, 11th ed. (Springfield, Mass.: Merriam-Webster, 2003), s.v. "heat."
4. Young Women theme, available at http://lds.org/pa/display/0,17884,6826-1, 00.html; accessed 15 September 2011.
5. Dieter F. Uchtdorf, "The Reflection in the Water," Church Educational System fireside for young adults, 1 November 2009; available at http://lds .org/ldsorg/v/index.jsp?locale=0&vgnextoid=22dfd7256ec8b010VgnVCM10 00004d82620aRCRD&year=2009; accessed 15 September 2011.
6. M. Russell Ballard, "Women of Righteousness," *Ensign*, April 2002, 69.
7. Ibid.
8. Henry B. Eyring, "A Living Testimony," *Ensign*, May 2011, 126, 127.
9. Neil L. Andersen, "A Gift Worthy of Added Care," *Ensign*, December 2010, 32–33.
10. Jay Evensen, "Why Don't the Japanese Loot?" *Deseret News*, March 20, 2011, G1.
11. Ballard, "Women of Righteousness," 70.
12. Oaks, "Desire," 44.
13. Young Women theme.
14. Spencer W. Kimball, "The Role of Righteous Women," *Ensign*, November 1979, 103–4.

LIKE A LIONESS AT THE GATES OF THE HOME

Margaret Dyreng Nadauld

The lioness at the gate of our home has left her post and nothing is the same anymore. In the early morning hours of July 3, 2010, just as the sun was beginning to tinge the sky with pale light, our mother took her last sweet breath and then she was gone. The dear little woman whose watchful eye and loving heart had blessed her family for over sixty years was stilled and our lives will never be the same again. She was just always there. She always had a word of encouragement, she was ever-interested, and nothing slipped past her without her knowledge. She desired to lift and build whoever crossed the threshold of her home, the door of our ward, or the borders of our community. She truly was like a lioness at the gate of our home.

We never left home without her sharing an inspirational thought with us. She lived to build and lift us.

Her lion heart was big and tender and kind and oh, so forgiving. She had a perspective on life that we thrived on and a sense of proportion that put the cares of life in their rightful place.

I'm reminded of the afternoon I needed her perspective as a mother myself. Three of our sons and the boy across the street who was their

Margaret Dyreng Nadauld was the eleventh general president of the Young Women organization of The Church of Jesus Christ of Latter-day Saints from 1997 to 2002. She and her husband, Elder Stephen D. Nadauld, a former member of the Seventy, are the parents of seven sons and the grandparents of twenty-eight grandchildren.

constant companion had been involved in campaigns for junior high and high school elections. Things had been abuzz in our home for days with posters and strategies and assembly skits being prepared. Excitement was high on the day of the final election. The grand crescendo was gathering up a bunch of dogs to walk on the stage at the assembly to illustrate the campaign theme: "If you elect me, I won't dog you." Very junior high! It was all quite the big deal.

I waited anxiously at home to learn the results of the voting. The news was a surprise—three of the boys had won and one had lost. Their dad was off already on a conference assignment so I tried my best to say and do the right thing for him and then the thought came—put them in the car and go home . . . home to where the lioness is protecting the gates. And so we did. Before we started the engine we prayed, as was our custom, and I was voice. I got out four words—"Our dear Heavenly Father"— and then I started to cry. Gradually regaining some composure, I poured out the feelings of our hearts to the Lord to the quiet accompaniment of sniffles coming from the back seat. It was a good thing. Then we drove the two hours to home where everything would be all better.

When we arrived, they were watching for us and greeted us at the door with open arms. Warm welcoming scents from the kitchen beckoned us inside, and we were home, home again from the wars of life, from the disappointments, the sting of defeat, the high of victory and we were grounded once again.

All the years of living and loving and watching and caring for family and others gave Mother and Daddy the right instincts for our little family crisis. In no time everyone was back on an even keel and the one who had lost the election was philosophical, even laughing again, and life moved forward.

How does it work? How do you have a home where magic happens? I believe that it begins with a good woman—a mother—on high alert with one goal in mind: the well-being of her family and those within the sphere of her influence, a mother whose desire is to build and strengthen others. When you have had your hand on the pulse of your family for a lifetime you can usually diagnose the trouble and find a treatment for what ails.

Mothers have their children convinced that they see all and know all, especially when it comes to the well-being of their children. I learned this on the occasion of our oldest son's kidnapping while he was serving as a missionary in Guatemala. We were sitting at home peacefully one Wednesday evening, watching the ten o'clock news and unwinding from the events of the day when the phone rang. It was unusual for that late at night. Slightly apprehensive, I picked up the phone and on the other end of the line was our missionary son. He said, "The mission president has given me permission and I just called to tell you that everything is all right and not to worry." All I could say—trying to sound as calm as possible as I started to tremble—was, "Tell me what happened." He then gave us the details of his harrowing experience and ended with this statement: "I know how you always seem to know when something is wrong, Mom, and I thought I'd better call to let you and Dad know what happened and that everything turned out okay."

There really is something about a mother's watchful care that seems to give her an extra sense of alertness to dangers or evils on behalf of her children.

A mother's responsibility is awesome and eternal and of utmost importance. The blessing of it all is that you were created and prepared for your earthly role in the premortal realms. D&C 138:56 teaches us: "[We] received [our] first lessons in the world of spirits and were prepared to come forth in the due time of the Lord to labor in his vineyard for the salvation of the souls of men."

And now here you are on earth, at your appointed time, to do what only you were sent to do, busily laboring in the vineyard of your home for the salvation of the souls entrusted to your care. You are an awesome instrument in the hands of the Lord to guide your share of this rising generation. Our Relief Society general president, Julie B. Beck, has encouraged mothers to be "like [a lioness] at the gate of the home."[1]

What can we learn from a lion?

Picture with me a scene on the Nature Channel of a mother lion and her cubs. She senses that there are dangers lurking on every hand and that her babies are vulnerable and so she keeps a watchful eye. She watches as they romp and play and she knows that should she turn away for a time and get distracted, her cubs could be dinner for the nearest predator. And so she is a protector. As she works with her cubs, they gradually grow strong and confident and independent. And so she is a preparer. Mothers are like lionesses. They too protect and prepare.

The predators lurking after your precious children are well-known to you. Therefore you keep a vigilant eye on what goes on. You don't let yourself be distracted by spending too much time with friends or trips or worthy causes or other things. You have a sense that if you keep a watchful eye your family will be strengthened. You monitor the TV programs they watch and the video games they play and that is easy to do because the television is in a common area of your home and not in the child's bedroom. The same with the computer—the screen is facing out into the family room for all to see what's happening. There is attention paid to cell phone use. You teach children the advantages and disadvantages of the cell phone.

Of course, watchful mothers do all they can to protect their children from the dangers of drugs. I remember being in a discussion about drug availability to teenagers. The mothers were rather passive regarding where drug dealers hung out, where kids were getting drugs, and so on. After sitting quietly and listening intently, one wise and experienced grandmother spoke up and said, "If there were a tiger loose in this town everyone would be on high alert; mothers would keep their children close to them; and the fathers would be out in a search party to track down the beast. They would unite to do everything in their power to keep their children safe from this imminent danger until he was caught. You know that drugs are even more dangerous to our children than a wild tiger!" Then she said, "Wake up, mothers!" I guess it's true that to be watchful you have to be wide awake!

Watchful mothers love the protection provided by our church programs and materials. The *For the Strength of Youth* booklet is a powerful source of protection for all of us.[2] You may be like we were. In our family home evenings we studied that booklet section by section as the children were growing up. We discussed each topic and pledged to follow the precepts taught. I was an eyewitness and participant when *For the Strength of Youth* was updated and revised. I can tell you from personal experience that every word was prayed over. It was read and reviewed and revised by prophets and Apostles. It is divinely inspired and a priceless tool for protection. I like to give it an additional subtitle: *Hints for Happiness*, or, *For the Strength of* YOU!

Another protection that wise mothers employ is role-playing. It is very useful in helping children figure out how to handle temptations that will come their way. Within the safety of your home they can practice what they will say when offered alcohol, or drugs, or are invited to participate in inappropriate activity with the opposite sex and so on. Watchful mothers protect their children from danger when they prepare them for dealing with temptation ahead of time.

Protect your family from birth with spiritual training. Teach them by your example and loving words to love the Lord, to worship Him, to follow Him. Show them how happy you are as you keep the commandments.

Prayer is a priceless protection. Teach your children to pray individually as they kneel by their bed.

The Church conducted a study several years ago for the purpose of learning what most influenced a young man's decision to serve a mission. They learned that the greatest influence was his private religious observance. This included personal prayer and personal scripture study.

How blessed are the children whose mothers teach and model modest behaviors. What a valuable protection that is for a family. Be oh, so careful about the fashion magazines you have in your home.

A wise mother *prepares* her children.

We tend to do things that we have been taught by example. On one of my assignments, I was in Brazil and staying at the home of a General Authority living in that country. After a long, tiring day of travel and training we returned home tired and hungry. The wife had been participating with us all day and now she had to prepare the evening meal. When I went in the kitchen to help her I found her and her two young teenage daughters busily working together like a well-oiled machine. They laughed and visited joyfully as they went about doing what I like to call "the wonderful work of women." They made room for me to help, but they really didn't need it. One of the girls quietly set a beautiful table. She knew the routine. No need to ask where the knife or fork went nor did she forget the napkins or a lovely centerpiece of flowers on the tablecloth. She knew, obviously from repeated practice.

I learned about the power of example again when two young adult sisters, living far away from home, volunteered to bring the pies for an event we were having. The pies were beautiful and delicious. I asked how they had learned how to make pies—in my opinion, one of the harder desserts to make. Allison replied, "I've never made a pie before in my life. But I just pictured my mother's hands as she made pies and then I tried to do just as I'd seen her do so many times." That is the power of example—my mother's hands: "I remembered my mother's hands."

The lioness knows by instinct that the very survival of her young depends on the preparation she has provided. She is no-nonsense.

We tenderhearted mothers have to remind ourselves to purposefully prepare our children to be strong physically and emotionally, self-sufficient, and independent. We have to be careful so that our children aren't so pampered that they become too soft to do hard things. What a blessing it is to learn to work hard.

I know a family whose children wanted to have paper routes when they were young. (That was in the days when there was such a thing.) The parents helped them apply and arrange for this job. It was fun for a few days. But soon the going got tough. The children grew tired of the hills they had to climb on their bikes with bags full of newspapers across the handlebars. They didn't think it was fun to do a paper route when it was raining or snowing or hot. And it was all so *daily*. All of a sudden something that had once looked fun seemed like a whole lot of work. In addition to delivering newspapers, they had to knock on the doors of their customers every month and collect the subscription money. Sometimes they got tips and that kept them going a little longer. Sometimes all they got was advice. It was hard! It was hard physically and it was hard emotionally. The mother could see how hard it was. Sometimes a mom would rather be a soft warm pussycat and keep her cute little kittens curled up with her on the cushions of life. But that's not the wise plan and the mother knew it. So she just kept encouraging them. She didn't believe in being a quitter and they began to accept that philosophy. Little by little they became stronger physically and emotionally. Before long, they'd earned enough money to buy a brand new go-cart on which they could ride to deliver some of their papers and the work began to be a little more like fun. Their work was rewarded—another valuable lesson for life!

When these children went on missions they missed their family so much it physically hurt and it was hard adjusting to a new and demanding way of life. But they had been allowed and encouraged to do hard things. It had given them the toughness they needed.

Scout camp and girls camp and youth conference are good opportunities for youth to get out on their own, away from the familiarity of family, but with trusted supervision. If they have trouble staying, then you have a strong signal that you have work to do to help them prepare for future independence—including missions and marriage. Time away from home at college or work is a nice preparation for the independence needed for a mission and marriage.

Personal Progress and Duty to God are programs for our youth which are designed to prepare them for the temple and future service in the Church and as mothers and fathers. These programs from the Church can be a marvelous asset to parents as you help your teens prepare for their future.

To you who are watchful mothers but have had disappointment with children, I want to say something: No matter how vigilant a mother is, life is filled with opportunities for exercising agency. Choices abound and children are not immune from poor choices no matter how carefully you have taught and how perfectly watchful you are. When a child makes poor choices, then disappointment becomes your companion and weighs heavily on the heart of the faithful mother. Please, in the face of disappointment, don't leave your post. Be ever-ready by the gates of your home with love and sure knowledge that your efforts have not been in vain and some day and some time and some place you will see that by small and simple things are great things brought to pass as you see a miracle unfold in the life of a repentant loved one. Brigham Young taught: "'I learned a long while ago not to die because my children go wrong. It has been revealed to me that every child and descendant will come to me some time, somewhere. What causes me great sorrow, however, is to know what some of them will have to go through before they get back.'"[3]

I began with a little story about my family. I will close with the story of the Dudoit family. The parents were married in their late teens in the Bern Switzerland Temple, but their schooling—his as a doctor, hers as a nurse—kept them too busy for the temple or the Church and they never went back again. Eventually they had five children. One day, a daughter was in the south of France and met the missionaries, who taught her the gospel. She returned home to Switzerland and was baptized in Lake Geneva in June. At the same time, her twin brother was studying in England and was taught the gospel and also returned home to be baptized. The father, seeing the wonderful influence of the gospel in the lives of his older children, asked the missionaries to teach the fourteen-year-old, and she was soon baptized. The parents went back to the temple for the first time with their son as he prepared to embark on a mission. Unbeknownst to the family, an older sister was secretly studying with the missionaries and independently decided to be baptized, like her sister, in Lake Geneva . . . in *January*. Nevertheless, on a freezing Sunday evening, she and an elder, both dressed in white, walked out into the lake without hesitation as twilight descended. As he raised his right arm to the square, the lights began to twinkle on across the shore and the majestic, snow-covered Alps stood in the background. He said the baptismal prayer and then immersed the fourth Dudoit child in the waters of baptism. It was an awe-inspiring moment in time. It was a scene I will always remember!

It was as though heaven had reached out over time and space to bring these children, who had been born in the covenant, back into the fold. It is now up to this blessed family to stay on the path they embarked on at baptism which will lead to their eternal happiness.

To mothers who may have times of doubt concerning the value of standing watch at your appointed post, like a lioness at the gates of the home, take courage! It is worth every effort, every pleading prayer, every personal sacrifice you make to labor valiantly and tirelessly in the vineyard of your home for the salvation of your children (see D&C 138:56). Please know that you are the one, now is the time, this is the place for every mother to have the courage to stand as one who protects and prepares her family. Bless your family with your love and your strength and one day, one day they will arise up and call you blessed. May you be blessed with encouragement and filled with peace as you go forward in your most valuable work.

NOTES

1. See Julie B. Beck, "What Is Your Mission?" in *Choose Ye This Day to Serve the Lord: Talks from the 2010 BYU Women's Conference* (Salt Lake City: Deseret Book, 2011), 1–13.

2. See *For the Strength of Youth: Fulfilling Our Duty to God* [pamphlet] (Salt Lake City: The Church of Jesus Christ of Latter-day Saints, 2001); also available at https://lds.org/youth/for-the-strength-of-youth?lang=eng; accessed 24 August 2011.
3. Cited in Susa Young Gates and Leah D. Widtsoe, *The Life Story of Brigham Young* (New York: Macmillan, 1930), 370.

"THINGS WHICH MATTER MOST MUST NEVER BE AT THE MERCY OF THINGS WHICH MATTER LEAST"

Silvia H. Allred

In the New Testament, we are introduced to a family of devoted disciples of Christ who lived in Bethany, a small town just a short distance from Jerusalem. We know the names of three members of that household: Martha, Mary, and Lazarus. In Luke 10 we read that as a friend and honored guest, Jesus Christ goes to pay them a visit. On this occasion, Lazarus is not mentioned, and we find only Martha and Mary visiting with Jesus. We assume that Martha was the oldest of the three siblings and the head of the household because we read that "Martha received him into her house" (Luke 10:38). In verse 39 it is implied that initially both sisters sat at Jesus' feet to hear His words. However, as head of the household, Martha felt the weight of responsibility for the comfort and attention given to her guest, and must have left to attend to what she felt Christ's needs would be. She became "cumbered about much serving" during Jesus' visit, while her sister Mary chose to remain listening to the Lord, and did not help her with any preparations.

This is where we must make a distinction. Martha was fulfilling her responsibility as a hostess, which was a valid and kind thing to do. She expected her sister Mary to assist her. When this did not happen, she went

Silvia H. Allred is the first counselor in the Relief Society general presidency. A native of El Salvador, she has served with her husband, Jeffry, as he presided over the Paraguay Asuncion Mission and the Missionary Training Center in the Dominican Republic. She and her husband are the parents of eight children and the grandparents of twenty-one grandchildren.

to the Lord in frustration and asked Him: "Lord, dost thou not care that my sister hath left me to serve alone? bid her therefore that she help me" (Luke 10:40). "And Jesus answered and said unto her, Martha, Martha, thou art careful and troubled about many things: but one thing is needful: and Mary hath chosen that good part, which shall not be taken away from her" (Luke 10:41–42).

When we read the words "much serving" and "careful and troubled about many things" we must ask ourselves: Was Martha overdoing what could have been a simple meal? Was her attention to Christ's temporal needs taking time away from moments she could have spent learning at His feet? It is clear she was a faithful disciple, with a strong testimony about His divine mission, as we can tell by her declaration: "I believe that thou art the Christ, the Son of God, which should come into the world" (John 11:27). She certainly understood how important His teachings were, so why was she not taking full advantage of this opportunity to learn from Him? Of course the answer must be she felt pulled in many directions: to show respect and love for her honored guest, to manage her household responsibilities, and to listen to her Lord's words. It was a full plate for any woman, and one to which each of us can relate.

Every day we are required to make many choices, some of which are easier to make than others. Our day is packed with a myriad of possibilities from the moment we wake up in the morning to the moment we fall asleep at night. Coping with these complex and diverse demands that surround us daily is a challenge for each of us. We all strive to maintain a balanced life of peace, harmony, and happiness, but can often feel overwhelmed. Demands from work, school, family, Church, and civic responsibilities press for our time and cause us to feel pulled in all directions. We become frustrated over our inability to manage our time, energy, and resources successfully. It is a constant tug-of-war between rewarding and demanding, or satisfying but stressful. Can peace, harmony, and happiness be found in a world that seems to pull us in so many directions at the same time?

We can and must learn to make wise choices about the use of our time and resources. Of paramount importance is having realistic expectations and realigning our priorities along gospel lines. Goethe said: "Things which matter most must never be at the mercy of things which matter least." How do we know which things matter most? Why is it important that we learn how to make wise choices? How do we make right choices? What are the consequences of the choices we make daily? How do we choose between two or more good things?

To answer these questions, we must consider the eternal significance of agency and how the choices we make on a daily basis affect the course of our life. The purpose of our mortal life is to gain exaltation. We are exalted in eternal family relationships. The plan of redemption was designed to help us accomplish this purpose. Heavenly Father's work and glory is "to bring to pass . . . eternal life" for His children (Moses 1:39). As part of His plan for us, we are given commandments, we are given agency, and we are given the gift of the Holy Ghost, all of which are instrumental in helping us gain exaltation.

Agency is the ability to choose and act for ourselves. It is a gift from God, and it is one of the most basic and important laws of the gospel. The right to choose is an eternal principle. We are free to choose our course of action, but we cannot choose the consequences of our actions. Consequences are a natural result of the choices we make. Elder Dallin H. Oaks said: "Our life's purpose to obtain experience and to develop faith would be frustrated if our Heavenly Father enlightened us immediately on every question or directed us in every act. We must reach conclusions and make decisions and experience the consequences in order to develop self-reliance and faith."[1]

Making righteous choices puts us on the path toward eternal exaltation, even if we get buffeted by life's winds. Our choices in this life will likewise determine our course in the eternities. Thus, our power to choose should be treasured above any earthly possession. If we use our agency wisely, it allows us to keep all of our choices open and improves our ability to make the right decisions in the future. Some choices are more important than others. Some choices have greater consequences than others. Some choices are relevant while others are trivial. Some choices are between two or more good things, while others are between good and bad. Regardless of the kind of choice before us, there is a consequence attached to the choice. Many of the choices we make determine to a large extent our peace, our happiness and our overall well-being, or our unrest, unhappiness and distress.

Think of the choices you have made so far today. Which of your choices was irrelevant? Which of the choices you made today was the most important? Which was the most far-reaching?

While making correct choices 100 percent of the time is not possible, when we follow gospel priorities, it becomes easier to make the right choice even between several good things.

How do we set our priorities in the proper order? And how do we soften our hearts to desire the priorities that we know are most important? Consider the words of the Savior to His disciples: "Seek ye first to build up the kingdom of God, and to establish his righteousness, and all these things shall be added unto you" (JST, Matthew 6:38).

We need to realize that seeking to have an eternal family is actually synonymous with seeking the kingdom of God. Bringing up our children in light and truth (see D&C 93:40), increasing faith and personal righteousness, strengthening families and homes, and helping those in need is indeed seeking the kingdom of God.

If you agree with me that our highest priority should be to seek first the kingdom of God, it becomes essential for us to make choices that will help us gain exaltation. Our highest priority must be the work of our own salvation, followed by the salvation of our families.

Think back to our original example of Mary and Martha. It was clear that Martha loved Jesus, and wanted to provide careful and loving service to Him. This was an admirable thing, a good choice. However, it was *more* valuable to receive lessons from the Lord's own mouth, a distinction which she must have realized when the Lord defended Mary's choice. We must also consider the value of our own activities. Are we choosing to clean the house because our visiting teachers are coming rather than doing a puzzle with our begging child? Are we spending an hour or more at the gym every day but can never find time for scripture reading or family prayer? Where must our priorities be? We must look at the activities and actions that fill our lives, and decide if individually they are leading us further toward God or doing nothing for us. Are the things we choose to do helping us fulfill our baptismal and temple covenants? When we fully understand that the purpose of our mortal existence is to gain exaltation, building and strengthening loving family relationships naturally becomes a top priority. This firm understanding will guide the many daily choices we must make.

Like God, our families are the most important things in our lives. In the family we experience the greatest joys and the deepest sorrows. These joys and sorrows affect everything else we do at work, school, or play.

Building an eternal family is an eternal quest which requires our full commitment. We must commit to do what is necessary to strengthen it in love, unity, and with faithful obedience to the commandments. The seemingly small choices we face daily have eternal consequences because they put us on a certain path. In a conference address, President Boyd K. Packer said: "Our lives are made up of thousands of everyday choices. Over the years these little choices will be bundled together and show clearly what we value."[2] I certainly believe this to be true. Each of the small things we do pushes us slightly in one direction or another.

Think of some of the small choices you face daily that affect your marriage. My eternal marriage occupies a position of high priority in my life, and many times I have had to forgo or postpone something that I would like to do in order to maintain a peaceful and harmonious relationship. It might be as simple as changing plans or rearranging schedules, or as complicated and difficult as choosing to be patient and forgiving when we really disagree on something. I also make sure that I spend time with my husband doing things that we both enjoy, such as walking daily and traveling together when we can. These are important things, and your spouse should feel that you value him enough to make nurturing your relationship a priority. Weekly date nights are a wonderful goal, as is attending the temple together at least monthly. Doing these things will help you keep balance in your relationship and provide a stability and happiness that will trickle down to all other areas of your life.

I would like to give you a personal example of prioritizing involving temple attendance. Early in our marriage we moved to Central America and for fourteen years the closest temple was in Mesa, Arizona. Because of this our trips to the temple were once or twice a year at best. Later we moved to Chile, and the temple in Santiago was dedicated shortly after. We now had a temple close by, but we also had eight children! We decided as a couple that we would try to go to the temple frequently, with our goal to go weekly. My husband's work required him to travel extensively, so Friday was our best chance to go to the temple together. I still remember how difficult it was for me to arrange everything so we could enjoy the blessing of temple attendance. It wasn't easy, and we didn't make it every week, but our determination helped us to go frequently. Our children learned that going to the temple was a high priority in our lives, and we benefited as a couple with increased closeness and guidance from the Spirit about raising our large family.

If you have children at home as well, are you so busy providing what you think are opportunities for them that you neglect things that truly do nurture family relationships? Are dance, sports, music, or art lessons getting in the way of daily family prayers, family scripture study, or enjoying family meals together? Are your choices of how you spend your time and resources affecting your spiritual progress? We need to weigh our choices against our priorities, and be intentional in including time and activities that bind our families and that are essential for our spiritual growth. In the honesty of our souls, we need to really think about whether we are trying to rear successful children in today's society, or righteous children? Sometimes these two things may not lead to the same choice of daily activities.

Research has actually shown that the strongest predictor of a child's academic achievement and of low behavioral problems is the amount of time families spend together, with the most important time being consistent family meals together. However, with an increase in our financial security, many of us choose to provide ever more extracurricular activities outside the home for our children. The result is a decrease in the amount of time families have together and a decline in the frequency of family meals. We should all reconsider the value of such a simple thing as eating together and sharing the events of the day.

When we give up family time for other seemingly worthwhile opportunities for our children or for ourselves, we are letting things which matter most be at the mercy of things which matter least. When we find ourselves with no time for prayer or scripture study, it might be time to evaluate and increase our efforts to prioritize. Is the way we use our time truly a reflection of what we value most? Are our choices aligned with our priorities?

President Harold B. Lee said: "The greatest work you will ever do will be within the walls of your own home."[3] This underscores the importance of nurturing and strengthening our families. We must remember that when we schedule the essential first, we will find time for the necessary and maybe the nice to do, but when we schedule the nice to do first, we might not have enough time to do the essential. For those of you whose children are grown and have their own families, or for our single sisters, what does strengthening families look like? Is it still a high priority? Or is it a priority at all?

Heavenly Father's plan of happiness is eternal and is for all His children. Qualification for exaltation comes only through obedience to the commandments and by receiving the necessary ordinances. All of us can fulfill the majority of those here on earth. Of course marriage is generally one of the first priorities, but not everyone will have that opportunity in this life. I know that this is a painful and difficult trial to bear if you are earnestly seeking marriage and keeping yourself worthy of it. If you continue to remain single, you will be happiest if you concentrate your focus on other worthy priorities, while at the same time maintaining your personal faith and testimony. Remember that the Lord is blessing you with extra time to serve in His kingdom in ways that many others are unable to. While it may seem small comfort, the Lord blesses many lives through the dedication of single sisters. You can also choose to strengthen friendships and extended family relationships. Remember that we are all children of God, and we can serve and love those around us and develop the attributes that will bless us when we have our own eternal families. This is a gift that our Father in Heaven promises every worthy woman and man in His timetable.

In addition, we have other important priorities. We have responsibilities that come with Church callings, with employment or education, and service to others. How do we choose to maintain balance between family, work, and church? Three scriptures come to mind.

Ecclesiastes 3:1 says: "To every thing there is a season, and a time to every purpose under the heaven."

In Mosiah 4:27, King Benjamin counsels: "And see that all these things are done in wisdom and order; for it is not requisite that a man should run faster than he has strength. And again, it is expedient that he should be diligent."

And in D&C 58:27–28, the Lord says: "Verily I say, men should be anxiously engaged in a good cause, and do many things of their own free will, and bring to pass much righteousness; for the power is in them, wherein they are agents unto themselves."

These three scriptures illustrate that although actively following our priorities is certainly important, God knows that we are not perfect. Sometimes our priorities shift and blur depending on the demands on our time. There have been many times in my life when my highest priority has taken first place when choosing what to do and that same priority has taken second place on a different occasion.

Serving a full-time mission has been one of those shifting priorities. When I was young and the opportunity to go on a mission presented itself, I chose to serve a mission over going to school. Later, I chose going to school over working full-time, which would have given me more income to buy nice things. Later in life, after my husband retired, we chose to serve another mission together over enjoying the leisure of retirement. All of those things were good things, but during those seasons of my life I was led to choose one over another.

Another good example has been my testimony of consistently doing my visiting teaching. I feel very strongly about my assignment as a visiting teacher. I see it as an opportunity to minister, help, and befriend other sisters. It has always been a high priority in my life. What has changed for me is how. When I had unresolved scheduling conflicts with my assigned companion, visiting our sisters occupied first place over going with my assigned companion. Thus, many times I have gone alone. Although preparing and discussing the monthly message is important to me, there have been times when my sisters needed a different message or even an act of service. On occasion, I have had the intention of taking some homemade cookies or a treat when visiting, but for some reason or another, I haven't found the time to bake. I have had to choose to make the visit to our sisters anyway and leave the cookies or treat for another time. What really mattered was that I was available to feel the Spirit and convey the love of God. My visiting teaching experiences have more clearly taught me what is essential, what is necessary, and what is nice to do in ministering.

Throughout my life I had many opportunities to host General Authorities in my home, and like Martha, I felt the responsibility to provide meals and comfort to our guests. I was also "cumbered about much serving," and "careful and troubled about many things," possibly at the expense of the "needful." I am still in the process of learning and reminding myself what all those "needful" things are, but I realize that balance, peace, and happiness are results of following gospel-aligned priorities. Personal spirituality and family ties should always be first. Continually reminding myself of this has enabled me to make better use of my time and resources, which in turn has given me peace and satisfaction. I have tried to prevent spending my discretionary time on ineffective activities that yield little spiritual substance. I have learned that how well we love, treat, and support each other within the family determines my truest happiness.

Always remember that there really is a time and a season for all things. The Lord doesn't expect us to run faster than we have strength, but He wants us to be diligent, and to always be engaged in a good cause. I know that agency and the right to choose are divine gifts that we have to learn to use correctly in order to gain eternal life and exaltation. Some of those choices are hard to make, but if we put them in the proper perspective, always seeking first the kingdom of God, the things which matter most for us will never be at the mercy of things which matter least. Strive to have your small daily choices show clearly what you truly value. I have a testimony that these things are true, and I pray that each of you will pray for the Lord's guidance in discerning which of life's choices will bring you the most lasting happiness.

NOTES

1. Dallin H. Oaks, *The Lord's Way* (Salt Lake City: Deseret Book, 1991), 36.
2. Boyd K. Packer, "The Choice," *Ensign*, November 1980, 21.
3. Harold B. Lee, cited in "Father, Consider Your Ways," *Ensign*, June 2002, 14.

"THY WILL I WILL DO; THY WORDS I WILL KEEP"

Kathleen H. Hughes

In late December, Dean and I received a call that our bishop wanted to meet with us. After years of experience in "meeting with the bishop," it can still be an experience that causes a bit of wonder and perhaps consternation. Since we had returned from our mission, I had not received a call in the ward, so my immediate thought was that perhaps now that time had finally come. But why would he ask Dean to come as well? He had just received a call. And so, as you can imagine, the speculation began. (Are you a speculator? I hope it's not just me!) Well, during our meeting, he called me to be one of two teachers for the Gospel Doctrine class. I smiled because that was a calling we had wondered about, and Dean thought either he or the both of us might be called. (I think he was a bit jealous when the call was just for me.)

It has been a hard but wonderful experience to teach those lessons. I am learning so much; I am thinking so much about the meaning of Christ's teachings contained in the New Testament. I am rereading and

Kathleen H. Hughes served as the first counselor in the Relief Society general presidency from 2002 to 2007. She earned a bachelor's degree in English education from Weber State College in 1966 and a master's in special education from Central Missouri State University in 1974. She worked in education for nearly thirty years, including working as personnel director, assistant superintendent, and director of special education for the Provo School District. She and her husband, Dean Hughes, are the parents of three children and the grandparents of nine grandchildren.

thinking in new ways about the meaning of those teachings in my own life.

To illustrate: In a recent lesson, we studied several parables. One of those is commonly called the parable of the sower. Some refer to it as the parable of the four kinds of soil. Remember that when the seed falls into the good soil, it grows and flourishes, being nurtured by rain and fertile ground. Interestingly, this ground still does not yield the same harvest. In fact, it says that in some places it yields "an hundredfold, some sixtyfold, some thirtyfold" (Matthew 13:8). In our class that day there was a lively discussion about the meaning of the "-folds"—the percentages. Did the amount refer to our capacity to produce, or did it refer to our commitment? My own opinion is that it refers to our commitment. A person with small capacity can still be fully committed.

As I thought about that discussion, my mind went back to a time in my own life when I was personally struggling to know where my own level of commitment lay. I was a young mother, and Dean and I were just beginning to get our heads above water financially after several years of graduate school. Things were to a point where I was feeling good about life and our ability to manage all the responsibilities we were facing. But then I began to feel a gnawing in my spirit. What was wrong? I felt as though I were doing okay with my church and spiritual life. But the more I thought about this, and the more I prayed, the realization of something became clear: I was holding back from the Lord. It wasn't holding back from serving Him; I had more than one calling. I wasn't holding back in my willingness to pay our tithes and offerings; we were doing well in that regard. It was me. Me, Kathy. I was not giving me—or more specifically, I wasn't willing to give my will to the Lord. I wanted to be in charge. I wanted to make the decisions about my life. He had been patient with me for many years, but now He was interested to know if I would give everything to Him. It became a matter of my heart and mind. And the question for me, obviously was, "Are you willing, Kathy, to give this one final part of you? Are you willing to commit 100 percent to Him?"

I believe that the Lord isn't so much interested in our capacity. He is interested in our commitment. Elder Neal A. Maxwell spoke often about submitting our will to the Father. In a January 1999 devotional address to Brigham Young University students entitled "Sharing Insights from My

Life," he stated: "I am going to preach a hard doctrine to you now. The submission of one's will is really the only uniquely personal thing we have to place on God's altar. It is a hard doctrine, but it is true. . . . When we begin to submit ourselves by letting our wills be swallowed up in God's will, then we are really giving something to Him. And that hard doctrine lies at the heart of discipleship." He then goes on to say: "It is the only possession we have that we can give, and there is no resulting shortage in our agency as a result. Instead, what we see is a flowering of our talents and more and more surges of joy. Submission to Him is the only form of submission that is completely safe."[1]

Is this always easy, this "submitting one's will to the Father"? I don't think it is, but I do believe that we can do it, and that when we do, our Heavenly Father will help us to know that we have done so.

Elder Maxwell stated in the same talk that it is often our minds that require the most discipline and testing in this effort to submit our will to the Father. Have you ever said something like this to Heavenly Father? "You know, I am willing to serve in the Primary (or Relief Society or Young Women) as the president, but please don't let me be called to serve in the nursery. I would rather do anything than serve in the nursery." In other words, I want to serve where I want to serve, and if I am not given the calling I want, then I won't serve at all! I've known of women who have said this and guess what? They didn't receive the blessing to serve anywhere!

I know a man who was called often to serve in the bishoprics of the wards in which he lived. He was a very willing servant, but he dreaded being called to serve as the bishop. In fact, he would pray that he would not receive this calling. However, when he finally knelt and asked the Lord to forgive him for his unwillingness to serve in that calling, he was called as the bishop in his ward. He served faithfully and fully and now describes that experience as one of the finest he has had in his years of membership in the Church. What I am trying to say here is that the Lord wants us to want to serve Him. Our minds and hearts need to be willing to do whatever He wants us to do, not what we want to do or what we think we want to do. My experience is that when we fully commit ourselves to the Lord's will, He increases our capacity to accomplish the task at hand.

Elder Larry W. Gibbons said in his conference address in October

2006 that some of us may be keeping a "summer cottage in Babylon."[2] It is so easy to do this: to want what *we* want; to want more of what the world values (clothes, homes, cars, money, fame, power—I call it "stuff"). But he went on to say that it is time we rid ourselves of this real estate and fully commit our lives to doing what Christ wants us to. Only then can we have hope of becoming what He wants us to become.

How can we know when we are making progress toward this goal? I am getting older. I hate to admit that, but my body is beginning to veto my secret desire to be thirty again. But getting older does allow me time to learn and contemplate some needful things. For example, I have always been curious when the scriptures admonish us not to ask for things we know are not good for us. My question was always, well, how can I know that? The scriptures, of course, do give the answer. We're told that the Holy Spirit will tell us what is right for us. The trouble is, that drops the dilemma right back in my lap. I still have to be in tune with the Spirit; I still have to understand the Lord's will for me.

What this need has caused me to do is to listen more intently for the voice of the Spirit in my mind and heart. As I prepared this talk, I prayed for the Holy Ghost to help me; then, as I sat at my computer, I listened for words and thoughts to enter my mind. Sometimes the words came easily and quickly; sometimes they did not. And it is painful when the words don't come. But what I have learned is to pay attention and to trust that when the words do come, it is the Spirit speaking to me, giving me "in the very hour, yea, in the very moment, what ye shall say" (D&C 100:6). I believe inspiration comes when we are willing to submit our will to that of the Father. I have come, in fact, to believe that the Holy Ghost consistently speaks to my mind and heart. What takes courage and submissiveness is the willingness to obey and act on the thoughts and impressions that come.

We need to examine the state of our hearts and minds. We must be willing to listen to the Spirit, but then, when we receive direction, we must be obedient and submissive to the Lord.

One of the great blessings I received as I served in the Relief Society general presidency was the opportunity to meet with women all around the Church. I particularly recall a time when I was invited to speak at a women's conference in Austin, Texas. As part of any travel or speaking experience, Bonnie [Parkin], Anne [Pingree], and I would ask to meet with small groups of women to ask them about their lives and how the gospel and Relief Society blessed their lives. We wanted to visit with members who represented the broad spectrum of women within the Church.

On this particular visit, I met two women whose stories have remained with me. I think of them often. One was a young married woman who had recently joined the Church. She and her husband had moved from the West, found the Church in Texas, and were discovering both the joys and difficulties that come with discipleship. Her mother was dumbfounded at her choice and often asked her to give up the Church and return to sanity. But this young mother said, "I felt like Alma: I had been spiritually born of God; I had received his image in my countenance. I had felt to sing the song of redeeming love." As I listened to her sweet, young yet strong testimony, my thoughts went forward to words from the same chapter of Alma: "If ye have felt to sing the song of redeeming love, I would ask, can ye feel so now?" (Alma 5:26).

I thought that afternoon of the state of my own heart and mind. Could I still feel how this woman felt? Was the gospel still as exciting to me as it was to her then as a newly baptized member? Did the gospel message bring me the joy she had received? Was I willing to serve the Lord wherever and in whatever capacity He asked?

Another woman, older, in that same group stayed in my heart for another reason. She and her husband lived in a small trailer in the country. They were both retired, living off the small Social Security checks they received each month. She described a life of hardship and work. But she also related to us a life that had demonstrated a commitment to the gospel and to serving the Lord. Even though she and her husband had to watch their finances very carefully, and they couldn't afford many of the things they might have liked to have, they made sure that they set aside money to put gas in their truck each week so they could drive to Church. Having the Church in their lives meant that much to them. Tears welled up in my eyes then (and they still do) when I recall her story, and I marvel at her heart and her commitment. "And [some] brought forth fruit, some an hundredfold, some sixtyfold, some thirtyfold" (Matthew 13:8). I believe hers was at least an hundredfold!

I recently spoke to a young mother who has been attending addiction classes sponsored by the Church. She had allowed prescription drugs to begin to take over her life. She was devastated by her choices and wanted nothing more than to put her life back on the path she had always followed. As I listened to her recount her story and the process of repentance and healing she had been through, I was touched by her simple statement of an eternal truth. She told me, "Obedience does free us; giving our lives over to the Savior is the most freeing thing we can do for ourselves." She was healing, spiritually and physically, and, obviously, the Atonement has been a significant part of her healing process.

Another woman, whom I have known well for many years, told me of her own experience of healing. She had, as a young woman, become pregnant out of wedlock. She married the young man and they have raised a good family. But she carried for over thirty years the burden of her regret over her transgression. Her husband, who is not of our faith, supported her in her church activity and was even willing to let her receive her temple endowment. Sadly, each time her bishop would talk with her about this, she would decline, always saying she was not ready. One evening, however, the bishop called her and when she met with him, he pushed her for a reason why she would not accept a temple recommend. Finally, after all those years, she confessed. And the result was remarkable! When she told me about this experience the morning after she had spoken with her bishop, she said, "I haven't felt this joy, this lightness of spirit, for many years. I felt it last night, and, Kathy, this morning, I still can feel it. If I would have only known what I've missed, of how I would feel, I would have spoken to my bishop long ago." Sin is painful. It weighs us down; and though we try to set it aside, it continues to plague us. Our sins own us until we confess them. But through repentance and the glorious Atonement, we can be free from the effects of our misdeeds and transgressions.

As we repent, obey, and submit our wills to the Lord, our spiritual eyes not only open, their vision becomes more clear. We begin to see God's power and influence in our lives more and more. Life becomes a miracle—a daily miracle. The Lord's love becomes constant; it becomes more and more apparent to us.

Shortly after I was called to the Relief Society general presidency, in the spring of 2002, our stake had a "Read the Book of Mormon" project, and in spite of my efforts, I had fallen behind in my reading. I had been working hard to catch up, and early one morning I came to some verses in Helaman 10. If you remember, this is where Nephi, the son of Helaman, begins preaching to the disbelieving Nephites. He has, in earlier chapters, exposed the murderers of the chief judge. Many have begun to believe in him as a prophet, but more of the people do not. In the beginning of chapter 10, we see Nephi leaving the mass of people who are now arguing with one another about the veracity of what they have both seen and heard. Nephi is "much cast down because of the wickedness of the people," but then the voice of the Lord comes to him and says, "Blessed art thou, Nephi, for those things which thou hast done; for I have beheld how thou hast with unwearyingness declared the word, which I have given unto thee, unto this people. And thou hast not feared them, and hast not sought thine own life, but hast sought my will, and to keep my commandments. And now, because thou hast done this with such unwearyingness, behold, I will bless thee forever; and I will make thee mighty in word and in deed, in faith and in works; yea, even that all things shall be done unto thee according to thy word, for thou shalt not ask that which is contrary to my will" (Helaman 10:3–5).

I had read these words many times before, but that morning the words jumped out at me, and it was as though I understood them for the first time: "And thou hast not feared them, and hast not sought thine own life, but hast sought my will, and to keep my commandments." I felt like I think Joseph Smith must have felt when he read James 1:5. Powerful emotions overtook me, and then, when I read the blessing given to Nephi because of his "unwearyingness" in keeping the commandments, I was overcome. "I will bless thee forever," says the Lord to Nephi. Whatever you ask, I will give "unto thee according to thy word, for thou shalt not ask that which is contrary to my will."

In the intervening days, I thought a great deal about those words, and tried to think about my own life and my relationship to the Lord. I still think about those words and their message for me. Have I sought my own life—to do what I wanted to do with my life—or have I always sought to live the commandments and do as the Lord wanted me to do? I know the answer. Sometimes I have tried to go my own way. I have been tempted toward belligerence. But I have kept trying to bring my will into compliance with the Lord's. I think that is what the Lord asks us to do. Keep trying.

There have been many times in my life when I had to have a conversation with myself to kick the "natural woman" out of my life and to listen to the spirit that taught me to be good to myself and to others. Out of these moments I have come to appreciate my genealogical connection to my Father in Heaven. We have no one in between us—He is my spirit's Father and it is He who will help my spirit grow as I yield my selfhood, my *will* to Him. That is what it means to "come to Christ."

Our lives are made up of small and simple things that put together create large and magnificent lives and blessings. Elder M. Russell Ballard has taught:

"When God asked who would come to earth to prepare a way for all mankind to be saved and strengthened and blessed, it was Jesus Christ who said, simply, 'Here am I, send me' (Abr. 3: 27).

"Just as the Savior stepped forward to fulfill His divine responsibilities, we have the challenge and responsibility to do likewise. If you are wondering if you make a difference to the Lord, imagine the impact when you make commitments such as the following:

"'Father, if You need a woman to rear children in righteousness, here am I, send me.'

"'If You need a woman who will shun vulgarity and dress modestly and speak with dignity and show the world how joyous it is to keep the commandments, here am I, send me.'

"'If You need a woman who can resist the alluring temptations of the world by keeping her eyes fixed on eternity, here am I, send me.'

"'If You need a woman of faithful steadiness, here am I, send me.'"[3]

And I would add, "If You need a woman who gives her life to Your will, here am I, send me."

I bear my witness to you that we will be blessed by obedience to the commandments, the first of which says, "Thou shalt love the Lord thy God with all thy heart, and with all thy soul, and with all thy mind" (Mark 12:30; see also Deuteronomy 6:5). I pray that we may be willing to give our selfhood—our will—to Him who is our Father for it is the only thing we really can give Him that is truly ours.

NOTES

1. Neal A. Maxwell, "Sharing Insights from My Life," in *Brigham Young University 1998–99 Speeches* (Provo, Utah: BYU Press, 1999), 112.
2. Larry W. Gibbons, "Wherefore, Settle This in Your Hearts," *Ensign*, November 2006, 103.
3. M. Russell Ballard, "Women of Righteousness," *Ensign*, April 2002, 70.

"THE BEST MEASURE OF TRUE GREATNESS IS HOW CHRISTLIKE WE ARE"

Kathy K. Clayton

On the wall just inside the door to my bedroom I have hung a pho-tograph of our seven children taken decades ago when the whole raucous crew counted on me for breakfast, lunch, and dinner. I catch a glimpse of that moment in time whenever I enter the room and it always makes me smile, both because that season was a demanding, treasured, fleeting one, that sometimes seemed would never end, and because of the details of interaction revealed in the photo.

Those children are dressed in pale pink and sky blue and profes-sionally arranged to create the perfect visual composition. One adorable daughter is seated right in the middle with her brothers and sisters be-hind her, on stools at her side, and on the floor at her feet. Undoubtedly aware of that trapped-in-the-middle predicament, she has grabbed the stool on either side and extended her arms to lift herself off her stool just a little to be sure that her head claims an altitude comparable to that of the older brothers and sisters beside her. Years after the photo was taken, she confessed to me that she was willing to tolerate the discomfort of

---

Kathy K. Clayton has served as an early-morning seminary teacher for ten years in California and Argentina as well as extensively at the ward and stake levels of the Young Women organization. She and her husband, Elder L. Whitney Clayton of the Presidency of the Seventy, are the parents of seven children and the grandparents of fourteen grandchildren.

hyper-extended elbows to manage an altitude in that photo that qualified her for an equal presence.

Already that little girl felt that unfortunate, nearly universal tendency to measure herself against others and think that she needed to take action to be adequate. She wasn't sure she was tall enough unless she was as tall as the others.

Did your grandmother have a door jamb littered with pencil marks as my husband's grandmother did? That darling woman used to invite her grandchildren to stand with their backs to the door jamb every time they came to visit. While they tried to gain a little extra altitude with their toes, she marked the door jamb to see how tall they were. Her desire was to recognize their personal growth, but my husband tells me that they were more often looking at how they measured up in comparison to their cousins than they were celebrating their own progress.

Taking stock of where we have been and where we are going is important for promoting forward and upward motion, but measuring can be a dangerous thing unless we are careful about what and whom we are measuring against. There is an element of comparison—and perhaps competition—implicit in measuring ourselves against others. If we assume that the scriptural injunction to be perfect means that we need to be better than someone else, we are likely to diminish our discipleship rather than enhance it. Seeking to be an ideal Latter-day Saint woman may not be as helpful a goal as seeking to be a worthy disciple of Christ. Using Christ as the measure is more helpful than comparing or competing with others. Additionally, being motivated by pleasing others is not as important as seeking to please God. President Ezra Taft Benson said, "The best measure of true greatness is how Christlike we are."[1] When He is our measure, His rewards are the result of our progress, not feelings of being taller in any sense of the word than anyone else. And His rewards, the fruits of the Spirit, are the blessed, soul-satisfying results of our quest: peace, joy, and love, not status, importance, or superiority.

So, if we are seeking to be Christlike, what then was Christ like? Certainly His attributes are broad and marvelous and include absolutely everything good. For now, however, perhaps we can consider a few of His innumerable notable characteristics in light of the two great commandments: loving the Lord our God and loving our neighbors as ourselves. That is what He was like. He did both perfectly.

Clearly the common denominator of that three-part injunction is love: love of God, love of others, love of self. All three of those types and focuses of heavenly mandated love work together. If we would desire to love God more convincingly, we would accomplish that partly by loving each other and ourselves more generously. If our goal is to feel a greater love for someone we're struggling to connect with, we might redouble our efforts to love God. And if we're having a hard time feeling at home with ourselves, addressing each other with greater kindness and bolstering our determination to show our love of God by more diligently keeping His commandments will increase our personal confidence and help us feel better about ourselves. The relationship among those three loves is certain.

The negative implications of that intricate relationship are inevitable as well. For example, if we are casual or sloppy about demonstrating our love of the Lord and doing what He wants us to do, our love of self, or our confidence, will always suffer. If we are impatient or unforgiving with others, we will feel uncomfortable both with ourselves and with God. And if we are relentlessly hard on ourselves or unwilling to treat ourselves with kindness, we will likely be hard on others too.

There is an important relationship between doing and being. Utilizing that relationship to change our hearts so that we will more ably love each other, ourselves, and the Lord, is powerful. At times it is just plain hard to love someone who seems difficult. On occasion, that person may even be our own child or husband. When that's the case, I recommend the "as if" principle. If we treat that annoying person as if she or he were our best friend, our hearts will change. What we do on the outside will affect what is going on inside. Because of that inevitable relationship between doing and being, with time, we will always begin to feel charity toward that person.

The same is true when we aren't so sure we are crazy about ourselves. Sometimes we are the person annoying ourselves! If we deliberately treat ourselves with patient kindness, we will begin to actually feel differently about ourselves. Did you know that it has been scientifically proven that if a person makes a decision to smile, regardless of whether or not she is happy, she will actually feel happier? Happiness or any other desirable characteristic can be affected from the outside in as well as reflected from the inside out.

With regard to spiritual characteristics, we know that feelings of faith promote faithful behavior. That's the inside out part. And faithful behavior builds feelings of faith. That's the outside in part. So if we want to strengthen our faith, we might make a decision to behave in more faithful ways. And if we want to behave in more faithful ways, we might increase our commitment to the doctrine or increase our faith.

As we consider the three dimensions of love that are the hallmarks of Christlike behavior, let's begin with the third: loving ourselves. That third mandate appears in verses again and again in every volume of the scriptures. Not surprisingly, Christ offered the perfect example of what appropriate loving of self looks like.

First, He knew who He was—and whose He was—and neither aggrandized (as if that were possible) nor minimized His identity. We, on the other hand, have such a hard time recognizing and remembering who we are and what that divine identity implies. Let me share a silly joke that I think makes a point. Once there was an elderly, prominent man who entered a grocery store looking for a particular product. Accustomed to special treatment, he was dissatisfied with the ordinary level of attention he received. Angry, he stormed up to the young woman at the cash register in the front of the store and protested, "Young lady, do you know who I am?" The busy young cashier promptly took her store microphone off its hook and nonchalantly broadcast to the store, "I have an old guy up here who doesn't know who he is."

Unlike that arrogant fellow, we, I fear, too often think too little of ourselves. We don't know who we are either, but our personal estimation of ourselves is less than the reality, not greater. I am convinced that personal confidence is an essential first step to generosity with others. After all, the injunction is to love our neighbors as ourselves, implying that we first love ourselves. The scripture suggests that measure almost as if loving ourselves were a given, but I fear that, for many self-critical women, it is not. I hope that when we read, "Thou shalt love thy neighbor as thyself" (D&C 59:6), we hear a heavenly mandate to love ourselves ringing in our ears. The commandment to love others as ourselves would be inappropriate if our love of self were weak. We women too often may have an easier time loving others than we do ourselves. It might be a good idea for us to say to ourselves, "Thou shalt love thyself with as much generosity as you do your neighbor." Too often we apologize for ourselves and minimize our efforts, saying, "I'm just a mom," or a wife, or a visiting teacher, and we shy away from honest compliments and resist legitimate opportunities to acknowledge the approval of the Spirit. Clearly, in order to more successfully love others, we must first love ourselves.

When President Joseph Fielding Smith returned from his mission, he applied at various places for employment. He was eventually offered a job as an inspector required to visit unsavory places to collect taxes. The work was respectable but the company he would have to keep was sketchy. After making a tentative decision not to take the job, he consulted his father, who wisely advised him to decline the offer, saying, "The best company is none too good for you."[2] As daughters of divine parentage, the best is none too good for us either. We can rightfully live for and cultivate the best of associations, as well as the best of gifts and blessings. In spite of our imperfections, we have been sent from our Heavenly Father and King not to be satisfied by anything unsavory, but to be refined and ennobled in every way. Is it a false modesty that prevents our claiming with certainty that "the best is none too good for us"?

Maybe our inevitable errors thwart our ability to maintain a posture of confidence. A popular radio host in earlier years named Paul Harvey used to tell some captivating, seemingly tragic stories about people who struggled and failed. Just when he had our full sympathetic attention, he added the essential postscript. That critical, concluding piece inevitably turned the tale of sorrow into one of triumph. It was his trademark "the rest of the story," after which he concluded with his signature, "Good day."

We, too, are works in progress whose stories might understandably seem like tragedies if we stop short and neglect to bravely complete "the rest of the story." Others, even scriptural greats, have been works in progress, too.

Think of Peter, who, in spite of his close association with Jesus, denied him three times. Think of Alma and the sons of Mosiah, who went about seeking to destroy the Church of God. Think of Paul, whose very purpose was to persecute the Saints. Think even of Adam and Eve, who were cast out of the Garden of Eden for their transgression. We know the blessed

The Denial of Peter (detail), Carl Bloch

"rest of the story" of each of those mighty disciples. We know that their stories didn't end with their errors but rather continued on to glorious conclusions. If any of them had stopped short, their place in the eternities might have been different—but they didn't. They are worthy heroes in spite of mortal errors. Picking ourselves up and pressing on with brightness of hope to complete the blessed "rest of the story" turns potential tragedy into triumph. Patient, determined endurance is part of the fundamental doctrine of Christ. We can love ourselves and remain hopeful, in spite of imperfections.

That determination to see beyond the immediate imperfections in ourselves enables us to maintain hopeful confidence in our ability to turn a page and begin a new chapter. When we are more patient with ourselves, we are more likely to see others through a more generous lens of charity. As we see ourselves as worthy, able, would-be disciples of Christ seeking to acquire and develop His characteristics, we are better able to see others with the same eye for potential and link arms with them on our mutual quest. Appropriate self-love equips us to better love others. The goal is to love them the way the Savior does: with a generous awareness of their divine parentage and a trusting confidence in their eternal potential.

An example of the way Christlike love for others looks in practice is illustrated by a story told in Exodus 17. The Israelites were fighting the Amalekites with Moses directing the Israelite effort. As we are today, those Israelites were united in battle against a fearsome enemy. Each of the Israelites had his own part to play in the drama. Exodus 17:9 tells us that

Victory O Lord! John Everett Millais

Moses was obligated to "stand on the top of the hill with the rod of God in [his] hand." When Moses held up his hand, the Israelites prevailed, but when his strength weakened, Amalek prevailed (see Exodus 17:11).

Here's where the lesson for us about the way we should love others begins. Aaron and Hur were on that hill with Moses. They saw what happened when Moses got tired, and because of their love for him and their desire for a favorable outcome in that battle, they wanted to help, but the charge to hold up his hand with the rod in it was Moses' charge. In spite of their love for Moses and their desire to help, they couldn't—and shouldn't—take away his task. It was his. But they could help as supportive friends and fellow fighters. What did they do? Exodus 17:12 says, "They took a stone, and put it under him, and he sat thereon." And when that wasn't enough, they stood on either side of him and held up his hands. The scripture says, "His hands were steady until the going down of the sun."

We work alongside others who bear burdens that, like Moses' rod, are theirs to bear. We neither can nor should take those burdens away, but neither should we neglect to find ways to help them bear them. After all, that's what Christlike love does—it strengthens us to enable us to meet the demands of our lives. It doesn't take our burdens away entirely, but it invites us to yoke ourselves with the Savior and share His strength. That's the enabling power of grace.

Our determination to help begins with compassion. True compassion is not a skill, but rather a Christlike quality of heart. The resulting behavior of that quality of heart is described in D&C 81:5 as a commandment to "succor the weak, lift up the hands which hang down, and strengthen the feeble knees." Compassion involves feeling what another feels even though we don't have her life experience. It impels us to act in loving, lifting ways. One of the marvelous, ironic results of lifting others is a lightened load for ourselves.

Elder Neal A. Maxwell said: "Looking for honest ways to lift another would . . . be more beneficial to our own self-esteem, for we would see more good in ourselves. We would cease to be so critical of our weaknesses and would find ways to allow our weaknesses to become strengths with God's help."[3] Lifting others lifts us—that's that relationship among the three fundamental loves in action again.

Loving others as He did also involves allowing them to bear their burdens and find the solutions to their problems in their own way. The Savior didn't and doesn't usurp anyone's agency to solve her problems for her and then claim all the credit. Remember when the young David offered to fight the fearsome Philistine giant Goliath? Saul had little confidence in that boy and his faithful determination. Skeptical, Saul proceeded to outfit the young hero in heavy armor, thinking that David really needed to do it

Saul's way. He had a hard time allowing David space to meet the demands of his battle in his own way. Christlike charity obligates us to believe in the capacity of others and seek to promote their success with Christlike allowance for their exercise of agency.

I personally know what that kind of Christlike love that champions and encourages the empowered use of agency in others looks and feels like. I didn't grow up in a home with the gospel but I never felt disadvantaged because of the empowering shepherding of others. My dad was a marvelous, mighty, integrity-filled father who took us kids with him to the Presbyterian church once annually for the Easter celebration. My gentle, pretty mom was a member of The Church of Jesus Christ of Latter-day Saints, but never attended during the time I lived at home.

My neighborhood, however, included wonderful, generous Saints whose faithful goodness fairly spilled over to bless me and many others with welcome and example. I walked to Primary after school every Wednesday with my little pals beginning when I was very young, and then to the church at the end of our street on Sundays where I always found a welcoming smile and a waiting bench. I knew I belonged. Because of the kind and broad embrace of those early, blessed shepherds, it never occurred to me that I was any kind of outsider. They included me as their own in their gospel conversations and at their family dinner tables. My faith took root and flourished as a result of their generous tutelage. When I married and began a family of my own, I knew through and through what the very best of an LDS home looked and felt like because I had been taking notes over the course of all those years when I had been welcomed into the living rooms and kitchens of the homes of my ward members and friends. Who was I, that little girl, after all? Really "one of the least of these" (Matthew 25:40). Those marvelous people who offered me such love did so like Christ, for Christ, and ultimately even perhaps *to* Christ: "Inasmuch as ye have done it unto one of the least of these, . . . ye have done it unto me" (Matthew 25:40).

That energetic type of shepherding is described well in Ezekiel 34. First, the Lord reprimands those who fail to serve beyond the bounds of their personal needs and those of their exactingly delineated flocks to bless those who are not specifically within their assigned boundaries. He says in verse 2: "Woe be to the shepherds of Israel that do feed themselves! should

Good Shepherd, Bernhard Plockhurst

not the shepherds feed the flocks?" My ward members and the families of my friends exemplified shepherds who fed random little lambs like me in addition to themselves and their genetic charges. I am forever grateful that they were so generous with their nurture.

The Lord goes on to offer in the subsequent verses all kinds of active verbs to describe the type of shepherding that is the result of Christlike love. The verbs include *strengthen, bind up, bring again, seek, search, deliver, bring them out, gather,* and *feed* (see Ezekiel 34:4, 8, 12–13). Several of those injunctions are restated many times in the course of a handful of verses. Clearly the Lord is serious about our rolling up our shirtsleeves and actively going to work to seek, serve, and save others. That's what Christlike love of others requires.

When my husband was called to serve in Salt Lake City, we moved from our longtime California home and purchased from my mother the home I had grown up in as a little girl. Many of the marvelous Saints who cared for me in that blessed neighborhood were still there. They were a little grayer and even more Christlike than they had been decades earlier.

Some time ago at a fast and testimony meeting in another ward, I listened to a grateful testimonial of Christlike love similar to that that had fed and blessed me. A tender young person, who had returned early from a mission, bravely stood and thanked with great emotion the many ward members who had generously extended a welcome home without judgment or reproof. I knew that the love that had served and sustained me all those years ago was alive and active. True Latter-day Saints all over the world are still serving as faithful shepherds seeking and saving grateful little lambs who need Christlike love.

My favorite lyrics in all the hymnbook are found in the second verse of "In Humility, Our Savior." As a request to heaven, they say, "Fill our hearts with sweet forgiving; / Teach us tolerance and love."[4] Christlike love is a gift. We must plead for it, even as we do all in our power to live as if we are constantly the possessors of it.

The third aspect of the love referred to in the two great commandments is to love God with all our heart, mind, and strength. Sometimes we speak of loving God in a more general way as "the love of God," or the love of Christ. I am fascinated by the linguistic ambiguity of that familiar phrase, "love of God." Defensibly, love of God could be the love that He has for us, as in "God's love for His children." We reference that sense of the phrase when we say, "I see evidence of the love of God in my life." It could also refer to a divine quality of love. That's what we refer to when we say, "We must seek to love each other as God loves us." Additionally, it might mean the love that we have for Him, as in, "Because I love God so dearly, I am seeking to do all that I do motivated by that love I feel for God." I suspect that it means all three.

"Thou shalt love the Lord thy God with all thy heart, with all thy might, mind, and strength" (D&C 59:5). That every-fiber-of-our-being kind of love is active, willing, hard-working, humble, energetic, obedient, submissive, trusting, patient, longsuffering. It is best characterized by Jesus Christ's willingness to serve as the Savior of all mankind. After Adam and Eve had partaken of the fruit and were to be cast out of the Garden of Eden, Jesus stepped forward to assume His foreordained role as our Redeemer. In Isaiah 6:8, we read of the Savior's willingness. In response to the voice of the Lord asking, "Whom shall I send, and who will go for us?" Jesus offered the response that should be the model for all of us who

The Annunciation, Carl Bloch

love God: "Here am I; send me." The quality and quantity of Jesus' love for both His Father and for us motivated Him to accept that responsibility that only He could assume. He meekly and modestly offered to unselfishly submit His will to His Father's with all the implications of that sublime deference.

Other scriptural heroes have sought to follow that divine example of Christlike love with a "Here am I, send me" inclination. Think of Mary when she was visited by an angel telling her of the favor she had found with God, and her subsequent calling to bear the Savior of the world. Certainly without understanding all the details or implications of that calling, she responded with a "Here am I, send me" statement. She said, "Behold the handmaid of the Lord: be it unto me according to thy word" (Luke 1:38). Think of the boy Samuel who, when he understood who was speaking to him in his dream, answered by saying, "Speak; for thy servant heareth" (1 Samuel 3:10). Samuel's willingness to listen certainly also implied his willingness to obey what he was told.

There are modern-day disciples who behave in a "Here am I, send me" way as well. Think of the missionaries of all ages who go to all kinds of unfamiliar places and eat all kinds of unfamiliar food and love all kinds of unfamiliar people because they have willingly stepped forward and said, "Here am I, send me." I love the example of the little girl at the dedication of the Sacramento California Temple who thrilled at the opportunity the prophet gave her to step forward to apply a bit of ceremonial mud to the cornerstone. Exultant, she exclaimed with her own version of the "Send me" attitude, "The prophet invited me to help him fix the temple wall!"

Willingness to offer ourselves in service and to take initiative are essential aspects of that Christlike "Here am I, send me" disposition. Years ago, in an attempt to teach our young children about that behavior, we staged an experiment. When no one was looking, we dumped a whole box of crunchy cereal in the hallway leading to the kitchen. One by one our children came home and walked down that hallway on their way to the refrigerator. Without even seeming to notice the mess, one child walked right through the crunchy pile undeterred, tracking bits of cereal as he went. Another saw the mess and, unwilling to slow his progress toward an after-school snack, simply walked around it. Two others came along later. They looked down at the giant spill and promptly called out in a loud voice as they kept walking, "Mom, there's a big mess in the hall. You had better come and clean it up." Another later arrival stopped briefly and hollered, "Yuck! Who made this big mess? Disgusting!" Then she hurried on. Only one daughter carefully detoured around the cereal to the broom closet. She took the dustpan and broom back to the problem and unceremoniously cleaned it up before she continued on to the kitchen.

Christlike love of God certainly begins with obedience to His commandments. We read in the scriptures the clear cause-and-effect directive, "If ye love me, keep my commandments" (John 14:15). Compliance with the commandments alone, however, is not the complete hallmark of true greatness. True greatness requires even more. It involves noticing, taking initiative, and doing more than is required. It implies a divine quality of heart, not just a series of check marks on a list of completed performances. That quality of Christlike love of God is referenced in a letter Paul wrote to Philemon in which he praised that early disciple by saying, "Having confidence in thy obedience I wrote unto thee, knowing that thou wilt also do more than I say" (Philemon 1:21). If Christlike love of God is the goal, then doing all and more than He has said with modest gratitude for the privilege reflects a heart full of that love.

"Jesus said unto him, Thou shalt love the Lord thy God with all thy heart, and with all thy soul, and with all thy mind. This is the first and great commandment. And the second is like unto it, Thou shalt love thy neighbour as thyself" (Matthew 22:37–39). As we seek true greatness, may we seek to be Christlike and to measure ourselves against that divine standard. May we consider the quantity and quality of our love for the Lord, our love for each other, and our love for ourselves as the yardstick by which we measure our likeness to Christ.

NOTES

1. Ezra Taft Benson, "A Sacred Responsibility," *Ensign*, May 1986, 78.
2. Joseph Fielding Smith Jr. and John J. Stewart, *The Life of Joseph Fielding Smith* (Salt Lake City: Deseret Book, 1972), 125–26.
3. Neal A. Maxwell, available at http://www.famousquotes.com/author/neal-a-maxwell/3; accessed 14 September 2011.
4. Mabel Jones Gabbott, "In Humility, Our Savior," *Hymns of The Church of Jesus Christ of Latter-day Saints* (Salt Lake City: The Church of Jesus Christ of Latter-day Saints, 1985), no. 172.

CALLED TO THE PRIMARY—
AT SEVENTY-EIGHT

Olene S. Walker

All my life I have been taught to accept Church callings, knowing that despite my inadequacies, with the Lord's help I could do my best. However, in September 2009, the bishop of our ward came over to our home for what my husband and I assumed was a friendly, get-to-know-you-better kind of visit. We were both completely stunned when he asked me, at age seventy-eight, to be the Primary president in the Bloomington Seventh Ward. My first response was, "Bishop, what are you thinking?" Why the surprise? My age aside, I informed him that I don't see very well, I don't hear very well, and I certainly don't breathe as well as I did when I was younger. The bishop explained to me that as he reflected upon a new Primary president, my name kept coming to his mind. Although he tried to dismiss the feeling, after praying about the matter, he still felt impressed to call me. He even went to the temple to pray about who should be Primary president, and the impression continued that I should be called to this position. And so when he came to my home and offered his

---

Olene S. Walker was born in Ogden, Utah, and obtained her bachelor's, master's, and doctorate degrees from Brigham Young University, Stanford University, and the University of Utah, respectively. She served as the vice president of Country Crisp Foods, a family company, from 1969 to 1992. She served for eight years in the Utah state legislature, including a term as majority whip. In 1992, she was elected as the first female lieutenant governor of the state of Utah, and was sworn in as the first female governor of Utah in 2003. She and her husband, Myron Walker, are the parents of seven children.

explanation as to why I was being called, I knew I could not say no. Could you say no, with such an explanation? Of course, when I told my daughter about the conversation, she said, "But did you tell him that you can't sing?"

I am not certain what inspired him to ask me to be Primary president, but I do know that I have been blessed to have the opportunity to serve in this capacity. It did not take long for me to realize that this calling is a greater blessing to me than it is to the Primary children. I was also blessed by being inspired to call capable and outstanding women to be counselors, secretary, teachers, and music leaders. In fact, our pianist is undoubtedly the most active nonmember in the whole Church.

Perhaps the greatest blessing has been the knowledge that our Heavenly Father loves these little children and wants them to be successful and happy as they grow in their testimonies of the gospel and their knowledge of the Savior. I have come to realize that we as leaders have the important responsibility of helping them build a strong foundation so that they will be able to endure the challenges that will come their way. We also have an important obligation to support parents and families as they strive to live the gospel on a daily basis and nurture the testimonies of their young children. At this young age their testimonies are simple; they have the understanding that they love God and want to follow the teachings of Jesus Christ. We have the wonderful opportunity to help them understand that God knows who they are and loves each and every one of them.

As Primary leaders, we hope that each child learns to pray and to read the scriptures daily, and learns to recognize the promptings of the Holy Ghost. We encourage them to learn the thirteen Articles of Faith, and to know the stories of the Book of Mormon, the Bible, and the Doctrine and Covenants. In Primary it is important that the children begin to gain a testimony of Joseph Smith and the restoration of the Church. Of equal importance is that they know that there is a living prophet of God on the earth today, President Thomas S. Monson, who leads and guides our church.

These sweet Primary children are also learning right from wrong. They are learning at a very young age that the choices they make have consequences. They need to make correct choices in order to find happiness in this life and return to live with our Heavenly Father. It is important that they not only read and hear about gospel principles, but that they actually apply them in their lives.

I look forward each week to greeting the Primary children. I want them to know how much I love them. As Primary leaders we must be aware that each child needs to feel that they are wanted and accepted, and that they have a place in Primary. I want the Primary children to leave each week knowing not only that they are loved by their Heavenly Father, but that their leaders and teachers love them and want the best for them, to have a positive feeling as they come each Sunday that will sustain them as their testimonies grow and are challenged.

Christ taught us that to enter the kingdom of God one has to become as a little child. In Matthew 18:1, the disciples ask Christ, "Who is the greatest in the kingdom of heaven?" Christ holds a little child on His knee and says, "Verily I say unto you, Except ye be converted, and become as little children, ye shall not enter into the kingdom of heaven. Whosoever therefore shall humble himself as this little child, the same is greatest in the kingdom of heaven" (Matthew 18:3–4).

Are we not all little children in the eyes of our Savior as we strive to learn and grow in the gospel? Christ is telling us that we must be humble, teachable, and have that same purity of spirit that little children have. In other words, the scriptures tell us we must become as Primary children—having faith in God and a willingness to follow in the footsteps of Jesus Christ. Just as Primary children have faith in God, we too must analyze our lives to assure that we are following the principles of the gospel and developing a strong testimony of our Heavenly Father and Jesus Christ.

The Lord has sent these precious spirits here on earth to be taught the gospel so they can return to the Savior's presence having been proven worthy. Throughout the Church, Primary teachers and presidencies are there to help parents and family in this critical assignment of teaching the children. It is the most important assignment both parents and Primary workers can have in the Church.

It is my firm conviction that a child comes with a testimony of Christ, for they have just left His presence. They have His light in their eyes. What is that light? President James E. Faust described it best when he told of the negotiations with leaders in Israel when an agreement was being reached to build the Brigham Young University Jerusalem Center. After the Church had agreed not to proselyte from the Center, someone asked, "But what are you going to do about the light that is in their eyes?"[1] He was speaking of the college students who had the light of Christ in their eyes. The sweet Primary children have that light and it is my hope and prayer that the light and knowledge of Jesus Christ will never disappear from their eyes.

Jean Stevens, first counselor in the Primary general presidency, talked about this light when she said, "These precious children of God come to us with believing hearts. They are full of faith and receptive to feelings of the Spirit. They exemplify humility, obedience, and love. They are often the first to love and the first to forgive."[2]

In Matthew 19:13–15, Jesus demonstrated the importance of loving and teaching the children. When the people brought their little children to Christ, "the disciples rebuked them. But Jesus said, Suffer little children, and forbid them not, to come unto me: for of such is the kingdom of heaven. And he laid his hands on them, and departed hence."

As Primary workers, we have the wonderful opportunity to love, nurture, and teach these children. In Mosiah 4:15, King Benjamin states: "Ye will teach them to walk in the ways of truth and soberness; ye will teach them to love one another, and to serve one another."

We also have the responsibility of teaching these principles by example. Children are very honest—for example, I recently gave what I thought was an excellent analogy of how we should take time to pray, ponder, and live the gospel. Sister Anderson, the second counselor in our ward Primary, had just won a club golf championship. I explained to the children that in her youth, Sister Anderson had spent many hours practicing so she could become a better golfer. I assured them that they too would become stronger in the gospel if they spent time studying the scriptures, praying, and being kind to others. To further illustrate my point, I explained that I rarely practiced golf and, as a result, I have never won a tournament. I then asked, "What is the difference between Sister Anderson and me?" I expected a brilliant answer of practice, study, and diligence. A seven-year-old was the first to raise his hand, and his answer was simply, "Age." Of course, we all laughed, for children often offer many moments of truth.

Another time, in an older class with five boys and one girl, it often became a tussle over who got the chair on the aisle. After the second occurrence, I asked this class to stay after Primary for a minute or two. I explained to them that they had a problem and if they didn't solve it, it would become my problem—and I didn't want it. The next Sunday, they came in very orderly and took their seats, but every ten minutes they rotated who sat on the aisle, which disturbed sharing time. I quickly said, "Please stay after a few minutes; I want to talk to you."

I explained that their plan of rotating seats so they all had a turn on the aisle was a great idea, but the execution needed improving. I suggested that we could keep their rotation plan, but we would try rotating on a weekly basis instead of every ten minutes. I had them draw numbers to determine the seat that they would sit in. As they came in, each sat in his or her assigned seat. This routine seemed to work. A few months later I was out of town and a counselor asked if she should provide numbers for the children to draw for their seat. I said that I thought the class had developed a pattern. However, I was told that a class member had made the numbers on her own. They drew out numbers and sat accordingly. The rotation schedule is still working to this day. This example illustrates that children have the ability to solve their problems. However, a little guidance and direction are needed.

Primary children learn from us and we learn from them. It is a great responsibility, but there are many moments of joy. I have never received so many hugs, or little waves, as the children walk down the aisle, or even knocks on my door at home from children wanting to say hello. (I really think they want a cookie.)

As a Primary president you are always concerned with the spiritual growth of the children, but the realities of life become all too apparent in both their faces and their behavior. You understand the pain of a child whose parents are going through a divorce. You understand the frustration of a fourth grader who still cannot read. You have empathy for the great-grandparents who are raising a boy that they adopted because the mother is still on drugs. And you know the hurt of a young girl with tears in her eyes because her mother is in the Utah National Guard and is leaving for Afghanistan. You have so many moments of sweet joy, but also feel the pangs of sorrow for troubles and problems that life can bring to these young children. Being involved in Primary gives you the opportunity to extend an additional amount of love and understanding for those who have special needs and are suffering because of the actions of others. You cannot always change their circumstances, but you can reach out to those who need a little extra help and understanding. It may just be in the form of a smile, an offer of help, or an extra hug. Primary workers know the importance of reaching out to every child with love and understanding.

I want you to know that even though I was surprised to be called as Primary president, I feel that this calling has been one of the greatest blessings in my life. I have often said there is a time and season for everything in life and this is true of service. You are never too old or too young to serve. When you put your faith and trust in the Lord, He will give you the strength and ability necessary to carry out your calling. In any position where we are called to serve, we can magnify that calling and grow individually in the gospel when we rely on our Savior. I love working in Primary. I am so grateful for the opportunity of working with some of God's choicest spirits. I pray that each of us may recognize the responsibility we have to love and teach the children.

NOTES

1. In James E. Faust, "The Light in Their Eyes," *Ensign*, November 2005, 20.
2. Jean A. Stevens, "Become as a Little Child," *Ensign*, May 2011, 10.

PATIENCE: KEY TO HAPPINESS

Gail Miller

Is there a connection between patience and happiness? We hear certain sayings all the time: "Patience is a virtue"; "He has the patience of Job"; "She has the patience of a saint." Yes, patience is a term we are all familiar with. It's something we all have to some degree. And I dare say it's something we have all struggled with at certain times in our lives.

Some of us are really good at practicing patience, and some of us are really bad at it. But the truth is we are not going to get out of this life without learning something about patience. Those who learn to make it a positive part of their lives will be happier in all areas than those who don't.

From personal experience I believe there is a very real connection between patience and happiness. On the surface, that may seem like an oxymoron. How can we be happy if we are always waiting for something?

First let me make a distinction here—I don't believe being patient means just waiting. Patience also involves a lot of hard work. It includes working toward a favorable outcome.

Gail Miller is the chairman of the advisory board of the Larry H. Miller Group of Companies. She is a graduate of West High School in Salt Lake City and attended the University of Utah. She and her husband lived in Colorado from 1970 to 1979. They then returned to Salt Lake City to start their own business, which has grown from one auto dealership to a consortium that includes over forty auto dealerships, several movie complexes, KJZZ Television, the Utah Jazz basketball team, a world-class racetrack, and a number of charitable organizations, including the Larry and Gail Miller Family Foundation. She and Larry are the parents of five children and have twenty-four grandchildren and four great-grandchildren.

"The dictionary definition of patience is to be undisturbed by obstacles, delays, or failures, to be able to bear strain and stress, to be persevering, and the ability to exercise forbearance under provocation."[1]

President Dieter F. Uchtdorf tells us, "Patience is not passive resignation, nor is it failing to act because of our fears. Patience means active waiting and enduring. It means staying with something and doing all that we can—working, hoping, and exercising faith; bearing hardship with fortitude, even when the desires of our hearts are delayed. Patience is not simply enduring; it is enduring well!"[2]

So how do we find happiness while exercising patience? When the foundations of the Church were being laid in this dispensation, Joseph Smith and the elders who were working with him to organize the Church were given a number of revelations because Heavenly Father knew they were going to need help in getting the Church established.

One of those revelations was given in February 1829 through the Prophet to his father and is recorded in Section 4 of the Doctrine and Covenants. It starts with the declaration that "a marvelous work is about to come forth among the children of men." And then goes on to say: "For behold the field is white already to harvest; and lo, he that thrusteth in his sickle with his might, the same layeth up in store that he perisheth not, but bringeth salvation to his soul; and faith, hope, charity and love, with an eye single to the glory of God, qualify him for the work. Remember faith, virtue, knowledge, temperance, *patience,* brotherly kindness, godliness, charity, humility, diligence. Ask, and ye shall receive; knock, and it shall be opened unto you. Amen" (D&C 4:1, 4–6; emphasis added).

In today's world of uncertainty, pressures, strains, and tribulation, *patience* is a very essential virtue. In 2 Timothy 4:2, those who preach and/or teach are given charge to do so with "all *longsuffering* [patience]" (emphasis added). This makes me think of mothers, who are the teachers of their children, and the patience that they exhibit. Patience comes easier when you think about God's timing rather than your own. It also comes easier knowing that it is through our trials that we can develop patience.

When some situation tries your patience, have a laugh over it, and it will seem less burdensome. God has a great sense of timing so it helps to be in tune with Him. When you practice spirituality it can help you develop patience—it's like you're exercising your patience muscles, you're adjusting your inner antennae.

When you look at a problem with your spiritual eyes it helps you to have a more balanced perspective and feel contentment as you work your way to a conclusion. You won't want mere relief of your anxiety or instant results; you'll want the matter resolved in as positive and correct a way as possible because you will see the eternal perspective instead of just dealing with things "in the moment of trial."

Every part of our lives is or will be touched by a need for patience. In other words, patience is a very real part of everything we do in this life, and perhaps in the hereafter as well. In the Doctrine and Covenants, the Lord tells us to "let the work of my temple, and all the works which I have appointed unto you, be continued on and not cease; and let your diligence, and your perseverance, and *patience,* and your works be redoubled, and you shall in nowise lose your reward" (D&C 127:4; emphasis added). This tells us that qualities necessary for success in the Lord's service (and I might add in our personal everyday lives) include faith, virtue, knowledge, temperance, and *patience.* And when we do our work well we will be rewarded.

Let's identify areas that require our patience:

- Think about prayer—patience is a key part of prayer. We, who demand instant responses, have to deal with the truth that any answer will come on God's schedule, not ours.
- As little children, we are at the mercy of others for all of our needs. We wait to have a diaper changed, or to eat, or to go to bed. As we get a little older, we must learn to exercise patience in developing skills like walking and talking and learning our lessons.
- As a teenager, we learn to exercise patience as we are trying to turn our awkward self into an attractive adult, crossing the threshold from childhood into adulthood.
- We exercise patience in dating and looking for a mate.
- As an adult, we have to exercise patience with our spouse

and our children as we shape and develop our eternal families.

- As a mother or father, we practice exercising patience while trying to juggle all the responsibilities of home and family and a career.
- As a grandparent, we are good at exercising patience with grandchildren.
- As a senior, we exercise patience with old age and infirmities and loneliness.
- In the Church, we exercise patience while developing a testimony, often leaning on someone else's while doing so.
- As a gardener, we have to wait for our crops to grow.
- As a teacher, we wait for our students to comprehend their lessons.
- As a neighbor, we practice patience in developing friendships or putting up with an unruly animal next door.
- In our politics we wait for the next group of leaders to appear to correct the mistakes of the last group.
- If we have a broken bone, we wait for healing.
- We wait for the seasons to change, for the snow to fall or the trees to blossom, for the birds to return and sing their songs.
- We wait for night to turn to day.
- To lose weight, we wait for the diet to work.
- When we correspond with someone, we wait for their response.
- We wait for things to improve in our difficult lives.
- We wait for a paycheck or a raise.

If we were inclined to do so, we could go on waiting until our life ended—the key is that we *could* just *wait*—but then again, waiting is not the same as being patient.

Patience requires action. The common denominator in all these things on our list is that they require action, work, effort, or growth to make them happen. If we merely wait, nothing happens. Developing patience requires that we work to make things happen.

The Lord, Jesus Christ, is our perfect example of patience. Though absolutely unyielding in adherence to the truth, He exemplified patience repeatedly during His mortal ministry.

He was patient with His disciples, despite their lack of faith and their slowness to recognize and understand His divine mission. He was patient with the multitudes as they pressed about Him, with the woman taken in sin, with those who sought His healing power, and with the little children. Finally, He remained patient through the sufferings of His mock trials and His crucifixion.

While being patient, He taught. While being patient, He showed us how to serve, and how to perfect ourselves. He showed us how to do His work. The Savior taught us to "continue in patience until ye are perfected" (D&C 67:13).

A certain amount of impatience may be useful to stimulate and motivate us to action, but most often a lack of patience is a major cause of the difficulties and unhappiness in the world today.

Too often, we are impatient with ourselves, our family members, and our friends. Sometimes we are even impatient with the Lord. We want what we want right now, regardless of whether we have earned it, whether it would be good for us, or whether it is right. Some of us want instant gratification or instant material wealth even if it comes through questionable investments or by dishonesty and with little or no regard for the consequences.

Being patient might be more difficult right now than at any other time in our history. Certainly the electronic age has made everything so readily available that waiting can be excruciating. I watched as my son was waiting for a site to load on his computer. Not more than ten seconds had passed when he said, "This is so slow!" When I commented on the absurdity of a ten-second time frame being slow, he said, "But I could be doing something else with my time."

Filling our time up with so many commitments can make us impatient and injure our chance to enjoy the fruits of our labors. It would be good to learn to be patient with ourselves. To recognize our strengths and our weaknesses, we should strive to use good judgment in all of our choices and decisions, to make good use of every opportunity, and to do our best in every task we undertake.

We should avoid becoming discouraged when we are doing the best we can even if it isn't as good as what someone else might do. We should be satisfied with our progress even though it may come slowly at times. Elder Richard L. Evans said, "There seems to be little evidence that the Creator of the universe was ever in a hurry. Everywhere, on this bounteous and beautiful earth, and to the farthest reaches of the firmament, there is evidence of patient purpose and planning and working and waiting."[3]

Elder Marvin J. Ashton said, "We do not have to worry about the patience of God, because he is the personification of patience."[4]

Adel Bestavros wrote, "Patience with others is Love, Patience with self is Hope, Patience with God is Faith."[5]

In my life I have had many opportunities to learn and practice patience. Sometimes it has felt like I was pulling on the reins of a runaway horse and it was all I could do to regain control of my life. At other times it seemed like I was pulling and couldn't get anyone to move forward and make progress. I didn't seem to be able to get the result I wanted when I wanted it.

I'd like to tell you some of the things that have taught me patience and brought me happiness. When Larry and I were dating it seemed to me that six years was a long enough courtship. He didn't seem to be able to think in terms of what the future held, so marriage was not on his radar.

That required that I take matters into my own hands—so I proposed to him. We were married for forty-four years. After we had been married for several years we found ourselves in debt because of some major medical bills with the children. Instead of getting discouraged, we went to work and concentrated on getting out of debt, which brought us great peace of mind.

Unfortunately this caused another problem—he was away a lot. He started working ninety hours a week and it seemed like we never had time with each other. I had to be creative to find ways to spend time together and let him be with the kids and them with him, so I decided I would gather the children up and take them to work to see him a couple of times a week, go to dinner, and then go home. It wasn't easy but it worked. I learned patience by fixing the problem where I had control.

Another area where I learned patience was with our children. Some of our children had a rebellious streak, to put it mildly. Patience, love, and understanding were big helps in this area. I decided that if I couldn't change them I would learn to accept them for who I knew they were—children of God. I would try to have faith that they would come through their difficult times and love them in spite of their rebelliousness. A lot of prayer was thrown into the mix as well. I didn't get instant results, but my patience finally paid off—I consider them my pride and joy.

All five of my children and their spouses and three married grandchildren will be able to go to the temple together for the first time in forty-five years. It took a lot of trusting patience and hard work to get to this point, but I can tell you that it was worth the effort. My feelings of happiness are overwhelming.

Just recently, I have acquired a new dog to keep me company since I am now an empty nester. Her name is Fezi. She is seven and a half years old and fully trained. I could see instantly that someone had a lot of patience to train her. She is very well-behaved and I am grateful for the effort that went into teaching her to be obedient. Since I haven't ever had a dog before, I hope Fezi will be patient with me.

One of my most recent experiences with patience was during Larry's illness. There were so many times when patience was the only thing that could get me through the day. Once he was out of the hospital, it seemed like all day, every day, was an endless round of doctor visits, treatments, physical therapy, shots, and making sure correct medications were given in the correct doses, all while trying to meet each other's emotional needs and struggling to maintain a household, do the laundry, and make nutritious meals.

Because of my eternal perspective and understanding that this life is but a moment and then all things will be made whole, I could endure what I was going through and try to help him to endure what he was going through as well. I was able to exercise patience because it was important for me to know I had done everything I could to make life good for him to the end without having any regrets. I have peace and contentment about our time together.

To develop patience and make it a positive force in our lives we need to carefully plan our activities and set realistic goals and objectives. Sound planning requires meditation, patience, and prayer. When patience is coupled with repentance, a changing of one's attitude, a controlling of one's temper, or some other action that corrects our behavior like prayer, faith, and works, we can overcome many kinds of obstacles.

Patience is closely related to persevering, and persevering means work—both mental and physical. When things are going well, people are inclined to overlook the importance of patience and then become impatient. It's easy to overextend oneself physically, mentally, financially, or in many other ways.

The Lord has told us, "Do not run faster or labor more than you have strength" (D&C 10:4). When we exercise patience we won't be inclined to run faster or labor more than our strength will allow us. Many of us want to take on big tasks before we are ready for them.

Elder Franklin D. Richards once said, "Survey large fields but cultivate small ones."[6] If we can concentrate on the task at hand while planning for growth, we are exercising patience—and patience is essential to progress. Don't expect too much too soon. Make the most of what you have. Practice exercising patience when you want to buy a new home, a new car, new furniture, or other important things. Get out of debt and stay out of debt. If you can practice patience in these things, it will reward you with peace of mind, happiness, and success.

One of the most important things Larry and I did was to get out of debt early in our marriage and never buy on credit again. If we couldn't afford it, we didn't need it until we could afford to pay cash. In that way we were able to plan for the future and be ready when the time came to go into business for ourselves. It's a good idea for a young person to plan and patiently prepare for a mission, for an education, and a vocation or profession.

Faith and patience are vital in the accomplishment of these objectives. When dating and courting, be patient in the selection of a husband or wife. Prepare for a temple marriage. Your patience will be rewarded with eternal blessings.

Having patience with our family members and loved ones can be difficult at times but it is the one area where we should have the most patience. I used to tell my children, "You need to treat your brothers and sister like they were your best friends, because they are going to be with you forever, but the friend down the street to whom you are so nice may one day move away. So be just as nice—or more so—to your family as you are to your friends."

Patience and perseverance in Church work also pays tremendous dividends. In D&C 64:33, the Lord told Joseph Smith and the elders of the Church to "be not weary in well-doing, for ye are laying the foundation of a great work. And out of small things proceedeth that which is great."

Missionary work would certainly fall into that category. It requires patience, love, and longsuffering. President Dieter F. Uctdorf said, "Patience—the ability to put our desires on hold for a time—is a precious and rare virtue. We want what we want, and we want it now. Therefore, the very idea of patience may seem unpleasant and, at times, bitter.

"Nevertheless, without patience, we cannot please God; we cannot become perfect. Indeed, patience is a purifying process that refines understanding, deepens happiness, focuses action, and offers hope for peace."[7]

Never give up on anyone. And that includes not giving up on yourself. The children of Israel waited forty years in the wilderness before they could enter the promised land. Jacob waited seven long years for Rachel. The Jews waited seventy years in Babylon before they could return to rebuild the temple. The Nephites waited for a sign of Christ's birth, even knowing that if the sign did not come, they would perish. Joseph Smith's trials in Liberty Jail caused even the prophet of God to wonder, "How long?" (see D&C 121).

Every one of us is called to wait in his or her own way. We must learn that in the Lord's plan, our understanding comes "line upon line, precept upon precept" (2 Nephi 28:30; D&C 98:12). In short, knowledge and understanding come at the price of patience.

Often the deep valleys of our present will be understood only by looking back on them from the mountains of our future experience. Often we can't see the Lord's hand in our lives until long after trials have passed. Often the most difficult times of our lives are essential building blocks that form the foundation of our character and pave the way to future opportunity, understanding, and happiness.

Sometimes as we are going through our difficult times we don't realize that our most valuable tool and the one we need the most is patience. It can be very hard to "be still" and hear the promptings and direction available to us when we are in the heat of our trials. Cultivate patience.

Patience is an eternal virtue. Heavenly Father loves you and wants you to be happy. Patience is the key to happiness.

NOTES

1. Franklin D. Richards, in Conference Report, April 1968, 13.
2. Dieter F. Uchtdorf, "Continue in Patience," *Ensign*, May 2010, 57.
3. Richard L. Evans, in Conference Report, October 1952, 95.
4. Marvin J. Ashton, "Patience Is a Great Power," in *Speeches of the Year: BYU Devotional Addresses, 1972–73* (Provo: BYU Press, 1973), 104.
5. Adel Bestavros, cited at http://en.wikiquote.org/wiki/Patience; accessed 22 September 2011.
6. Richards, in Conference Report, October 1964, 77.
7. Uchtdorf, "Continue in Patience," 56.

BELIEVING CHRIST

Gaye Strathearn

In 2001, I was at Lake Powell camping with some of my friends. We arrived in the morning, set up camp and were starting to play on the water. I was on my wave-runner watching some of my friends parasail. This was something that I had always wanted to do, but the older I've gotten, the less adventurous I've become. As I watched the others, I kept telling myself that it looked so easy and I could certainly do it as well. So I girded up my loins, fresh courage took, and went and got into the harness. The boat took off and I took a couple of steps and then I was in the air, but then something went wrong. Instead of going higher into the air, I started going sideways, and I could see that I was on a collision course with my wave-runner, which I had moved off to the side so that it wouldn't be in the way! As I came closer I desperately pulled my legs up under me, trying to avoid the collision, but to no avail. I hit, and my first thought was, *Ooh—that hurt!* and then I looked down and saw that my tibia was protruding about two inches out of my leg—then I thought, *Whoa, that really does hurt!* As I lay in the water for the thirty to forty minutes that I

Gaye Strathearn was born and raised in Australia. She holds bachelor's and master's degrees in Near Eastern studies from Brigham Young University and a PhD in New Testament from the Claremont Graduate University. She is an associate professor of ancient scripture at BYU, and a popular presenter at BYU Education Week. She is the co-author of He Will Give You Rest: An Invitation and a Promise *(with Richard Neitzel Holzapfel) and the co-editor of* The Sermon on the Mount in Latter-day Scripture: The 30th Annual BYU Sidney B. Sperry Symposium.

waited for the rescue people to come, a number of bullet-point thoughts went through my mind.

- I have to start teaching in two weeks! How am I going to do that now?
- I'm going to be teaching the New Testament Gospels, and one of those days we're going to discuss Jesus' miracles.
- In one of those miracles Jesus was teaching in a house in the seaside village of Capernaum. The crowds listening to Him were so great that a group of four men climbed onto the roof and then let down a paralyzed man on a bed so that Jesus could heal him. Jesus said to the man, "Arise, and take up thy bed, and go thy way into thine house." The Markan account said that the man "immediately . . . arose, took up the bed, and went forth before them all" (Mark 2:11–12).
- As I lay in the water I imagined Jesus walking on the beach, and seeing me, stopping and saying to me, "Gaye, arise and walk." I have always, it seems, believed in Jesus, that He is the Christ, the Son of God. At that moment I wondered if I would have *believed Jesus* enough to respond to His invitation in the same way that the paralyzed man had.

That thought has haunted me ever since—haunted in the sense that I have often reflected upon it and used it as a kind of spiritual mirror to hold up and evaluate where I am in my spiritual journey. But the thought has also come to me that although Jesus' miracles were an important part of His mortal ministry, they were not central to it. He is the great healer, but the focus of His mission was to reach out to the spiritually sick. So, the question I often reflect on is whether, when it comes to spiritual matters, I only believe in Jesus, or do I also really believe what He says to me?[1]

So in the short time that we have together today, I would like to reflect on just one of those times when Jesus speaks to me, and to all of us, and ask the question, do I really believe this? One scholar has described the passage as "perhaps the most important verses in the Synoptic Gospels,"[2] and Elder James E. Talmage describes it as "one of the grandest outpourings of spiritual emotion known to man."[3] It is found in Matthew 11:28–30, which I have formatted in its chiastic structure:

1. Come unto me, all ye that labour and are heavy laden,
    2. and I will give you rest.
        3. Take my yoke upon you, and learn of me; for I am meek and lowly in heart:
    2. And ye shall find rest unto your souls.
1. For my yoke is easy, and my burden is light.

If these verses really are the "most important verses in the Synoptic Gospels," then why is Matthew the only one to include them? Why are they *so* important to Matthew? After all, Luke includes the verses that precede them, in which Jesus speaks about knowing the Father (Luke 10:21–22) and both Mark and Luke include the story that follows in chapter 12 about plucking the grain on the Sabbath (Mark 2:23–28; Luke 6:1–5). May I suggest that these verses are important to Matthew because they are an important counterpoint to his emphasis on works-righteousness. In contrast to the other gospels, the concept of righteousness is at the heart of Matthew's gospel. He uses the Greek term for righteousness, *dikaiosunē*, seven times, whereas Mark doesn't use it at all, Luke uses it only once and John only twice (see Matthew 3:15; 5:6, 10, 20; 6:1, 33; 21:32; Luke 1:75; John 16:8, 10). For Matthew, writing to a Jewish audience, salvation is about righteousness and that comes about by what a person *does*. These expectations are focused to a large extent in the Sermon on the Mount and include commands such as: "except your righteousness shall exceed the righteousness of the scribes and Pharisees, ye shall in no case enter into the kingdom of heaven" (5:20); "let your light so shine before men, that they may see your good works, and glorify your Father which is in heaven" (5:16); "whosoever is angry with his brother without a cause shall be in danger of the judgment" (5:22); "judge not, that ye be not judged" (7:1); and "Be ye therefore perfect, even as your Father which is in heaven is perfect" (5:48). In some ways Matthew's gospel epitomizes an approach to righteousness that some of us struggle with today. We want so desperately to be righteous that we fall into the same trap that Paul said the Jews had done: "For I bear them record that they have a zeal of God, but not according to knowledge. For they being ignorant of God's righteousness, and going about to establish their own righteousness, have not submitted themselves unto the righteousness of God" (Romans 10:2–3).

Then, as now, the injunction to become perfect through righteous acts can be a heavy burden to carry. Frankly, we all live busy lives, and we live in a world of expectations. We have expectations from employers, spouses, children, friends, communities, and from God. As Elder Dallin H. Oaks has said, "Most of us have more things expected of us than we can *possibly* do."[4] Then, as now, if we're not careful we, like Martha, can get to the point where we are "cumbered about [with] much serving" (Luke 10:40). Somehow, we have to be able to find a balance, without becoming overwhelmed with expectations. It's in this context of works-righteousness that Matthew 11:28–30 stands out as a counterpoint and a reminder, that we must not only believe *in* Christ, we must also believe Him when He promises us that He will give us rest and that His yoke and burden are light!

In discussing this passage of scripture, I realize that its profundity is much greater than I can ever discuss in the short time allotted today. But I would like to briefly discuss the invitation and two of the promises.

INVITATION

First, Jesus invites everyone who labors and is heavy laden to come unto Him. I think that it is fair to say that every one of us has experienced times of labor and feelings of being heavy laden. I love what Elder Jeffrey R. Holland has said: "We all have highs and lows, but such times come and they usually always go. Kind neighbors assist. Beautiful sunshine brings encouragement. A good night's sleep usually works wonders. But there are times in all of our lives when deep sorrow or suffering or fear or loneliness makes us cry out for the peace which only God Himself can bring. These are times of piercing spiritual hunger when even the dearest friends cannot fully come to our aid."[5] It is at these times that we must not just believe in Jesus, but believe Him enough to respond to His invitation to come unto Him. In Matthew's gospel the invitation to "come" is a frequent call to discipleship. Jesus invited Peter, Andrew, James, and John to "follow me," to which they responded immediately (Matthew 4:19–22). But Jesus also extended the same invitation to the rich young man. In contrast, he rejected the invitation and "went away sorrowful" (Matthew 19:21, 22). In Matthew 11, however, Jesus is inviting us not just to follow Him, but to come unto Him, so that He can minister unto us during our times of struggle. Perhaps one of the saddest scriptures is Jesus' lament during the last week of His mortal ministry, when He declared, "O Jerusalem, Jerusalem, . . . how often would I have gathered thy children together, even as a hen gathereth her chickens under her wings, *and ye would not!*" (Matthew 23:37; emphasis added). Why, when we need it most, do we sometimes turn away from the Savior's invitation? Who doesn't need to experience the promises that He extends?

JESUS' PROMISE OF REST

Jesus' promise of rest is two-fold, as seen in the chiastic format of the invitation. In verse 28 He promises that *He* will give us rest, and then in verse 29 He promises that *we* will find rest. The fact that it is repeated twice adds emphasis and reinforces the reality that, regardless of our personal struggles, finding rest is indeed possible. For many who feel burdened it is sometimes difficult to even imagine a time when life could be better. Therefore, Jesus' double emphasis is meant to give hope—"a perfect brightness of hope" (2 Nephi 31:20) that, as Elder Neal A. Maxwell taught, "permits us to 'press forward' even when dark clouds oppress."[6]

In his first promise, Jesus reminds us that *He* is the source of rest: "I will give you rest" (Matthew 11:28). Contrary to the myriad of advertisements that constantly bombard our physical senses, we will not find lasting meaningful rest in the enticements of the world, the philosophies of men, or even in clearing our busy calendars. Jesus is the great physician, the healer of our souls. And so He invites us to come unto Him because He, and only He, is the source of the rest we seek. Thus Enos testifies, "For I know that in [my Redeemer] I shall rest" (Enos 1:27). But note that Jesus' promise does not necessarily guarantee an immediate reward. Although it is certainly possible to receive instantaneous relief, He does not use the present tense of the verb; rather, He uses the future tense. His promise is *real*, but it is important to remember that it will be realized on *His* timetable, not ours. Thus the Psalmist implores us to "rest in the Lord, and wait patiently for him" (Psalm 37:7).

In the second promise of rest, Jesus shifts the focus from *His* steward-ship to *our* responsibility. In addition to promising that He will give us rest, He also promises that *we will find rest*. In this instance the emphasis is not on what He will do, but on what we must do: "take [His] yoke upon [us] and learn of [Him]" (Matthew 11:29). His words invite us to become active seekers rather than passive supplicants. Thus although His rest is available to all, it is, in part, contingent upon our coming to Him. Here is the first of a couple of paradoxes in this passage: Can we really find rest if we are required to work to find it? The answer is absolutely yes! But we do have to make sure we know what "rest" is.

In the scriptures there are places where "rest" means a cessation of work: the conclusion of the creative period is perhaps the most obvious. But Doctrine and Covenants 84:24 gives a definition of rest as "the fulness of [God's] glory." This is the rest that Jesus promises to those who respond to His invitation to come unto Him. If we're looking for rest only as an absence of work or trials or disappointments, we may fail to recognize the Lord's hand in our lives. This is why the Savior stresses that, although He is the source of this rest, we have a responsibility to be active seekers of this rest.

Sisters, I hope that we will recognize that this type of rest, the fulness of God's glory, is not just something that we can anticipate only in the next life. Mormon hopes that his people "have obtained a sufficient hope by which ye can enter into the rest of the Lord, from this time henceforth until ye shall rest with him in heaven" (Moroni 7:3).

JESUS' PROMISE OF A LIGHT BURDEN

Before we discuss some specific burdens that Jesus promises to make light, it is important to understand a principle taught in Mosiah in the Book of Mormon that will help us recognize when Jesus lightens our bur-dens. Here we find two different groups that were experiencing heavy bur-dens from Lamanite oppression: the people of Limhi and also the followers of Alma the Elder. Both groups cried mightily to the Lord for deliverance (see Mosiah 21:14; 24:10), and the Lord responded to their prayers, but in different ways. In the case of King Limhi's group, the Lord softened the hearts of the Lamanites so that they eased their burdens. In contrast, the Lord strengthened the people of Alma so that they could bear their burdens with ease. It is probably fair to say that most people, when they pray for the Lord's help to lighten their burdens, hope that He will respond in the same way He did with King Limhi's group: remove some of the burdens. We would like Him to remove the burdens of financial stress, physical illness or limitations, a guilty conscience, or the cravings of an addiction. Sometimes He does answer our cries for deliverance in this manner, but the story of Alma's group shows that He does not always respond in this way. The reality is that many times the Lord makes our burdens lighter not by removing them but by strengthening us so that we are better able to bear them. For example, He may not always send us an unexpected check in the mail when we are burdened with financial stress, but He may help us to develop a simpler lifestyle or put people in our path who can help us find ways to make ends meet with the money we have available to us. Again, if we are not careful, we may fail to recognize the hand of God in our lives because we have preconceived expectations about how He should lighten our burdens.

Recognizing this important principle about how Christ can lighten our burdens, we can now discuss the questions, "What are the burdens Jesus promises to make light?" In some ways this is a difficult question to answer because in Matthew 11 Jesus does not elaborate. I would like to briefly discuss two possibilities: the burden we may feel in accepting and fulfilling Church callings; and the burden with which we struggle on account of sin.

There are times when a call to serve in the kingdom of God may feel like a burden that is too heavy to bear. We may feel inadequate to fulfill the responsibilities of the calling, or it may be that those responsibilities will take us out of our comfort zone. Certainly this is how Enoch and Moses felt when they received their prophetic calls. Enoch's response was, "Why is it that I have found favor in thy sight, and am but a lad, and all the people hate me; for I am slow of speech; wherefore am I thy servant?" (Moses 6:31). Moses' response to his call was simply, "Who am I, that I should go unto Pharaoh, and that I should bring forth the children of Israel out of Egypt?" (Exodus 3:11). Some of us may even feel as Jonah did, who tried to escape the burden of the prophetic call and sought to flee from the responsibility (see Jonah 1:1–3).

Of course the feeling of inadequacy is not limited to prophetic callings. The burden may also feel overwhelming, for example, for people who are called to play the piano in Primary when they have limited piano skills, or who are asked to teach Gospel Doctrine when they do not view themselves as gospel scholars. But the Lord responded to both Enoch and Moses in ways that showed that He recognized their weaknesses and that He would help them. He promised Enoch that He would protect him and guide him in the things that he should teach. In Moses' case He gave signs to prove to the people that God was indeed with him. Of course the promise to lighten these burdens did not mean that either prophet would be carefree for the rest of their prophetic ministries. Jesus' promise in Matthew 11:30 is not that He will necessarily remove the burdens—only that He will make them bearable. Both Enoch and Moses continued to face challenges, but after these initial experiences they were able to move forward with confidence that the Lord would continue to make them equal to each new burden as it confronted them.

Likewise, the Lord promises that He will lighten the burdens that accompany modern callings in the Church. President Thomas S. Monson teaches: "Some of you may be shy by nature or consider yourselves inadequate to respond affirmatively to a calling. Remember that this work is not yours and mine alone. It is the Lord's work, and when we are on the Lord's errand, we are entitled to the Lord's help. Remember that whom the Lord calls, the Lord qualifies."[7] In other words, just as He did for Alma and his people, Christ helps us to become equal to the task. He helps us to develop the skills that we need. He will help the shy person find the courage to stand up in front of a class and teach or give a talk or knock on someone's door. He will help magnify an individual's talents and skills as he or she continues to work to develop them. Sometimes these transformations are immediate, as they seem to have been when Paul was baptized. "And straightway he preached Christ in the synagogues, that he is the Son of God. But all that heard him were amazed, and said; Is not this he that destroyed them which called on this name in Jerusalem, and came hither for that intent, that he might bring them bound unto the chief priests? But Saul increased the more in strength, and confounded the Jews which dwelt at Damascus, proving that this is very Christ" (Acts 9:20–22). More often, however, the transformation proceeds over a period of time. Sometimes we may not recognize the hand of the Lord until we are looking back in hindsight. Nevertheless, the scriptures give us confidence that the Lord will indeed make our burdens light as we have the faith to accept His call. Elder Neal A. Maxwell taught, "God does not begin by asking about our ability, but only about our availability, and if we then prove our dependability, he will increase our capability!"[8]

Another kind of burden comes through sin. All mortals, to a greater or lesser extent, carry this burden. Paul taught the Romans, "For all have sinned, and come short of the glory of God" (3:23), and the apostle John declared, "If we say that we have no sin, we deceive ourselves, and the truth is not in us" (1 John 1:8). Perhaps the greatest scriptural example of how Jesus lightens the burden of sin is that of Alma the Younger. In his account, Alma describes in some detail the physical, spiritual, and emotional burden of sin as well as the lifting of that burden when he finally recognized his need to come unto Christ. In his vivid description of the burden of his sins, Alma told his son Helaman: "I was racked with eternal torment, for my soul was harrowed up to the greatest degree and racked with all my sins" (Alma 36:12). As serious as his sins were (Alma likened them to spiritual murder in verse 14), the real emphasis of the account is the power of Jesus Christ to remove the burden of guilt:

"And it came to pass that as I was thus racked with torment, while I was harrowed up by the memory of my many sins, behold, I remembered also to have heard my father prophesy unto the people concerning the coming of one Jesus Christ, a Son of God, to atone for the sins of the world.

"Now, as my mind caught hold upon this thought, I cried within my heart: O Jesus, thou Son of God, have mercy on me, who am in the gall of bitterness, and am encircled about by the everlasting chains of death.

"And now, behold, when I thought this, I could remember my pains no more; yea, I was harrowed up by the memory of my sins no more. And oh, what joy, and what marvelous light I did behold; yea, my soul was filled with joy as exceeding as was my pain" (Alma 36:17–20).

Not only did the Atonement lighten Alma's burden of guilt, it also transformed him from a being who once despaired at the idea of coming into God's presence (see Alma 36:15) into one who longed to be with God (see Alma 36:22). Alma's experience is proof of what the author of

Hebrews hoped for all Christians: "Let us therefore come boldly unto the throne of grace, that we may obtain mercy, and find grace to help in time of need" (Hebrews 4:16).

This power is real, and it is just as real today as it was in Alma's day. Elder Dallin H. Oaks describes two powerful experiences of persons who were burdened with their own sin or with the sin of a loved one. In both of these instances the individuals' burdens were lightened as they turned to the Savior for help: "A man wrote a General Authority about how the power of the Atonement helped him with his problem of same-gender attraction. He had been excommunicated for serious transgression that violated his temple covenants and his responsibilities to his children. He had to choose whether to attempt to live the gospel or whether to continue a course contrary to its teachings.

"'I knew it would be difficult,' he wrote, 'but I didn't realize what I would have to go through.' His letter describes the emptiness and loneliness and the incredible pain he experienced from deep within his soul as he sought to return. He prayed mightily for forgiveness, sometimes for hours at a time. He was sustained by reading the scriptures, by the companionship of a loving bishop, and by priesthood blessings. But what finally made the difference was the help of the Savior. He explained:

"'It [was] only through Him and His Atonement. . . . I now feel an overwhelming gratitude. My pains have been almost more than I could bear at times, and yet they were so small compared to what He suffered. Where there once was darkness in my life, there is now love and gratitude.'"[9]

In a second instance the burden came because of the sin of a loved one. These burdens are also very real. "A woman whose marriage was threatened by her husband's addiction to pornography wrote how she stood beside him for five pain-filled years until, as she said, 'through the gift of our precious Savior's glorious Atonement and what He taught me about forgiveness, [my husband] finally is free—and so am I.' As one who needed no cleansing from sin, but sought a loved one's deliverance from captivity, she wrote this advice:

"'Commune with the Lord. . . . He is your best friend! He knows your pain because He has felt it for you already. He is ready to carry that burden. Trust Him enough to place it at His feet and allow Him to carry it for you. Then you can have your anguish replaced with His peace, in the very depths of your soul.'"[10]

It is important that modern disciples do not get caught up in a sense of false security, thinking that because they have committed no major sin, they have no need for the Atonement. Remember Paul's teaching: "All have sinned" (Romans 3:23). All of us need the redemptive power of the Atonement in our lives. Even the righteous can be burdened with sin. We find an example of this situation in Nephi's psalm. When Lehi died and Nephi realized that the prophetic mantle was now upon him, he keenly felt the burden of his sin and wrote:

"Notwithstanding the great goodness of the Lord, in showing me his great and marvelous works, my heart exclaimeth: O wretched man that I am! Yea, my heart sorroweth because of my flesh; my soul grieveth because of mine iniquities. I am encompassed about, because of the temptations and the sins which do so easily beset me. . . . Why should I yield to sin, because of my flesh? Yea, why should I give way to temptations, that the evil one have place in my heart to destroy my peace and afflict my soul?" (2 Nephi 4:17–18, 27). In some ways it is hard to even imagine what sins Nephi could have committed that would cause him to lament in this way. After all, Nephi was the good son, unlike his brothers Laman and Lemuel. Speaking of Nephi's lament, Elder Maxwell taught, "The prophet Nephi, who had progressed and advanced spiritually to a remarkable degree, still lamented about 'sins which do so easily beset me.' (2 Nephi 4:18.) Obviously, Nephi's sins were not major. But just as God cannot look upon sin with the least degree of allowance (D&C 1:31), *as we become more like Him, neither can we.* The best people have a heightened awareness of what little of the worst is still in them!"[11]

Nephi also came unto Jesus seeking a lightening of his burden: "O Lord, wilt thou redeem my soul? Wilt thou deliver me out of the hands of mine enemies? Wilt thou make me that I may shake at the appearance of sin? . . . O Lord, wilt thou encircle me around in the robe of thy righteousness! O Lord, wilt thou make a way for mine escape before mine enemies! . . . O Lord, I have trusted in thee, and I will trust in thee forever. . . . Yea, I know that God will give liberally to him that asketh. Yea, my God will give me, if I ask not amiss; therefore I will lift up my voice unto thee; yea, I will cry unto thee, my God, the rock of my righteousness.

Behold, my voice shall forever ascend up unto thee, my rock and mine everlasting God" (2 Nephi 4:31, 33–35). Even a righteous man such as Nephi carried burdens from sin, which the Lord was able to ease when Nephi came unto Him heavy ladened.

In our discussion thus far we have concentrated on how *our* burdens can become lighter as we come unto Christ. But Jesus does not specifically teach that *our* burdens will be light; rather, He teaches, "Take my yoke upon you, and learn of me . . . for . . . *my burden* is light" (Matthew 11:29–30; emphasis added). Here is an important principle that we must not overlook: although they are very much a part of us, the burdens we experience do not belong to us. Jesus redeems us through His atonement, which means that He has bought and paid for us. As Paul taught the Corinthians: "What? know ye not that . . . ye are not your own? For ye are bought with a price" (1 Corinthians 6:19–20). In redeeming us, Christ has not only bought us, or our sins, but has also bought our burdens. They belong to Him, so we must not try to hang on to them. It is only as we turn them over to Him that He can lighten our burdens. In inviting us to come unto Him, Jesus is asking us to hand our burdens over to Him. Just as He did for Limhi and his people, He can lighten our burdens by removing them from us.

CONCLUSION

The turning point in the chiasmus of Matthew 11:28–30 is Jesus' invitation for us to take His yoke and to learn of Him. I have chosen to be an active seeker of Jesus Christ. In doing so, I willingly submit to His yoke and I actively endeavor to both learn of Him and to learn from Him. As I have made my small efforts to do so I have personally experienced a lightening of my burdens. Sometimes I have felt those burdens being removed from me, but more often I have felt an increased ability to carry them. I testify that these blessings are very real. I also testify of the power of Christ to bestow His rest upon us. I realize that His rest can come in many forms. One example, I believe, happened to me not long ago after a very hectic Sunday. I was in meetings most of the day and then spoke at a fireside that night. After it was all over I went home. I was exhausted, but I took my dog YoYo for a walk. As we were walking, suddenly I experienced an overwhelming feeling that is difficult to describe, but I remember thinking, "I LOVE the gospel of Jesus Christ! I love being a part of it." On that day there was no time for physical rest, but I believe that in a small, but important way to me, I experienced a portion of His rest.

As I look back and think about my experience at Lake Powell, with the benefit of hindsight, I can now say, I believe! I believe Jesus is the Christ, that He is the Son of the living God. But I also believe Jesus has both the *power* and the *desire* to reach out to me in my most difficult times to lighten my burdens and help me find rest as I respond to His invitation, "Come unto me."

NOTES

1. See Stephen E. Robinson, *Believing Christ: The Parable of the Bicycle and Other Good News* (Salt Lake City: Deseret Book, 1992).
2. A. M. Hunter, "Crux Criticorum—Matt. XI.25–30—A Re-appraisal," *New Testament Studies* 8 (1962): 241.
3. James E. Talmage, *Jesus the Christ* (Salt Lake City: Deseret Book, 1914; reprint, 1982), 242.
4. Dallin H. Oaks, "Good, Better, Best," *Ensign*, November 2007, 104; emphasis added.
5. Jeffrey R. Holland, *Trusting Jesus* (Salt Lake City: Deseret Book, 2003), 84.
6. Neal A. Maxwell, "'Brightness of Hope,'" *Ensign*, November 1994, 35.
7. Thomas S. Monson, "Duty Calls," *Ensign*, May 1996, 44.
8. Maxwell, "It's Service, Not Status, That Counts," *Ensign*, July 1975, 7.
9. Oaks, "He Heals the Heavy Laden," *Ensign*, November 2006, 8.
10. Ibid.
11. Maxwell, *Notwithstanding My Weakness* (Salt Lake City: Deseret Book, 1981), 16–17.

BEYOND STATISTICS

Mary Ellen Edmunds

When I received this assignment to speak about visiting teaching, I made special arrangements so that no one I have ever been called to visit would be allowed to attend. I have prayed and pondered a lot about what to share with you today and pray that the Spirit of the Lord will teach each of us something that will make a difference in our lives and in our service in Relief Society.

I love the quote from President Julie B. Beck, "A sister in this Church has no other responsibility outside of her family that has the potential to do as much good as does visiting teaching."[1] She has taught us that this is a work of salvation, of service, and of becoming a holy people, and that "much of the *essential* Relief Society work we do *doesn't happen in meetings*."[2]

These are profound statements.

Many of the best, most spiritual, happifying, and tender experiences happen when we visit someone—in their home—when we're listening, feeling, caring, and praying like the dickens for guidance as we minister to a child of God.

Since tomorrow is the last day of April 2011, we have all completed our visiting for the month. . . . And there are some things we may have

Mary Ellen Edmunds is a former member of the Relief Society general board, a former director of training for the Provo Missionary Training Center, a nurse, and the author of several books.

shared which I'd like to repeat. Sister Beck reminded us that "the Lord expects us to increase our offering. He expects us to fulfill the purpose of Relief Society as never before."[3]

How shall we do that—increase our offering? I think each of us must search our heart and make a very personal commitment as to what we will do.

I love the invitation as recorded in the Book of Mormon: "And now, my beloved brethren, I would that ye should come unto Christ, who is the Holy One of Israel, and partake of his salvation, and the power of his redemption. Yea, come unto him, and offer your *whole souls* as an offering unto him, and continue in fasting and praying, and endure to the end; and as the Lord liveth ye will be saved" (Omni 1:26; emphasis added).

How different our lives can be when there are others watching out for us, caring about us, wanting to know and understand us. This feels like an offering that is beyond statistics. Do those we visit *know* that we love them? That we *care*? What do they sense from our interaction with them?

Do our phone conversations sound like this:

"Hi, Jo, can we come over in half an hour and visit you? Yeah, we *do* need to come today. I know, it's the 31st—oh! Thirty days hath September? We missed? Well . . . we'll stay twenty minutes and call it good for October too. How's that grab you?"

I'll tell you about something that grabbed me. In 1976, I was called on a mission to Indonesia. They'd not yet had lady missionaries, and the president wanted us to see how Relief Society was doing. We were assigned to the branch in Solo, in Central Java. Our branch Relief Society president, Ibu Subowo, was a tiny package of thorough conversion. We didn't yet have the Book of Mormon in the Indonesian language, let alone a Relief Society handbook.

But someone had come up with the words for Relief Society: *lembaga pertolongan*—"the society of helpfulness." With these two words, Ibu Subowo helped miracles happen. She asked the sisters in the branch to put aside a spoonful of rice before they cooked in the morning.

Each week, all the sisters would bring their little plastic bags of rice to church and they were put on a shelf in the home we used as our chapel. I can still feel the emotion I felt as I looked at those little bags. It was a storehouse, and there was so much love on the shelf along with those bags of rice.

After Relief Society, Ibu Subowo would gather us together and ask someone to pray and ask Heavenly Father who needed us to visit. An impression would come, and we all would walk together to go visit one of the sisters in the branch who couldn't come that day. And they would take a few of the bags of rice, according to what they felt was needed.

I received a strong impression not to meddle with what was happening. It was a very distinct message: "Edmunds, do not disturb what is happening here. This is a higher, purer form of visiting teaching than you have yet experienced. Just watch, and feel, and learn, and *remember*."

Ibu Subowo knew a little bit of English, so she borrowed our Relief Society handbook and other materials and did some studying, using her English-to-Indonesian dictionary.

One day she came to me with a problem. She said that in something she had read there was the recommendation that you call the sister to make an appointment to visit her. I knew what the problem was, but I wanted to hear her tell me about it. She said, "Tidak ada phone." ("No one has a phone.")

No phones! Well, that pretty much is going to keep you out of the celestial kingdom, eh? (You know that's not what I thought—or said!)

I asked, "So what do you do?"

"I pray." (What a great idea!)

She said, "I ask Heavenly Father who needs me to visit them. Then I ask Him if they need rice. And then I get on my bicycle and go to visit them." She told me that many times they'd be waiting, knowing that she'd come.

This incredibly wonderful Relief Society president, the mother of twelve children, serving in a tiny branch in central Java, Indonesia, is one of my heroes, an incredible example.

Years ago I imagined that I was in an interview with the Savior. He was asking me about some of my activities while I was an earthling.

"I heard you were a visiting teacher."

"Oh, yes, wasn't everyone?"

"Probably not everyone. Not many of the men, I'd guess."

"Oh. Yeah."

"Did you enjoy that calling?"

(And I'm thinking, I can't lie! He knows my thoughts!)

"Uh . . . I had some times that I did pretty much come close to almost nearly enjoying it."

"But not all the time?"

"Not all the time. Sorry."

"Why not?"

"Well, sometimes I wasn't in the mood."

"But you *had* to go?"

"Sure—they keep records. We were always trying to get 100 percent."

"And how did you reach 100 percent?"

"By everyone being visited or contacted or something like that."

You can see that the whole imagined interview just went down, down, down. It was as if I kept digging myself deeper and deeper into a hole.

I've thought a lot about that interview that never happened. What if it *had* happened? What if it *might* happen someday? I'd like it to go better than it did in my imagination. My friends, I am convinced that we will *never* be asked to do anything stupid—anything that doesn't *really* matter.

And visiting teaching really matters!

We are *not* called to serve each other in this Church just to keep us busy, stressed, and annoyed! Can you imagine the Savior saying, "This is really going to bug her; let's get her called as a visiting teacher"?

There must be a reason—a good reason! And there is!

We are asked to care for each other, to watch over each other, as "true undershepherds"[4] to Heavenly Father's children. Jesus could visit everyone Himself. He could round up a few angels and get some beautiful work done. Why does He let us help?

Because . . .

> *The errand of angels is given to women;*
> *And this is a gift that, as sisters, we claim:*
> *To do whatsoever is gentle and human,*
> *To cheer and to bless in humanity's name.*[5]

We are called to the work of lifting and comforting, of teaching and encouraging, of loving and serving in Christ's name (see D&C

59:5–6). You'll remember what the Savior taught in Matthew 25:35–36 about visiting:

"For I was an hungred, and ye gave me meat . . ." (I was hungry for love and attention, for kindness and compassion, and you came.)

"I was thirsty, and ye gave me drink . . ." (I was thirsty for companionship, for someone to listen to me, to lift my spirits, to be nice. And you came.)

"I was a stranger, and ye took me in: naked, and ye clothed me [I was without protection or defense; I was vulnerable, and you gave me protection; you clothed me with your friendship and your genuine charity]: I was sick, and ye visited me: I was in prison, and ye came unto me."

What was Jesus teaching us?

Certainly what He was teaching us is a reminder that we serve others the best we can in His name. We try to do what He would want us to do, but then He uses the word "inasmuch." He helps us to understand that yes, we do things for Him—we seek to be true disciples—but in some holy and sacred way, it's as if we've done those things *to* Him!

In a way, He's saying, "Inasmuch as ye have visited one of the *least* of your ward members, your neighbors, and have responded to their hunger and their thirst and their nakedness, ye have done it unto Me; you have clothed Me; you have comforted Me; you have visited Me! And I will bless you forever."

Can this make a difference in how we accept and carry out our assignments as visiting teachers? Can it make a difference in the way we welcome *our* visiting teachers into our homes and lives?

Elder David McKenzie, who served as president of the Scottish Branch of the British Mission and as Secretary to the First Presidency under Brigham Young, taught: "It is no trifling thing, my brethren and sisters, to be a Saint. What does it require of us? It requires of us our whole heart, our whole purpose of mind, and correspondent actions. . . . We are to manifest our religion by our works. We are not simply to say how lovely it is to feed the poor, to clothe the naked, to visit the sick and the afflicted, to cheer and console them.

"It may be all very well to talk about this; but the thing is to practice it in our lives, and by that practice create our own characters."[6]

What are some things that would make a difference for you as a visiting teacher?

Would it make a difference if you prayed more earnestly and often to know what is needed by those whom you visit, mentioning them by name?

Would it make a difference if you remembered a birthday, followed up on how someone was doing after a crisis, sent a card at Christmastime or any other time, sent an e-mail, dropped by with something you know they'd enjoy (soup, flowers, a book, a hug . . . possibly a zucchini)?

What our Heavenly Father and the Savior are asking is that we love one another as They have loved us. Of course, in our service there are some things that don't change, including principles and ordinances and doctrines. But with programs, there is a need for flexibility. President Spencer W. Kimball reminded us that "people are more important than programs."[7]

With visiting teaching, we adapt to a large variety of circumstances in which women live, and in which they serve as visiting teachers. As I've pondered all of this, I've asked myself some questions:

- What am I willing to do to be a more effective representative of the Savior as I visit?
- What might Heavenly Father have in store for me that I'm resisting by not responding more completely to His promptings about my call as a visiting teacher?
- In what ways might I be blessed if I make a commitment to step up to a higher level (with His help) as I serve others?

We're building trusting relationships with those whom we visit. If you don't trust me, you won't share your heart with me. What a difference it makes to be able to trust someone to look on your heart, to withhold judgment, and to keep your confidences. (As my neighbor says, "Keep your heart open and your mouth shut.")

Several years ago, I was teaching a group of missionaries about bringing people back into church activity. I mentioned something Elder Neal A. Maxwell had said, "Sometimes reaching out is like trying to pat a porcupine."[8] (Which I like to pronounce "porky-pine.") A lady missionary who was probably in her early thirties raised her hand and said, "I was a porcupine!" And then she shared her story.

She went away to college when she was eighteen. It was her first time away from home, and she loved the idea that she could make her own choices. She said that some of her decisions weren't very wise. She began skipping Church activities, eventually becoming, as she described it, "totally inactive." She told her bishop she didn't want *anyone* to visit her from the Church. She said it embarrassed her and made her uncomfortable.

"I don't want *you* to visit, I don't want home or visiting teachers, priests or teachers gathering fast offerings—no one!"

And it worked. No more visits from people from the Church. Until one day when there was a knock on the door, and she opened it to find a smiling lady standing on the porch.

"Hello! I'm your new visiting teacher!"

She was *so* upset.

"I don't want you here! I told the bishop I didn't want *anyone* to visit me! I don't want a visiting teacher!"

Anything could have happened at this point. Her visiting teacher could have said, "Well, I have never been treated like this. You don't need to worry that I'll ever come back!"

She could have gone back to the Relief Society president and told her she almost lost her life, and not to ever send anyone to visit that porcupine again! But no. When she heard, "I don't want you here! I don't want a visiting teacher," this brave, wonderful, rescuing soul, said, "Oh, good! Then I can just be your friend!" And she walked right in!

And they became *friends*. She was her "un"-visiting teacher for about eight years, as I remember it. Then one day the porcupine called her up and said she wanted to come back to church, and asked, "Will you help me?"

Her friend, her "un"-visiting teacher, said of course she would, and they grew even closer to each other. A little over a year later, the young woman called her friend, her visiting teacher, and told her she was preparing to go on a mission. Was it worth hanging in there for eight years? Was it worth the courage and love it took to respond the way she did at the door that day?

You know, it's a good thing that angels are silent notes taking,[9] because I think you have no idea how much of a difference you make in the lives of those you visit, even when you may not be in the mood.

One important role of Relief Society leaders is to know the needs of women and their families. They work as a team with priesthood leaders, and their input is critical in the ministering that takes place in wards and branches.

President Spencer W. Kimball shared this: "One of the most important responsibilities Relief Society leaders have is to really know the sisters in their wards—know what their circumstances are—and thereby serve them better. We need to have a keen awareness of each sister's situation in order to make the programs of Relief Society helpful to each one. Leaders should always have a 'why' for everything they do. The 'why' is found in the needs of the sisters."[9]

Leaders, how are *you* doing? Does the thought of visiting teaching sometimes make you want to move to Timbuktu? (That's in Africa.) Have you figured out some things that help you in your calling?

How do you orient your visiting teachers (and new members of Relief Society)?

Are they given information about their companion, and those whom they'll be visiting? (This would seem so much more helpful than a piece of paper with only names, addresses, and phone numbers.)

Do they know how much you want and need to hear about how the sisters and their families are doing? Do they have a way to contact you directly if there are matters that need your attention?

Are your visiting teachers asked about more than just "did you get it done"? That is one of the most ineffective questions a visiting teacher can be asked. It doesn't seem to hold much motivation for doing anything different than just "getting it done."

I've wondered if it would make a difference if you let your visiting teachers know what you want to have happen as they visit. Maybe you'll think of some questions you'd like them to ask so you can find out how the sisters in your ward or branch are doing.

What if they were to ask things like:

• What is something you're looking forward to?
• Can you share a concern that you have at this time?

- What would you consider to be one of your greatest needs in this season of your life?
- How could a visiting teacher make more of a difference for you?
- How could Relief Society meetings and activities make more of a difference for you?

You'll think of other questions which would help you *and* the visiting teachers to get to know the sisters better.

Asking questions—real questions—and then listening is a way to strengthen relationships and build bonds of trust and friendship. If I have a specific question to ask, and if someone is going to want to know how "my sisters" are doing, I think I'll visit differently—I think I'll be much more likely to go beyond statistics.

Many years ago, a friend of mine whom I'll call Debbie (because that's her name) was at home, sicker than a dog with the flu. She'd been down and out for several days. Her husband was a student, so he was gone most of the time. Her mother-in-law had taken their four little boys for a few days. But the laundry was piling up, along with the dust and the dishes, and Debbie was just trying to get better.

There was a knock at the door. She wasn't going to answer it, but then she remembered it was getting close to the end of the month, and the ward had a goal of 100 percent visiting teaching.

She thought, Oh! it might be them! And they might help me!

So she made it to the door.

"Oh, Debbie, you don't look too great."

"I've been really sick with the flu, but I'm over the worst part. I'm mostly just sleeping and resting to get better."

"Well, then, we'll just hurry and give you the lesson so you can get back to bed."

And they did. And then they left.

And she did go back to bed. And she wept, partly because she was desperate for some help, but also because she wondered if *she* had ever done that to anyone in her years as a visiting teacher.

She was pretty sure the ward got 100 percent, but what did it mean? What was the purpose of their "visit"? They were right there in her home where they could have seen and felt so much more. Maybe they did, and they just ignored it.

How could this experience have been different? What could have changed the outcome and blessed not just Debbie, but the two visiting teachers? Could there have been some sacrifice—maybe they could miss a lunch date, or a TV program, seeing a soccer game, or even postponing something they had planned to do at home. So many miracles are waiting just beyond statistics.

A friend of mine who was close to delivering her fifth child was in a head-on collision. She lost the baby and nearly lost her own life. Her visiting teachers and home teachers didn't wait for her to get out of the hospital to ask her if there was anything they could do to help. Chances are they prayed to know what would help her the most at that time of great sorrow and loss.

They organized a cleaning team, got in her home, and cleaned it top to bottom, even organizing closets. (And no, I don't have their names and phone numbers.)

When the Relief Society was first organized, the Prophet Joseph Smith shared his vision of its purpose: "This charitable Society is according to your natures, it is natural for females to have feelings of charity. You are now placed in a situation where you can act according to these sympathies which God has planted in your bosoms. If you live up to your privileges the angels cannot be restrained from being your associates. This Society is not only to relieve the poor but to save souls. . . . You should be armed always with mercy. If you would have God have mercy on you, have mercy on one another."[10]

I *know* this is true—that angels *will* serve with us and help us in this holy work. Visiting teaching is the errand of angels, and Relief Society *is* the Lord's organization for women—it is no less than that!

President Joseph F. Smith shared such tender thoughts about our responsibilities for ministering: "[Part of our duty] is to look after the spiritual welfare and salvation of the mothers and daughters of Zion; to see that *none is neglected*, but that all are guarded against misfortune, calamity, the powers of darkness, and the evils that threaten them in the world."[11]

Let's make sure that no one is neglected. Let's help to guard each other through our watchcare and our genuine love. Let's put the *relief* back in the *society*. Our motto is "Charity never faileth."

Let's do our best to make sure that's true—that it *never fails!* It may getteth tired, it may be weary or even discouraged at times, but let's do all we can to make sure it doesn't *fail.*

Ask yourself what you can do and be that will make a difference in how you feel about being a visiting teacher and about carrying out that calling. The change will begin in our hearts and in our souls.

President Boyd K. Packer gave a talk entitled "The Circle of Sisters" and shared these promises: "Service in the Relief Society magnifies and sanctifies each individual sister. . . . You sustain the cause that will bless every woman who comes within its influence. . . .

"This great circle of sisters will be a protection for each of you and for your families. The Relief Society might be likened to a refuge—the place of safety and protection—the sanctuary of ancient times. You will be safe within it. It encircles each sister like a protecting wall."[12]

Visiting teachers help this happen—*you* help this happen. You help to provide safety for individual women and their families. You help provide a protecting wall.

So, why do we do visiting teaching? Your answer may be similar to the one given by Eve and Adam when they were asked why they offered sacrifice: "I know not, save the Lord commanded me"! (Moses 5:6).

I admit I don't know all the reasons we are asked to visit and teach, but this I do know: We've been asked to love God and to love our neighbors as ourselves, and to serve them in the name of Jesus Christ. May we do this the best we can, with all our hearts, and with the help which angels are waiting to give us.

NOTES

1. Julie B. Beck, "Relief Society: A Sacred Work," *Ensign*, November 2009, 113.
2. Ibid.; emphasis added.
3. Beck, "The Purpose of Relief Society," *Ensign*, April 2011, 7.
4. Mary B. Wingate, "Dear to the Heart of the Shepherd," *Hymns of The Church of Jesus Christ of Latter-day Saints* (Salt Lake City: The Church of Jesus Christ of Latter-day Saints, 1985), no. 221.

5. Emily H. Woodmansee, "As Sisters in Zion," *Hymns,* no. 309.

6. David McKenzie, in *Millennial Star,* 4 April 1895 (vol. 57, no. 14): 211–12.

7. Spencer W. Kimball, "Living the Gospel in the Home," *Ensign,* May 1978, 101.

8. Neal A. Maxwell, "'According to the Desire of [Our] Hearts,'" *Ensign,* November 1996, 22.

9. "Do What Is Right," *Hymns,* no. 237.

10. Kimball, Regional Representatives Seminar, 1978.

11. Joseph Smith, cited in "Historical Events in the Relief Society," *Relief Society Magazine,* August 1927 (vol. 14, no. 8): 390.

12. Joseph F. Smith, *Joseph F. Smith* [manual], in the Teachings of Presidents of the Church series (Salt Lake City: The Church of Jesus Christ of Latter-day Saints, 1998), 185; emphasis added.

13. Boyd K. Packer, "The Circle of Sisters," *Ensign,* November 1980, 110.

LINE UPON LINE: THROUGH PERSONAL REVELATION, ALL THESE THINGS SHALL GIVE US EXPERIENCE

Cathy Chamberlain

Joseph Smith's small decision to "ask of God" in a grove of trees was the beginning of the great restoration of all things. If there is one thing we have learned from the Prophet Joseph's experience in the Sacred Grove, it is that God will actually talk to His children. He actually will talk to you and me!

In my years of public opinion research with both Latter-day Saints and people of other faiths, significant questions—that I call questions of the soul—arise:

- Does God know me personally?
- Will He communicate with me?
- Does He have a plan for my life?
- Why does He allow bad things to happen to good people?

When Joseph walked from the grove of trees, he had clear answers to two of those questions and soon would have answers to them all. Remember Joseph's words, "When the light rested upon me I saw two

Cathy Chamberlain is the managing director for market strategy at Deseret Book. She was previously the owner and CEO of CTC, Inc., a communications and re-search firm and a vice president at Wirthlin Worldwide in Washington, DC, primar-ily involved in communication, branding, and positioning strategies for corporations, organizations, and political candidates. She is a member of the National Advisory Council for the Marriott School of Management at Brigham Young University and a member of the Board of Trustees for Southern Virginia University.

Personages. . . . One of them spake unto me, *calling me by name* and said, . . . *This is My Beloved Son. Hear Him!*" (Joseph Smith–History 1:17; emphasis added).

Then, line upon line, through the spirit of revelation, the Lord laid out His plan for Joseph's work. In the words of Elder David A. Bednar, "the fundamental truths of the restored gospel were not delivered to the Prophet Joseph Smith all at once in the Sacred Grove. These priceless treasures were revealed as circumstances warranted and as the timing was right."[1]

We know the work was fraught with tough and painful challenges. Joseph himself said, "I was hated and persecuted for saying that I had seen a vision, yet it was true. . . . I knew it, and I knew that God knew it" (JS–H 1:25). "It seems as though the adversary was aware . . . that I was destined to prove a disturber and an annoyer of his kingdom; else why . . . the opposition and persecution that arose against me . . . ?" (JS–H 1:20).

Joseph had to learn to trust the Lord! He had experienced in his youth that if a man lacked wisdom he could ask God. Over time, his experiences taught him that God would pave the way for anything that He asked him to do.

We all know the significance of the Restoration, but I wonder if we've thought much about the process of how the Lord did it. The pattern the Lord used—line upon line through personal revelation—is *exactly the same pattern* He uses in each of our lives today. Remember, personal revelation requires that the Lord knows you. And just as He knew Joseph, He knows you—your circumstances, your needs, and your desires. He directed the work Joseph came to do and He will direct the work you and I came to do. Years of personal experience—mired with mistakes and heartache—have taught me that as I grow closer to our Father in Heaven it becomes easier to see the hand He has played in my life.

Receiving personal revelation line upon line means that we often have to walk to the edge of the light and be willing to step into the dark—both believing and trusting in the Lord: believing that He won't ask us to do anything for which He hasn't already prepared the way and trusting that we will be led by the Spirit even if we don't know exactly what the next step is.

Because the daily grind can often feel overwhelming, and some challenges insurmountable, the Lord has warned us, "Be not weary in well-doing, for ye are laying the foundation of a great work. And out of small things proceedeth that which is great" (D&C 64:33). Regardless of how tough the going gets, "all these things shall give thee experience, and shall be for thy good" (D&C 122:7). During your difficult times, stop and ask yourself, "What does the Lord want me to learn?"

Just before Joseph was taken to Carthage, where he was martyred, Emma asked him to give her a blessing. Joseph said there wasn't time and suggested that she write out the best blessing she could think of. He promised to sign it when he returned. In a most difficult and trying time, one of the things she wrote was "I desire the spirit of God to know and understand myself."[2] We know that Joseph never returned, but I believe the Lord honored Emma's desires, and I believe He will do the same for you and me.

Emma's desire—to understand and know who she really was—is as much or maybe even more critical for you and me today. We live in a world that confuses our true identity, devalues our divine role, and validates in ways that never satisfy. We can become easily distracted from the work the Lord needs us to do at this time, our time. The work He is counting on us to do is both essential and eternal.

So where do we begin to seek this same blessing that Emma desired?

Several years ago I was diagnosed with an illness called "chronic fatigue syndrome." It was something new that the doctors weren't sure how to treat. In my search for help, I met Dr. McGarey, who taught me some profound truths about healing—both physically and spiritually. This is a story she told: "Picture spring in the Arizona desert, and imagine the glory in the colors as the desert breaks into bloom. As wonderful as this is, what is truly marvelous is how the desert tree will withstand the heat and drought of the Arizona summer sun and then the cold of the winter. Some of the desert trees will not survive. This has nothing to do with the variety of the plant or even where it is located. The desert tree, when it puts its roots down, soon hits a caliches layer, a hard soil layer cemented by calcium sometimes called hardpan. When this happens, the tree has two options. The first option is to spread its roots to the side looking for nourishment and water in the area surrounding it, in which case it dies. The second option is to put all of its energy into its taproot. The tree then focuses all of its energy to work and fight its way through the caliches layer. *When it breaks through that layer and hits its source, nothing can knock it over.* It now has made contact with a depth of nourishment that is not affected by conditions on the surface. It will withstand heavy winds, drought, freezing conditions, and even flooding. Because it is secure in its source of energy, it will bloom again in the spring."[3]

Just like the trees in the Arizona desert, we all seek nourishment. One form of nourishment we seek is validation, the feeling that our lives have value, that what we do matters. Research indicates that this is one of the main drivers of our behavior. We can seek validation, like the water in the story, from two sources: externally, where we spread ourselves in many directions seeking things the world validates, or internally, where we quietly and steadily put our energy into doing the things the Lord has asked us to do. Here's the truth about external validation: *you can't get enough!* In the constant search for it, you will soon forget who you really are. You can't be cute enough, skinny enough, have enough clothes, a big enough house, or be loved and admired enough. It's like an artificial sweetener that increases your appetite but never satisfies.

Compare that with searching and finding the well of living water—the source the Savior promised will never run dry, and despite conditions on the surface, will keep us from being knocked over. This well provides the nourishment that assures we will bloom again eternally.

Dr. McGarey's story hit home with me. I had just moved from Washington, D. C., after spending several years spreading myself in the "thick of thin things"[4] seeking the validation of the world. I became defined by titles, possessions, and the accolades of men, which create a false image that's hard to keep up. Even Church callings, if we are not careful, can define us in ways that, when they no longer exist, may cause us to forget who we really are. When I got sick, those things were gone. So, who would I be if I wasn't who I thought I was?

My desire was the same as Emma Smith's—I wanted the Spirit to help me know who I really am and whose I am. I had prayed often to understand how the Lord saw me—something I had heard Sheri Dew mention in many talks. But nothing happened. Then one day, an answer came in an unexpected way. Before I share that answer, let me ask you a question: Have you ever felt like others didn't see you the way you wanted to be seen? If we are really honest, most of us have probably worked hard to protect an image we wanted others to have of us. It comes from the need to be validated.

On this particular day, the image I wanted to portray didn't happen. As I sat stewing, I softly heard these words in my mind, "Cathy, Cathy, don't you care more how I see you than how other people see you?" Wow! Did I really care more how others saw me than how the Lord did? The sad truth was I did! I was so busy seeking validation from others, I *couldn't* see what the Lord wanted me to see. What a waste of time and energy. Suddenly a sweet feeling of reassurance filled my heart. The Lord did know me, He was communicating with me, and I knew that He loved me. At that moment, nothing else mattered. I had experienced personal revelation, and it changed my life.

This experience didn't mean that my life would now be free from challenges, or that my mission would be clearly laid out. In fact, in some ways it was just the opposite. But I was equipped now with the knowledge and strength I needed to deal with the trials and uncertainties of life. I was learning to trust the Lord and to recognize the promptings of the still, small voice. It gave me the courage to start to walk away from the things of the world. In mortality, we will probably always struggle with being in the world but not of it. But we always need to be working at walking away from the world.

In 1873, Eliza R. Snow spoke to the women gathered in Ogden: "When I am filled with that spirit [the spirit of the Holy Ghost] my soul is satisfied; and I can say in good earnest, that the trifling things of the day do not seem to stand in my way at all. But just let me loose my hold of that *spirit and power of the Gospel,* and partake of the *spirit of the world,* in the slightest degree, and trouble comes; there is something wrong. I am tried; and what will comfort me? You cannot impart comfort to me that will satisfy the Immortal mind, but that which comes from the fountain above."[5]

What is it about this incredible spirit that Emma and Eliza sought? In the April 2011 general conference, Elder David A. Bednar taught us that "revelation is communication from God to His children on the earth and one of the great blessings associated with the gift and constant companionship of the Holy Ghost."[6] He went on to teach about the ways the Holy Ghost illuminates our hearts and minds: "The gradual increase of light radiating from the rising sun is like receiving a message from God 'line upon line, precept upon precept' (2 Nephi 28:30). . . . Sometimes the sun rises on a morning that is cloudy or foggy. Because of the overcast conditions, perceiving the light is more difficult. . . . But on such a morning we nonetheless have sufficient light to recognize a new day and to conduct our affairs."[7]

The Holy Ghost is the member of the Godhead who can be with us continually in mortality. Elder Jeffrey R. Holland says that "perhaps all disciples of Christ . . . should pray for the influence and guidance of the Holy Ghost as that heavenly gift 'which they most desire.'"[8] His most important mission is to bear witness, to all who seek, that Jesus is the Christ, the literal Son of God. This is the most important personal revelation you and I will ever receive. After receiving this witness, one of the most important revelations you should seek is to find out how your Father sees and feels about you.

Years ago, President Spencer W. Kimball told the women of the Church: "Remember, in the world before we came here, faithful women were given certain assignments. . . . While we do not now remember the particulars, this does not alter the glorious reality of what we once agreed to."[9]

We can't possibly fulfill these premortal assignments without learning to hear and then follow the "still, small voice."

- We must pray and ask for the Spirit.
- We need to purify our hearts—what we think, watch, hear, read, how we dress—and we need to stop judging and gossiping.
- We need to be diligent in keeping all of the commandments, and not ignoring the ones we think don't apply; this is our protection against the ever-constant distractions of the adversary.
- We need to learn to recognize God's voice by doing the things that He inspires and instructs us to do and then watching for the confirmation.

President Boyd K. Packer has said, "These are sobering times. . . . You won't survive spiritually unless you know how to receive revelation."[10]

The scriptures teach us that the Holy Ghost can

- Teach us the truths of His kingdom (Moroni 10:4–5).
- Give us words to speak in the very moment we need them (D&C 100:6).
- Carry our message to the hearts of people we speak to (2 Nephi 33:1).
- Warn about things that might harm us (D&C 89:4).
- Comfort us in times of need (John 14:6; D&C 88:3).
- Guide and direct us in fulfilling everything we promised to do in our premortal existence (John 16:13).

Think of these promises as they relate to the essential work Joseph outlined for the women of the Relief Society—to save souls and bring relief, both spiritually and temporally, to the Lord's children—just as the Savior did. It makes me think of the last words my grandmother spoke to her older daughters just before she died: "Take care of my babies." She left in their care very young children—one of whom had Down's syndrome— and they have faithfully fulfilled that promise to their mother. I believe those are the words our Father wants His daughters to hear today, and the promise He wants us to make—take care of My babies and bring them safely home. *That* is the errand of angels given to women!

At this conference we have thousands of women gathered from around the world, seeking to receive personal revelation for ourselves and our families. I feel like Eliza R. Snow when she spoke to a Relief Society group in Lehi in 1869: "We want to be ladies in very deed, not according to the word as the world judges, but fit companions of the Gods and Holy Ones. . . . I know we like to be appreciated but if we do not get all the appreciation which we think is our due, what matters? We know the Lord has laid high responsibility upon us, and there is not a wish or desire that the Lord has implanted in our hearts in righteousness but will be realized."[11]

In closing, may I share my testimony of the things I know to be true:

1. God knows you by name.
2. He has a specific plan for your life, which will unfold line upon line.

3. If you live up to your privileges—magnifying the gifts God planted in your heart as a woman and a mother—angels can't be restrained from being your companions.

4. When you enter His holy temple and make sacred covenants, you leave armed with His power—all the power you need to fulfill your mortal mission.

5. While the challenges of mortality can be tough, the Savior has promised that you do not need to bear your burdens alone. He has promised that, in time, all things will turn to your good.

6. If you keep the sacred covenants you have made with Him, one day you will see Him and you will be like Him. Imagine the feeling as He enfolds you in the arms of His love forever!

Because of all this precious knowledge that was restored as a result of Joseph's small decision to ask God in a grove of trees, I, like Eliza R. Snow, feel to say that "'my heart is fixed'—I know in whom I trust"![12]

May each of us, like Emma, seek the Spirit of God to know and understand ourselves and then have the courage to walk away from the validation of the world.

NOTES

1. David A. Bednar, "The Spirit of Revelation," *Ensign*, May 2011, 88.

2. Cited in Gracia N. Jones, "My Great-Great-Grandmother, Emma Hale Smith," *Ensign*, August 1992, 34.

3. Personal conversation with Dr. Gladys McGarey.

4. Thomas S. Monson, "What Have I Done for Someone Today?" *Ensign*, November 2009, 85.

5. Eliza R. Snow, in *Woman's Exponent*, September 15, 1873, 62; emphasis added; available at http://contentdm.lib.byu.edu/cgi-bin/showfile .exe?CISOROOT=/WomansExp&CISOPTR=15696&filename=15697.pdf; accessed 14 September 2011.

6. Bednar, "The Spirit of Revelation," 87.

7. Ibid., 88–89.

8. Jeffrey R. Holland, *Christ and the New Covenant* (Salt Lake City: Deseret Book, 1997), 278.

9. Spencer W. Kimball, "The Role of Righteous Women," *Ensign,* November 1979, 102.

10. Boyd K. Packer, commencement address, BYU–Hawaii, 17 December 2005; available at http://devotional.byuh.edu/node/363; accessed 14 September 2011.

11. Snow, cited in Julie B. Beck, "'And upon the Handmaids in Those Days Will I Pour Out My Spirit,'" *Ensign,* May 2011, 12.

12. Snow, "Lines, Suggested on reading the Author's first Letter in the Series," in Orson Spencer, *Letters Exhibiting the Most Prominent Doctrines of The Church of Jesus Christ of Latter-day Saints* (London: Latter-day Saints' Book Depot, 1852), 242.

Balancing Work and Family— and Other Polite Fictions

Emily Watts

I want to begin by declaring this area a no-guilt zone. If you're going to insist on feeling guilty about the choices you've made, I'm going to have to ask you not to read this chapter. I was so grateful to hear Elder Quentin L. Cook offer a similar sentiment in general conference. Let me just remind you what he said about the topic of mothers and working:

"These are very emotional, personal decisions, but there are two principles that we should always keep in mind. First, no woman should ever feel the need to apologize or feel that her contribution is less significant because she is devoting her primary efforts to raising and nurturing children. Nothing could be more significant in our Father in Heaven's plan. Second, we should all be careful not to be judgmental or assume that sisters are less valiant if the decision is made to work outside the home. We rarely understand or fully appreciate people's circumstances. Husbands and wives should prayerfully counsel together, understanding they are accountable to God for their decisions."[1]

Notice to whom we are accountable for the decisions we make: not to the neighbors, not to the ward members, but to Heavenly Father. So that question—should I feel guilty about working or not working?—gets to be

Emily Watts is a senior editor at Deseret Book Company, for whom she has worked for more than thirty years. During much of that time she worked part-time from home so she could devote the lion's share of her attention to her husband, Larry, and their five children. She holds a B.A. in English from the University of Utah and is a Relief Society teacher, the author of several books, and, best of all, a grandmother.

put to rest. What we really want to do here is figure out, if we've made the decision that being employed outside the home is what we're going to do, how we're going to make that work.

I told my mother that I had been invited to speak at the BYU Women's Conference on the topic of balancing work and family, and she said, "Oh—do you think you'll be doing it by then?" Bolstered by that vote of confidence from the woman who gave me life, I wasn't sure how I felt about my qualifications to speak on the subject. But I have come to understand that my mother was right about my lack of balance: If you think of "balance" as a capacity to make all things equal, there is no such thing. All we really can hope for and work toward is a carefully crafted system of priorities that allows us to understand what needs to be getting the weight at any given time. We need to decide, and we need help with this.

Fortunately, where priorities are concerned, we have scriptural help, because Heavenly Father says it: "Seek ye first . . ." Anyone who is reading this can finish that scripture: "Seek ye first the kingdom of God, and his righteousness; and all these things shall be added unto you" (Matthew 6:33). To me this simply means that if you're seeking the kingdom of God, everything else falls into priority the way it needs to.

And of what does "the kingdom of God" consist? Elder Jeffrey R. Holland has taught: "There might be wards and stakes in heaven—I don't know anything about them—or there may well be some other organization that we don't know much about. What we *do* know will exist in heaven is families. And most of what has been revealed about our afterlife, our eternal life, our celestial life, focuses on family organization."[2]

To me, seeking first the kingdom of God means serving our families. And there are many ways that we serve our families. Sometimes women serve their families best by being stay-at-home moms, and sometimes women serve them better by being working moms. I fall in the latter group, so my current task is to learn how best to serve my family in this circumstance.

There are some principles I have learned about being a working mom, mostly from having done things wrong most of my life. It is said that we learn best from our mistakes, so I guess I could say I'm sort of a genius about these things because I've made a ton of mistakes. I want to share with you some of the things I've learned in hopes that maybe you will be wiser than I have been and not have to make the same mistakes I have made.

The first principle I want to give you, and to me it's the one that trumps everything, is this:

PRINCIPLE NUMBER 1: WORK WILL TAKE IT ALL, IF YOU LET IT.

Work will take every ounce of time and energy you have. That is not because work is some big, evil monster out to wreck your life. It's because, by definition, work is never done. If your work is done, you're out of a job! And so, you don't necessarily want work to be done, but then you have the dilemma that it doesn't *feel* done, and thus it will continue to take all your time and your energy.

What do you do about this? You have to decide. You have to understand clearly where your boundary is that says, "*For today,* my work is done." Try to picture Fred Flintstone at the beginning of each cartoon when the whistle blows and he slides down the back of that dinosaur yelling, "Yabba dabba doo!" He's done—for that day. He'll be back tomorrow. Those rocks are still going to be there tomorrow.

It's the same with your work. You have to decide where to put your boundaries around it so that it does not consume your life.

I had a great opportunity to have a little metaphor happen in my life recently. I was at work, and, spring in Utah being what it is, I was rather injudiciously running a space heater along with my computer and microwave oven, all on the same circuit. This blew the circuit breaker.

If you pop a circuit breaker at my office, it turns out, you can't just go in and push the button to fix it. You could—you're perfectly capable of it—but it makes the people who own the building really mad. I couldn't find anybody in the building to turn the circuit breaker back on so that I could have my computer to do my work. They had to call the property management company to send someone over to push the button, and it was an hour and a half before I could do any more work on my computer. Why did this happen? Because I tried to do too many things at one time.

If you try to make yourself do more than you can do, you'll pop. And sometimes you can push the button to reset your life yourself, and sometimes you have to wait and wait before you can regain some sanity and working order in your life. And so I would suggest to you to learn to understand how to put a boundary around your work and make sure that it doesn't take more than you really want to give it.

PRINCIPLE NUMBER 2: WORKING AT HOME, ALTHOUGH IT MAY SEEM LIKE A PERFECT SOLUTION, MAY NOT BE RIGHT FOR YOU.

I went to work in the editorial department at Deseret Book right out of college, and then when I started having children I went home and continued to work out of my home for the next fifteen years. Many people thought I was the luckiest woman alive: I could do the work I had been trained to do and still be there for my children and participate in all the things that they wanted to do. It *was* a blessing in so many ways.

But before you think that you need to hurry out and find a job that you can do at home, let me just tell you a couple of things about working at home.

One is that when you work at home, your work is *always there*. It's constantly playing in the background, making it impossible to escape the thought that you need to be working instead of . . . whatever you're doing. This is especially true if your budget is tight (and let's face it, there's never really enough money, is there?) because you figure you could just put in a couple more hours and try to make a little more money. When vacations roll around, you don't go on vacation, because this is a golden opportunity to get in some extra work since you don't have to get your kids dressed and ready for school—they can be with Dad, and you can work.

Another challenge is that, unless you have a nice, big house with a private office in it for you, you'll probably have to do your work right in the thick of things. I always had to dig my papers out and spread them over the kitchen table, where they sometimes got watercolored on or spilled on or smeared with dinner remnants or Play-Doh. This is not ideal—especially when it comes time to turn those papers in.

Sometimes it's hard to be patient with the children when a work deadline is looming. I realized this most poignantly when I was watching my youngest child playing with one of her dolls, and all of a sudden she picked it up and looked into its eyes and said, "Listen! Can't you see Mommy is trying to work?" I felt like such a fabulous example. It led me to realize, *Walt Disney spends more time with this child than I do.* I thought that if I had placed her in day care, and the person I had hired to provide day care for her was providing the kind of care I was providing, I would *fire* that person. This happened because, referring back to principle number 1, work will take it all if you let it. So I had to stop and realign my priorities again and recognize how much work I could do and how much I couldn't do and just needed to set aside. Working at home was a blessing, but it was not an unqualified blessing.

PRINCIPLE NUMBER 3: WORKING OUTSIDE THE HOME IS NOT AN IDEAL SITUATION EITHER.

I remember when I was considering going back to work at the office full time, my husband and I approached it prayerfully and carefully, as Elder Cook has suggested. We went to the temple. We thought about it and prayed about it for a few weeks and decided that the time was right. That was in 1995.

I remember the first week of work in my own office: I thought it was heaven. I couldn't believe how amazing it was to be able to go into a quiet space and find there my books and my papers and my red pens, exactly where I had left them the night before. Nobody asked me for a drink of water all day long. And when I left the office, I left it all behind. I went home, and it was done, and I just thought that was so wonderful.

It became a little less wonderful as time went on, partly because I was laboring under the illusion that what needed to happen now was that I just needed to be more organized. I could arrange my life better and be more on top of things, and since the kids were in school most of the day anyway, they probably wouldn't even notice I was gone. In fact, I was *determined* that they would not notice my absence.

I don't know in what universe I was living to think that I could pull a nine-hour block of the day right out of the middle of my family's life and not have them notice. I think now that that was sort of an absurd expectation, and I can tell you—yeah, they noticed. They saw that I wasn't there all the time anymore, and they had to make some adjustments.

But one of the traps that it's easy to fall into if you are working is that you don't want to impose a greater burden on your family by your being away (that guilt again), and so you still try to do everything that you were doing before you worked—well, maybe *you* don't. But *I* did. My husband finally sat me down one day and said to me very calmly, "Sweetheart, you know these children are perfectly capable of doing their own laundry." I'm embarrassed to confess that such a thing had not even occurred to me. My oldest daughter was fifteen—of course she was capable. But when her father said that, all I could think was, "Mom does the laundry."

No! Not necessarily. I developed a new philosophy: Wash a kid a sock, and you clothe him for a day. Teach a kid to wash a sock, and he can never complain again about not having any clean socks. Of course, the difficulty comes when you have one child who steadfastly refuses to wash his own socks and so wears unwashed socks, leading to a whole different can of worms I don't care to open at the moment.

The important thing to understand is that if you are working, your children have the opportunity to learn some pretty important life skills. I would suggest to you that you delegate everything that can be delegated. Everything you can find that can be done by somebody else in your home, let them do it. There's no guilt in that. Give your children the glorious op-portunity of contributing to your family so that you can continue to make your own contribution by working. View them as an asset—and let them know how much you value their help.

PRINCIPLE NUMBER 4: SEEK THE BLESSING OF A FAMILY-FRIENDLY WORK ENVIRONMENT.

I know that we don't always have choices in the kind of work we do or the kind of employer we end up with. But I can tell you that your chances of finding flexibility in your job will improve if you become very good at what you do. If you become an important and valued commodity, it's like-lier that employers will be happy to have you for those few hours a week that they can get.

I was blessed to feel valued by my employer enough that I was com-fortable taking my children into the office when I simply had to be at a meeting. I can still picture my littlest ones writing on the bottom two inches of the whiteboard during some of our weekly tracking meetings.

One occasion I remember most clearly: I had my two-year-old daugh-ter sitting on my lap in this meeting, and I was wearing a pair of those clip-on sunglasses that flip up and down over your regular lenses. My little girl was entertaining herself quietly by flipping my sunglasses up and down, up and down, and I was explaining my progress on the project I was currently working on. I happened to glance up and see the manager who was in charge of the meeting looking at me with an incredulous expression on his face that seemed to say, "How are you even thinking, let alone talking?" I should point out that he was a man—that was part of why he didn't get it. All I could think was, "If a little thing like a child playing on my lap were enough to stop me from working, I'd be in serious trouble." That's the Mom Multitasking Power coming out, and most women I know possess it.

You learn to work with what you have, and if you can make it good, there will be a market for it, and you won't have to work as many hours. My daughter is a nurse—she's a good nurse—and she only has to work one shift a week at the hospital because they'll take whatever they can get. They're happy to have her skills. So I would suggest that you find a way to become astonishingly good at what you do. And if you can, find an opportunity to work at something that doesn't leave you so exhausted and wrung out that you have nothing left for your family when you go home.

Every choice you make will have sacrifices. Every time you decide to go through one door, there are several other doors you have automatically decided *not* to go through. That's the nature of our choices in this world, and because we live in a time when we have more choices, we have more sacrifices that we get to make. Sometimes your family has to sacrifice if you have something at work that really needs to be done. But I hope— and I think it's true—that my children knew that if they were the ones who required the sacrifice, the work would always come second. Be sure your children know that when they need you, you will be there. And be sure also that they know you are trusting them not to need you all the time.

PRINCIPLE NUMBER 5: BE VIGILANT ABOUT PROTECTING YOUR FAMILY.

If I had teenagers who lived at home right now, and I was at work, I would make a rule that the computer was not on when Mom was not home. I would password-protect the computer so that the children could not get on. There's not one thing they need to be doing on that computer that can't wait until I get home from work. I would not trust a filter of any sort to keep my family safe for me. I have never yet met a fail-safe filter for the Internet.

That is just the harsh reality of the world in which we live, and we have to be tough about enforcing such rules because kids can get into so much more trouble now than we could when we were teenagers. Unbridled watching of *Gilligan's Island* reruns, that was about as mind-rotting as it got for me. Granted, that can rot your mind pretty seriously—view enough sitcoms and you won't have a whole lot of active brain cells left—but it's not the same kind of trouble that a kid can get into now.

Protect your family as much as you can, in every way that you can, while you're away. Now, they'll whine. They're not going to be happy about that. That's okay. You do what you need to do.

PRINCIPLE NUMBER 6: TRUST THE LORD TO MAKE YOU ABLE TO DO THE THINGS THAT YOU NEED TO DO.

One November I was attending a conference out of town and had gotten sick while there. I had to have a couple of my colleagues give me a priesthood blessing before I could even get on a plane to come home, but fortunately, I did make it home. It was Sunday, and I dragged myself into bed and fell fast asleep. After a few hours, my husband cautiously opened the bedroom door and whispered, "Honey, the bishop wants to talk to us. He really wants to talk to us today, and he wants to talk to both of us. Do you think you can do it?"

I mumbled something like, "Yeah. Yeah, sure. Do I have to wear stockings?"

"No, just put on a dress, he doesn't care."

So I put on something and staggered over, and the bishop said to me, "Heavenly Father would like you to be the Young Women president in our ward." And because I was weak and sick, I said, "Okay." No, actually the first thing I said was, "You know I don't do camp, right?"

Well, camp was a long way away, so he sort of hemmed and hawed around that one and didn't really address it. So I said, "You get that I'm really, really busy, right? You get that I'm not going to do this the way the previous Young Women president did? Because she had the cute gene that I somehow didn't stand in line for. She did darling handouts and invitations and refrigerator magnets and everything that just gets really close to young women's hearts that I have *no skill in*. You get that I'm not going to be her, right? Because the girls are already going to be mad that I'm not her, and if you expect me to be her, I can't do that." I guess I must have sounded pretty hysterical by that point.

The bishop said, "No, we don't want you to be *her*, we're calling *you*. And it's not my idea. It's Heavenly Father's idea."

So I said, "Okay. I'll do it."

A few months later, I received an assignment at work that I could probably most accurately describe as the most difficult and personally challenging assignment of my professional career. It was on a short time frame, a great deal was at stake, there were a lot of personalities involved, and it really required every skill I had at work—and in the middle of it came girls camp. I had two counselors and one advisor, no additional board, because we had a very small Mutual, and both of my counselors were pregnant. I understand that's putting the right priority first, but I was not being very gracious about it because it meant that the camp director and the one advisor and I were the only women who could go from our ward to girls camp that year.

I prayed about this and got the inescapable feeling that, impossible as it seemed, I should go to camp. I was right in the middle of this incredibly taxing project, and I said, "I don't know how I'm going to do this. I don't see how I'm going to get this done." My optimistic husband said, "Well, I'll come with you, and I'll be your priesthood support," and he came and stayed the whole time. He pitched my tent. The girls had to pitch their own tents, but he pitched mine, thank goodness, and I did all the usual camp things. I slid down to the bottom of the stupid mummy bag several times during the night. I had girls complaining outside my tent flap at midnight and yelling at each other through their tent flaps. I went on the five-mile hike that they *said* was a three-mile hike until we got to the end of it and then they said, "Oh, ha-ha, that was a five-mile hike," thank you so very much. I did all the things that you do at girls camp that make it such a wonderful experience. Then I came home and went back to the office and picked my project back up.

Now, here's a really interesting thing. I didn't have time to go to girls camp. I didn't have any inclination to go to girls camp. I didn't have any desire to go to girls camp. But I had to go to girls camp. And when you do something for the Lord, even if it's something that you really don't want to do, if you put yourself in His hands and say, "I'm going to do this," He will make you able. In fact, He will even consecrate that for your gain. Looking back, I can tell you that for three days I miraculously didn't think once about that project at work. Not once. And so, when I got back to it, I came to it fresh and had the blessing of being able to attack it again with a new vigor.

A fascinating postscript to this story was that later on in the summer, when it was time for youth conference, I received absolutely no prompting that I needed to attend. I told the bishopric counselor to whom I reported, "I am not feeling like I need to be at youth conference, and I don't see how I can anyway," and he said, "Yeah, we talked about that; we don't think you need to be there either."

It was amazing to me that Heavenly Father knew where He needed me and where He did *not* need me. He allowed the right priorities to surface *every single time*. That's better than balance. Priority is better than balance. I testify to you that, whatever circumstance you find yourself in, if you put your trust in Him and do what He asks you to do, whether or not it suits your skill set or your inclination, if you try to do it with all your heart, He will make you able.

He will *not* make you perfect. I tell my children I have given them the gift of an imperfect mother so that they will not enter marriage with unrealistic expectations. I hope it gives them the opportunity to see that imperfections are not something to panic about but something to be patient with.

I am not perfect—but my Savior is. I testify to you that when we walk with Him, in His light and by His grace, He will help us do what He needs us to do. And when we're doing what He needs us to do, we will find the happiness He means us to have.

NOTES

1. Quentin L. Cook, "LDS Women Are Incredible!" *Ensign,* May 2011, 21.
2. Jeffrey R. Holland, in *Worldwide Leadership Training Meeting: Building Up a Righteous Posterity* (Salt Lake City: The Church of Jesus Christ of Latter-day Saints, 2008), 12.

PRAYER: A SMALL AND SIMPLE THING

Virginia H. Pearce

Our conference theme comes from Alma 37:6, a verse we all know well, memorable in its alliteration and paradoxical in its promise. Alma, speaking to his son Helaman about the importance of keeping the scriptural record, said, "Now ye may suppose that this is foolishness in me; but behold I say unto you, that by small and simple things are great things brought to pass" (Alma 37:6).

Isn't that comforting in our world, where extravagant, larger-than-life events and expectations are before our eyes continually? I have a tiny sign on my computer at home—it's not embroidered, cross-stitched, or framed. It's just a little sticky note that says:

"KEEP IT SMALL.
"KEEP IT SIMPLE.
"GIVE IT TIME."

Reading these words—sometimes out loud—never fails to settle me down.

Virginia H. Pearce was the first counselor in the Young Women organization of The Church of Jesus Christ of Latter-day Saints from 1992 to 1997. She is the author of several books, including Prayer Time *(with Kathleen H. Barnes)*, A Heart Like His, *and* Through His Eyes. *She and her late husband, James, are the parents of six children and the grandparents of twenty-six grandchildren.*

One of our great Relief Society forebears, Emmeline B. Wells, said it much more poetically:

"Faith urges on the weak, and gives them grace,
"And thus we often see the fragile ones outdo
"Those who were strong when starting in the race."[1]

Given time, our very smallness—our fragileness—actually allows God's grace to work in us and to triumph over those who might have seemed stronger and larger in the beginning.

My mother wore a simple gold band on her finger. As she grew older, with arthritic hands, she often wore the ring on a chain around her neck. She and I went out to lunch one afternoon a couple of years before her death. We were talking about nothing in particular when she stopped and asked me if I knew the story about the gold band. "It's 18-carat gold, you know, more than 100 years old, and I want to be sure you know its story." And then she proceeded to tell me about my great-grandmother's ring.

Martha Elizabeth Evans was seventeen years old when she first met George Paxman. He was new in town, lean, with a fine bone structure and deep-set blue eyes. She was a petite, five-foot-two young woman with smooth skin and an abundance of fine hair, unbelievably soft to the touch.

They fell in love. Two years later, in the fall of 1885, as they made eternal promises to one another, he put a gold band on the fourth finger of her left hand.

The hopeful young couple moved into a two-room adobe house with a dirt roof while George's carpenter skills played their part in building a majestic white limestone temple, towering on a hill above the little adobe village of Manti, Utah. The young husband worked eight hours a day and received scrip for a weekly four dollars' worth of goods in the local store and produce from the tithing office. It was a sweet way to begin married life.

On a June evening in 1887, a month before their first little girl turned one, George came home from working on the temple where he had helped hang the large east doors. He was in terrible pain. Alarmed,

Martha loaded him in a wagon and made the strenuous trip through the mountains to a hospital, where he died three days later of a strangulated hernia. Eight months later Martha gave birth to a second little girl—my grandmother—whom she named Georgetta after her beloved George.

A twenty-two-year-old widow with two little girls, her faith in God, and a gold band on her finger, Martha faced the future.

Now comes the story my mother wanted to be sure I knew. Several years after George's death, Martha was invited by a neighbor one day to replenish her tick with new straw. In Martha's words: "Just as I finished filling the tick, I looked at my hand and my ring was gone. I could have cried. When I got home I spread sheets out on the floor and went through the straw piece by piece, but no ring was there. I decided to go back [to the neighbor's] anyway and look around the straw again. I prayed that I might find it."[2] The neighbor helped her look, but it seemed to be of no use. Just as she had given up, she kicked the straw with the toe of her shoe and the ring appeared.

Martha told and retold this story to her daughters and their children. Her grandmother's story convinced my mother that prayers are heard and that prayers are answered. This ring is a loving link honoring marriage and eternal loyalty, but to me it is a reminder about the power of prayer.

I believe in prayer, and have felt impressed to discuss this small and simple practice by which great things are brought to pass. Prayer is certainly the most basic religious ritual of all faiths. All those who believe in God seek Him in some form of prayer. It is the earliest religious behavior we teach to our children. And yet the process of prayer cannot be fathomed by the human mind. None of us understands how it works even though we have had a lifetime of experience with it.

But we do know some things:

The first thing we know is that *prayer rests on the principle of faith*. We have faith in the doctrine that we are children of a Heavenly Father; that we are separated from Him during this time of mortality; and that our goal is to become like Him so that we can once again return to His presence. Think about that. When we understand that God is our Father and we are His children, then prayer becomes natural and instinctive.[3]

We also know that *prayer is an expression of agency*. Earnest, sincere, heartfelt prayer is a deeply personal choice. No one can force us to reach out with all of our hearts. No one can compel us to feel after our Maker. I love the way Isaiah expresses this heartfelt desire to pray: "With my soul have I desired thee in the night; yea, with my spirit within me will I seek thee early" (Isaiah 26:9).

And so our small and simple choice to pray allows God to unlock the powers of heaven in our behalf. The Holy Ghost is free to fill our minds and hearts, leading us towards Him and our eternal destiny. I can think of no greater thing.

We know that *prayer grows out of humility*. When we pray, it signals a recognition that we cannot live this life alone, that we are dependent upon the Father and His Son for our very breath. I know some very smart people. I know some gifted and highly skilled people. I know some very wealthy people. But I have never met any person who has sufficient resources to meet all the demands of this life on his or her own. We need God. And if our troubles can take us to God, we can be thankful for them.

I was recently awed by the exhibition of Carl Bloch's art titled *The Master's Hand;* in particular, I loved the painting *Christus Consolator*.[4] It, along with other magnificent pieces, was on display at the Brigham Young University Museum of Art from 12 November 2010 to 7 April 2011. I love to look at this painting, at each individual who seeks consolation from Christ. You can see the troubles of mortality on their faces. These are they who know they cannot do it alone. Bloch described the joy we can take in adversity when we know it brings us to Christ. He said: "'When things are at their worst they then become their absolute best. I think then that I have so much to thank God for, and it would be foolish to demand that one should be happy in this life. By that I mean always sparkling, always seeing the ideal under the light sky. No, grey skies and rain splashing are part of it—one must be washed off thoroughly before one goes in to God.'"[5]

I like that image—being washed off thoroughly by the gray skies and rains of life as we kneel in humility, in our fragileness, asking for God's help. "Be thou humble; and the Lord thy God shall lead thee by the hand, and give thee answer to thy prayers" (D&C 112:10).

I have a good friend whom I will call Jane. Jane is a covenant-keeping member of The Church of Jesus Christ of Latter-day Saints. Her life has many facets: Church service, full-time work, devotion to family, neighborliness. She is smart and funny and faithful. And, like all of us in mortality, she confronts heart-rending challenges—the greatest of which concerns her family. As her children matured, some of them began to choose different paths. She witnessed them making choices that she knew would lead to unhappiness, and she was heartbroken—and frantic. She constantly reviewed her past parenting decisions and was filled with guilt. Maybe it was all her fault. She found herself anxious and fearful, wondering what she could say and how and when she could say it so that her errant child would see the light and return. She worried about every interaction with the child—her own, her husband's, the ward members', the neighbors'—everyone's! It would be accurate to say she felt tormented and out of control.

And she prayed. My, did she pray! Her heart was "drawn out in prayer unto him continually for [her own] welfare, and also for the welfare of [her children]" (Alma 34:27).

One afternoon in fast and testimony meeting, she listened to a friend she admired describe how she had been troubled with a particular problem with one of her children and had determined to go to the temple once a week. The friend then testified in gratitude that after many months her prayers had been answered—her problem had been miraculously solved.

Jane was touched, returned home, kept praying, and felt inclined to make a personally ambitious yearly goal of temple attendance. She felt sure that the Lord would honor such a significant sacrifice.

I am going to interrupt the story here to point out some of the things we have discussed. Jane had faith. She understood her relationship to her Father in Heaven. She exhibited humility, an understanding that she needed divine help. She made an individual personal choice to pray. As she continued her very personal conversation with the Lord, kept her covenants, and went to church, the Holy Ghost sent the words of her friend's testimony deeply into her heart. Continuing to pray, Jane acted on the promptings she received to attend the temple more often.

To continue with her story, I quote Jane: "After ten years of increased temple attendance and constant prayer, I am sorry to say that my children's choices have not changed."

And then a pause . . .

"But *I* have. I am a different woman."

"How?" I asked.

"I have a softer heart. I am filled with compassion. I can actually do more and am free of my fear, anxiety, guilt, blame, and dread. I have given up my time limits and am able to wait on the Lord. And I experience frequent manifestations of the Lord's power. He sends tender mercies, small messages that acknowledge His love for me and my children. My expectations have changed. Instead of expecting my children to change, I expect these frequent tender mercies and am full of gratitude for them. I have a new openness and sensitivity to the Spirit and no longer worry myself to death over what I will say and how I will say it. If I feel inclined to speak, I don't hesitate, and the words feel as if they are given to me.

"All of my relationships are better, especially with my children and my husband. I can do and say things that I could never do or say before. My children are respectful of my temple devotion. They are sweet and supportive of me, as is my husband. He and I are cemented together by these difficulties rather than blaming and pulling apart. Our marriage has never been more joyful. My ability to appreciate and enjoy the good things of my life is heightened. I am simply more present.

"My prayers are changed. I express more love and am more thankful. I pray to be equal to the tasks before me. I pray for an increase of charity and patience and faith. I am grateful for the trials that led me here. I wouldn't change a thing that has happened. The Lord works in marvelous ways and I truly am filled with the 'peace . . . which passeth all understanding' [Philippians 4:7]."

Prayer and temple attendance are not dramatic, sensational, or one-time activities. But, repeated day by day and year after year, they are small and simple things by which great things come to pass. In fact, this gradual process of change seems to be the way the Lord often works with us. Yes, we have scriptural stories of seemingly sudden and complete change, but more often we become "new creatures" (Mosiah 27:26)—like those in the City of Enoch—"in process of time" (Moses 7:21).

I find the word *consecration* intriguing. It means to make holy and sacred, and to sanctify. Consecration means that we dedicate our thoughts, our actions, our very lives to God. In turn, He can consecrate our experiences—sanctify them, make them holy—no matter how difficult, foolish, or destructive they may be.

It is written: "In everything give thanks; waiting patiently on the Lord, for your prayers have entered into the ears of the Lord. . . . He giveth this promise unto you, with an immutable covenant that they shall be fulfilled; and *all things wherewith you have been afflicted shall work together for your good,* and to my name's glory, saith the Lord" (D&C 98:1–3; emphasis added).

All things shall be for our good? How does *that* work? I don't know, but I believe the words of Nephi: "Ye must pray always, and not faint; that ye must not perform any thing unto the Lord save in the first place ye shall pray unto the Father in the name of Christ, that he will consecrate thy performance unto thee, that thy performance may be for the welfare of thy soul" (2 Nephi 32:9).

When I listened to Jane, I felt how the Lord had consecrated her difficulties with her children to the eternal welfare of her soul. Wasn't it something to read her description of those changes? I thought I could see before my very eyes someone who had prayed with all the energy of her heart and who had been filled with pure charity—a gift bestowed freely on all true followers of Christ (see Moroni 7:48).

How could this not also be helpful to her children?

Nephi talks about his prayers for his people. Think of Jane and her prayers for her children. Think of yourself and your prayers for those you love.

"But behold, there are many that harden their hearts against the Holy Spirit, that it hath no place in them. . . . I pray continually for them by day, and mine eyes water my pillow by night, because of them; and I cry unto my God in faith, and I know that he will hear my cry. And I know that the Lord God will consecrate my prayers for the gain of my people" (2 Nephi 33:2–4).

I don't know how He will do this—individual agency must be exercised—but my faith tells me that someday when those loved ones make a choice to come to Christ and His atonement begins to operate in their lives, our prayers will be part of a miracle that can not only change their future but can consecrate their past experience to the welfare of their souls. Rather than creating torment and bitterness and despair, their past sins will become experiences that deepen their compassion toward others and their gratitude for their Savior. Isn't that an amazing transformation, possible only through the Savior's infinite power?

Like Jane, we often add fasting, temple worship, and priesthood blessings to our prayers as we importune the Lord in times of exceptional need. I don't know how that works, either, but as I have added these things, I have personally experienced the power of increased consecration and felt my heart open wider to receive the will of the Lord. One of the great outcomes of effective prayer is that through it, the will of the Father and my will become one and the same.

I also know that as others have joined their prayers, fasting, and temple worship on behalf of me and mine, I have indeed felt an increase in the Lord's presence. And why would that not be so? Faith coupled with pure charity—the love we extend when we pray, fast, and add names to the temple rolls—makes a difference. It unifies us with one another. It unifies us with the Lord.

Sister Julie Beck encourages us as Relief Society sisters to pray. She said, "Think of our combined strength if every sister had sincere prayer every morning and night or, better yet, prayed unceasingly as the Lord has commanded."[6]

Praying for one another brings strength. It knits our hearts together in unity and love. And this pure love, charity, opens our hearts to receive the blessings that the Lord desires to give us, "but that are made conditional on our asking for them."[7]

Sometimes answers to prayer are quite clear, simple, and direct. But often prayer becomes a long and personal conversation. We continue to pray and work and find that, in inexplicable ways, our problems are gradually resolved or changed. Sometimes even our righteous and heartfelt desires are modified. Gradually, our desires become His will. Our pleading becomes part of the experience.

Elder Neal A. Maxwell taught that the Lord works on us through the very process of prayer:

"Some have difficulty with the reality that prayers are petitions even though God knows all and loves all anyway. True, we are not informing God, but we are informing ourselves by reverently working through our real concerns and our real priorities and by listening to the Spirit. For us merely to say, ritualistically, 'Thy will be done' would not be real petitionary prayer. This would involve no genuine working through of our own feelings. There would be no experience in agonizing, in choosing, and also in submitting."[8]

And so the power of praying is more than saying at the end of a prayer, "Thy will be done." It is actually finding that His will has become our will. Often the change in our part of the conversation is almost imperceptible. It is simple and small and occurs over time. It is difficult to talk about because by its very nature it is personal and unique—something that is happening between the Father and the individual. And it is unpredictable. He may answer me so immediately and distinctly at one time and so gradually at another time that I may think that nothing is happening. But if I make the choice to keep believing, and I demonstrate that choice by continuing to pray, I am quite sure His will *will* be made manifest, and it will, in the end, seem to me to be just right.

Sometimes we may feel we are simply left on our own to do the best we can. I believe that if we were to wait to act until we recognized a clear answer every time we prayed, most of us would be waiting and wasting a good part of our lives.

Elder Richard G. Scott asks the question, "What do you do when you have prepared carefully, have prayed fervently, waited a reasonable time for a response, and still do not feel an answer?" He continues: "You may want to express thanks when that occurs, for it is an evidence of His trust. When you are living worthily and your choice is consistent with the Savior's teachings and you need to act, proceed with trust. . . . God will not let you proceed too far without a warning impression if you have made the wrong decision."[9]

President Gordon B. Hinckley had a personal motto that is quite practical. He taught it in many settings: "Things will work out. If you keep trying and praying and working, things will work out. They always do."[10]

And so we have to pray and then keep moving forward, trusting that if it is a direction that will *not* be for our good, the Lord will help us know.

Otherwise, we trust that the Lord is bound to own and honor the decisions we have made using our own best judgment.[11]

My great-grandmother Martha Elizabeth Paxman prayed for her ring. She looked down and found it. She acknowledged the answer. I think of other prayers Martha Elizabeth must have offered—many much more critical to her future than the one about the ring. I think of the desperate prayers she must have offered as she drove her husband in the carriage in search of a doctor. That prayer was not answered as Martha would have hoped. Somehow it was not part of His plan for Martha and George that they should have a full lifetime together.

But on the day that Martha lost her ring, God granted her prayerful desire. However, I believe that finding the ring was a minor miracle when compared to the real message. The real message to Martha was that God was aware of her sadness and love for her long-gone sweetheart whom the ring represented. He was telling her that He knew and loved her and that He was there for her. And, stunningly, this reassurance of His presence and love is much greater than any other possible outcome.

My friend Jane talked about receiving those kinds of messages from Heavenly Father. She said, "I experience frequent manifestations of the Lord's power. He sends tender mercies, small messages that acknowledge His love for me and my children. My expectations have changed. Instead of expecting my children to change, I expect these frequent tender mercies and am full of gratitude for them."

In Martha's life, in Jane's life, surely in yours, and most certainly in mine, God has not always granted those things that we have wanted or even asked for desperately. But He frequently puts His divine signature[12] on small events of the day. And His presence—the indescribably settling quality of His great love—more than recompenses for all tragedies and disappointments. He says, with these tender mercies, "I am here. I care about you. You are living your life with my approval. Everything will work together for your good. Trust me."

The miracle of prayer doesn't reside in the ability to manipulate situations and events, but in the miracle of creating a relationship with God.[13]

Think about that carefully, would you? What does it do for you to have an assurance that the Lord is with you?

In October 2008, my husband and I were busily preparing to respond to a mission call. It had been a year of perpetual motion for us. My father had died in January, necessitating the business of dividing and distributing all of his stuff. Oh, we do leave lots of things behind, don't we? Just as we were finishing that, my husband retired from his medical practice, and we were loading and unloading more boxes of stuff. There were lots of family events, some travel, and the preparation of our mission papers. And then there we were with a mission call, making arrangements to rent out our home—yes, moving more stuff—when everything stopped.

Responding to some symptoms that were becoming increasingly problematic, my husband went in for tests and was diagnosed with a fatal and untreatable disease. He lived just short of one year from the day of diagnosis.

It was a unique year for us—one of quiet and slow living—of unbusyness. President Dieter F. Uchtdorf explained, "When growing conditions are not ideal, trees slow down their growth and devote their energy to the basic elements necessary for survival." He continued, "It is good advice to slow down a little, steady the course, and focus on the essentials when experiencing adverse conditions."[14]

We did just that.

We talked, we cried, we read and reread verses of scripture, we pored over talks from the brethren, we spent sweet time with family and friends. We went to bed every night and got up every morning. Most of all, though, we prayed. We prayed together, we prayed separately, we prayed vocally, we prayed silently. We prayed with loved ones. We fasted and prayed. We went to the temple and prayed. We prayed constantly. We pled with our Father in Heaven in the name of His Son, Jesus Christ.

I tell you this by way of personal testimony. Prayer works. It does indeed call down the powers of heaven. It reconciles our will with the will of the Father. It consecrates even our most aversive experiences to the welfare of our souls. Through combined prayer we experience love, unity, and power that is impossible to describe. We may not be granted that which we desire, but we end up grateful with all of our hearts for that which the Lord gives us.

And along the way we experience tender mercies over and over—those unmistakable messages from Him: "I am here. I love you. You are living your life with my approval. Everything will work together for your good. Trust me."

Even though we may not see from minute to minute that we are moving forward and making progress, I believe we will be able to one day look back at our lives and see that we were, in fact, doing just what we needed to be doing at just the right time in just the right place. We can trust that the Lord will work in and through us. Mormon expressed it beautifully: "And now, I do not know all things; but the Lord knoweth all things which are to come; wherefore, he worketh in me to do according to his will" (Words of Mormon 1:7).

Like Mormon, I do not know all things, but I do know that the Lord works in faithful, prayerful people to do according to His will. I know that by small and simple means are great things brought to pass.

NOTES

1. Emmeline B. Wells, "Faith and Fidelity," in *Musings and Memories*, 2nd ed. (Salt Lake City: The Deseret News, 1915), 221; available at http://ia600408.us.archive.org/13/items/musingsmemories00well/musingsmemories00well.pdf; accessed 12 August 2011.
2. Personal history in author's possession.
3. See Bible Dictionary, s.v. "Prayer," 752–53.
4. *Christus Consolator*, in Dawn C. Pheysey and Richard Neitzel Holzapfel, *The Master's Hand: The Art of Carl Heinrich Bloch* (Salt Lake City: Deseret Book, and Provo: Brigham Young University Museum of Art, 2010), 114.
5. In ibid., 55.
6. Julie B. Beck, "What Latter-day Saint Women Do Best: Stand Strong and Immovable," *Ensign*, November 2007, 110.
7. Bible Dictionary, s.v. "Prayer."
8. Neal A. Maxwell, *That Ye May Believe* (Salt Lake City: Bookcraft, 1992), 178.
9. Richard G. Scott, "Using the Supernal Gift of Prayer," *Ensign*, May 2007, 10.
10. Sheri Dew, *Go Forward with Faith* (Salt Lake City: Deseret Book, 1996), 423.
11. See *Journal of Discourses*, 26 vols. (London: Latter-day Saints' Book Depot, 1854–56), 3:205, in which Brigham Young taught: "If I ask Him to give me wisdom concerning any requirement in life, or in regard to my own course, or that of my friends, my family, my children, or those that I preside over, and get no answer from Him, and then do the very best that my judgment

will teach me, He is bound to own and honor that transaction, and He will do so to all intents and purposes."

12. See Gerald N. Lund, *Divine Signatures: The Confirming Hand of God* (Salt Lake City: Deseret Book, 2010).

13. See Bible Dictionary, s.v. "Prayer."

14. Dieter F. Uchtdorf, "Of Things That Matter Most," *Ensign*, November 2010, 19.

INDEX

INDEX

243